Modern Confessional Writing

Modern Confessional Writing offers the first comprehensive and scholarly account of this popular and influential genre. The essays in this collection take as their subject confessional literature from the mid-twentieth century to the present day, including the writing of John Berryman, Anne Sexton, Ted Hughes, Dave Eggers and Njabulo Ndebele.

Drawing on a wide range of examples, the contributors to this volume evaluate – and in most cases critique – conventional readings of confessionalism. Orthodox humanist notions of the literary confession and of its assumed relationship to truth, authority and subjectivity are challenged. In their place a range of critical perspectives and practices are adopted, utilizing the insights of contemporary critical theorists. *Modern Confessional Writing* develops and tests new theoretically-informed perspectives on what confessional writing is, how it functions, and what it means to both writer and reader. When read from these new perspectives, modern confessional writing is liberated from the misconception that it provides easy authorial release and readerly catharsis and is instead read as a discursive, self-reflexive, sophisticated and demanding genre.

Jo Gill is Lecturer in American Literature at Bath Spa University College.

Routledge studies in twentieth-century literature

Modern Confessional Writing

New critical essays

Edited by Jo Gill

Routledge
Taylor & Francis Group

LONDON AND NEW YORK

First published 2006
by Routledge
2 Park Square, Milton Park, Abingdon, Oxon OX14 4RN

Simultaneously published in the USA and Canada
by Routledge
270 Madison Ave, New York, NY 10016

Routledge is an imprint of the Taylor & Francis Group

Typeset in Garamond by Wearset Ltd, Boldon, Tyne and Wear
Printed and bound in Great Britain by MPG Books Ltd, Bodmin

British Library Cataloguing in Publication Data
A catalogue record for this book is available from the British Library

Library of Congress Cataloging in Publication Data
A catalog record for this book has been requested

ISBN 0-415-33969-3

Contents

vi *Contents*

Contributors

Tracy Brain is Senior Lecturer in English and Creative Studies at Bath Spa University College. She is the author of *The Other Sylvia Plath* (2001).

Jo Gill is Lecturer in American Literature at Bath Spa University College. She is the editor of the *Cambridge Companion to Sylvia Plath* (2005) and has published articles on Anne Sexton, Ted Hughes and the contemporary confessional memoir.

Leigh Gilmore is a visiting professor of Women's Studies at the University of California, Berkeley. She is the author of *Autobiographics: A Feminist Theory of Women's Self-Representation* (1994) and *The Limits of Auto-biography: Trauma and Testimony* (2001). She is completing a book on privacy, self-representation and global publics.

Elizabeth Gregory is an associate professor of English and Director of Women's Studies at the University of Houston. She is the author of *Quotation and Modern American Poetry: 'Imaginary Gardens with Real Toads'* (1996) and is at work on a manuscript entitled *Why Tell?: Situating the Confessional Mode in Twentieth-Century Poetry*.

Leah Guenther is a doctoral candidate at Northwestern University. She has published articles on English Renaissance rhetoric and Shakespearean film. She is currently working on a project studying figures of headship in English Renaissance politics and drama.

Deirdre Heddon is a lecturer in Drama at the University of Exeter. Her writing has appeared in *Performance Research*, the *New Theatre Quarterly*, *Feminist Futures?* (2005), and *Women, Theatre and Performance: Auto/biography and Performance* (2004). She is the co-author of *Devising Perform-ance: A Critical History* (2005).

Ann Keniston is an assistant professor of American poetry at the University of Nevada, Reno. Her book *Overheard Voices: Subjectivity and Address in Post-modern American Poetry* is forthcoming from Routledge; a volume of poems appeared in Spring 2005 from David Robert Books. Her essay on Rich is part of a new book on memory and ghosts in postwar American poetry.

Yianna Liatsos was awarded a Ph.D. in Comparative Literature at Rutgers University, where she completed her dissertation on the idea of historical catharsis in post-apartheid public discourses and the post-apartheid South African novel. She is currently Assistant Professor in the English Department at the University of Oklahoma.

Bran Nicol is Senior Lecturer in English Literature at the University of Portsmouth. He is the author of *Iris Murdoch: The Retrospective Fiction* (2004), *D.M. Thomas* (2004) and editor of *Postmodernism and the Contemporary Novel: A Reader* (2002).

Susannah Radstone is Reader in the School of Social Sciences, Media and Cultural Studies at the University of East London. She is the co-editor of *Contested Pasts* and *Regimes of Memory* (2003) and edited *Memory and Methodology* (2000). She is currently completing *On Memory and Confession*: *The Sexual Politics of Time*.

Ruth Robbins is Senior Lecturer in English at Leeds Metropolitan University. She is the author of *Literary Feminisms* (2000) and *Pater to Forster, 1873–1924* (2003). Her book, *Subjectivity* is due for publication in 2005.

Acknowledgements

I would like to thank the School of English at the University of Gloucestershire where this book had its origins, the University of Exeter which sustained it during its middle period and Kingston University whose generous offer of a Research Fellowship ensured its completion. Particular gratitude to Professors Peter Widdowson, Stan Smith, Avril Horner and David Rogers, and to Alice Entwistle, Shelley Saguaro, Sarah Sceats, Mark Whalan, Stacy Gillis, Margaretta Jolly, James Annesley, Victoria Stewart, Tony Simoes da Silva, Jeannette Gill and Sheena and Ray Hennessy, to Jo Whiting at Routledge who commissioned the book and Terry Clague who succeeded him as editor. Thanks, too, to all of the contributors and those who offered papers which, for reasons of space, I was unable to include. Final thanks go to Neil, Jacob, Freya and Keziah, of course.

Introduction

Jo Gill

> We don't really know what we think of confessions or what we want them
> to be or to do.
>
> (Brooks 2001: 86)

On turning our attention to modern confessional writing, we are faced
immediately with a sense of its complexity, its indeterminacy and its apparent incomprehensibility. We are faced with numerous questions: who confesses? Why do they choose so to do? Is there an element of choice or is
confession coerced in some specific and individual or general and social way?
What, if anything, distinguishes confessional writing from other forms of
confession (psychoanalytic, legal, religious?) What, if anything, distinguishes *modern* confessional writing from the writing of the past? Is confessional writing to be thought of generically (that is, as having a distinctive
style or structure which transcends time) or as a historically specific form?
The titles of two previous essays, Laurence Lerner's 1987 'What *is* Confessional Poetry?' and Diane Middlebrook's 1993 'What *was* Confessional
Poetry?' (my emphases) strike at the heart of this particular debate. (Both of
these essays focus on poetry, however they do address issues germane to
prose; differences between the two are teased out in some of the contributions to the present volume.) To think about confession is, paradoxically
given confession's apparent proximity to truthful revelation, to enter into
profound uncertainty. As the original essays in this collection show, to think
about confession is to abandon conventional and hitherto dependable
notions of reliability, authority and authenticity and to embrace, and find
new ways of addressing, the difficulty and slipperiness – which is also the
fascination – of modern variations on the form.

This collection offers the first critical survey of this diverse and challenging field. My intention in assembling these essays is to bring the frequently
used, but rarely interrogated, term 'confession' under scrutiny, to appraise
not only contemporary examples of confessional writing but emergent
approaches to its study. In this respect, *Modern Confessional Writing: New
Critical Essays* is not simply a companion to recent confessional writing, but

a critical guide to new ways of reading it; it is not only a history of modern confession, but a history of modern confessional criticism. The aim of the collection is to stimulate debate about this contested and continually evolving subject; for this reason none of the essays attempts to impose a determinate definition of 'confession' although most do posit characteristic features, or contexts, or effects.

The essays which follow, all of which were commissioned for this volume, take as their subject a wealth of influential texts, writers and issues. Chronologically, these range from the beginning of what, for the purposes of this book, I am defining as the modern era of confessional writing (that is, the period from the late 1950s when the 'confessional' mode of poetry was first defined (Rosenthal 1959: 154)) through to the present day. The collection opens with Tracy Brain's provocative essay, 'Dangerous confessions: the problem of reading Sylvia Plath biographically'. Drawing on Plath's poetry, fiction, journals and letters, and offering a close comparative reading of numerous biographical accounts of her life and work, Brain raises important questions about the legitimacy of reading confessionally. Thereafter, Elizabeth Gregory in 'Confessing the body: Plath, Sexton, Berryman, Lowell, Ginsberg and the gendered poetics of the "real"' looks back to the confessional poetry of the 1950s in her nuanced analysis of the dynamics of modern confessionalism. She argues that, while ostensibly the site in which 'truth' about the self is asserted, confession turns out to be the place where received definitions of gender, family roles, and the mind/body relation are challenged. Chapter 3, Ann Keniston's '"To feel with a human stranger": Adrienne Rich's post-Holocaust confession and the limits of identification' examines the fusion in her work of a personal voice with one which is public and politically conscious – a fusion which Keniston sees as enlarging the scope of confession. Jo Gill's essay '"Your story. My story": confessional writing and the case of *Birthday Letters*' (Chapter 4) reads Hughes's book as an exemplary confessional text in its profound self-consciousness. It argues that it is the process and difficulties of confession as much as the 'story' ostensibly at its heart which are its primary concern.

In the next chapter '*Bridget Jones's Diary*: confessing post-feminism' we turn to contemporary popular fiction, and Helen Fielding's *Bridget Jones's Diary* which Leah Guenther reads in the light of successive 'waves' of modern feminism. Guenther sees the personal diary as the site of self-scrutiny, and of self-evasion. Also on contemporary prose, Bran Nicol's '"The memoir as self-destruction": *A Heartbreaking Work of Staggering Genius*' addresses the obsessively ironic reflexivity, or metafictionality, of Eggers's memoir. Nicol asks whether, or in what ways, such irony is commensurate with the authenticity hitherto regarded as the defining feature of the form. Chapter 7, Yianna Liatsos's 'Truth, confession, and the post-apartheid black consciousness in Njabulo Ndebele's *The Cry of Winnie Mandela*' asks what the practice has to offer to the new South Africa. Like Keniston, above, Liatsos is absorbed by the complex and contested relationship between 'private' and 'social' confessions. In Chapter 8, 'Personal performance: the resistant confessions of Bobby Baker', Dee Heddon proposes that the work of contemporary performance artist Bobby Baker resists dominant models of confession through a process of strategic performance which illuminates its performed (artful) nature and undermines its apparent truth-value.

The final three chapters of the book think in broad and abstract terms about the detailed issues and questions encountered thus far. Chapter 9, Ruth Robbins's 'Death sentences: confessions of living with dying in narratives of terminal illness', considers a number of contemporary narratives of illness and dying. Robbins is interested in the apparent inadequacy of the 'abstractions of theory' to account for what we see and feel as we read these accounts. In response to this impasse, she proposes a new critical practice appropriate to the demands of the contemporary form. Susannah Radstone's 'Cultures of confession/cultures of testimony: turning the subject inside out' traces the emergence of, and relationship between, discourses of confession and of testimony. She points to the disjunction between the practice of recent confessional fiction and the insights of confessional theory and suggests that a similar critical distance – a sense of the mode's impossibility – is regrettably absent in testimony theory. In the topical and polemical essay which closes the collection, 'How we confess now: reading the Abu Ghraib archive', Leigh Gilmore looks to recent events in Iraq. She argues that experience there has much to teach us about the nature of confession: principally that the truths it produces are unstable and are shaped within specific practices and specific power relations – with repercussions for confessant and confessor alike.

As this summary indicates, *Modern Confessional Writing* rethinks the meaning and the possibilities of 'confessional writing' – often in the light of poststructuralist and/or postmodern challenges to our sense of the reliability of language, the coherence and authority of the subject, and the accessibility and desirability of authentic truth. As David Attwell puts it in an interview with J.M. Coetzee; 'it is logical that you should bring deconstruction to bear on the analysis of confession where the problem of the self's residence within language is so visible' (Coetzee 1992: 245). Nevertheless, there is no orthodoxy of critical practices here. Just as the collection covers a diversity of confessional genres from a range of contexts it also exemplifies and tests a range of theoretical perspectives and strategies drawn from a broad range of related genres (including autobiography and the literature of trauma and testimony) and disciplines (law and psychology, for example). For most of the critics collected here, modern confessional writing is not hermetically sealed from its historical and cultural contexts. Instead its development coincides with new cold war cultures of privacy and surveillance, with therapy/pop psychology culture, with the falling away of modernist and 'New Critical' approaches to art and literature, with the rise of the television talk show and the cult of the celebrity. These are studies of modern confessional writing in the world – in South

Africa, in post-Holocaust contexts, in relation to changing gender dynamics, and finally in contemporary Iraq. This variety notwithstanding, a common theme throughout the collection, one to which I will return, is that it is precisely the uncertainty and strangeness of its own endeavour which is modern confessional writing's major preoccupation.

It is difficult today to contemplate such writing without recourse to Michel Foucault's work, primarily in the hugely influential *The History of Sexuality* but also in his essays 'Truth and Power' (1986) and 'Technologies of the Self', where he describes confession in terms of 'specific techniques that human beings use to understand themselves' (1988: 18). Foucault offers an account of the origins and continuing importance of confession: 'in justice, medicine, education, family relationships, and love relations, in the most ordinary affairs of everyday life, and in the most solemn rites' and, of course, in literature (1981: 59). For Foucault:

> The confession is a ritual of discourse in which the speaking subject is also the subject of the statement; it is also a ritual that unfolds within a power relationship, for one does not confess without the presence (or virtual presence) of a partner who is not simply the interlocutor but the authority who requires the confession, prescribes and appreciates it, and intervenes in order to judge, punish, forgive, console, and reconcile.
>
> (1981: 61–2)

Confession, then is not a means of expressing the irrepressible truth of prior lived experience, but a ritualized technique for producing truth. Confessional writing is poietic not mimetic, it constructs rather then reflects some pre-textual truth. It is not the free expression of the self but an effect of an ordered regime by which the self begins to conceive of itself as individual, responsible, culpable and thereby confessional. Most importantly, confession takes place in a context of power, and prohibition, and surveillance. It is generated and sustained not by the troubled subject/confessant, but by the discursive relationship between speaker and reader (confessant and confessor) or, for Leigh Gilmore, developing Foucault's model, by the triangular relationship between 'penitent/teller', 'listener' and 'tale' (1994: 121).

Before exploring the implications of this model in more detail we need to look back to the ancient origins of confession and to early spiritual and philosophical practices. It is from these sources that other secular forms of confession (legal, psychoanalytical and so on) have arisen. The 'technologies of the self' which Foucault identifies in Western culture since the middle ages have their roots in the development of early Greek and Roman philosophies and primitive Christianity (Foucault 1988: 18, 19). In this period, the *Confessions* of St Augustine (397–398 CE) retain a crucial place. Here, in a three-fold confession, Augustine recounts his youthful sins and his persistent temptation, confesses his faith and avows God's glory. The text is significant as a model partly because of its structure, with its repeated use of apostrophe and its perpetual questioning of self, faith, and God, and partly because it offers an example of the development and representation of a unique, unified subject (the confessing 'I') in dialogue with an other (Tambling 1990: 12 ff.).

In the pre-Reformation period, the Christian Church in Western Europe was Roman. Of vital importance in this period to the shape of confession – as a religious practice and thereby as the source in this period and later of legal authority – is the fourth Lateran Council (1215). This, for the first time, prescribed annual confession and penance for the faithful, making it a condition for admission to Easter communion (Bossy 1985). During the fifteenth century, monthly or more frequent confession was introduced. An understanding of penance as both palliative and reformative in its effects also became more widespread during this time.

In the sixteenth century, challenges to the ideological, spiritual and material dominance of the Roman Church in the West began to rise (from Martin Luther, John Calvin and others), and new Protestant practices began to emerge. The Council of Trent (1545–1563) took the fundamental step of codifying the place of confession in the Roman Church. Confession, one of the seven sacraments, was determined to be of 'divine origin and necessary for one's spiritual salvation' (Brooks 2001: 18). In other contexts, for example in emerging Protestant, Calvinist, Puritan and later Quaker traditions, developing through into the seventeenth and eighteenth centuries, confession took different forms. Primarily understood to be a private, *written*, practice of self-examination (although as Patricia Caldwell demonstrates, the American strand of Puritan confession diverged from the English one in its promotion of a public, shared, oral declaration or '"performance"' of private experience (Caldwell 1983: 50)) it looks back both to the practice of Ancient Greek cultures which Foucault describes in 'Technologies of the Self' and forward to the autobiographical and confessional writing of the modern age. Ian Watt notes the influence of this Protestant tradition of 'self-scrutiny' and 'introspection', even or especially when 'religious conviction weakened', on the writing of Daniel Defoe and his contemporaries, and thus its importance to the rise of the novel (2000: 74, 75). Lawrence Stone, too, comments on the importance of what started out as a religious practice of individual, private self-examination to the rise of 'secular individualism' and hence to the growth of 'a *literature* of self-exploration' (1990: 155, 154, my emphasis).

Here, we find the beginnings of the sense of the value and distinctiveness of the self and its stories which is crucial to, for example, Jean-Jacques Rousseau's *Confessions* (1781) (a text which is interesting not simply as a self-authorized account of one man's failings but as an early exemplar of the strategies of evasion, denial and self-conscious artfulness to be found in much recent confessional writing) and to the rise of Romanticism. Susan Sontag sees as instrumental to the 'modern idea of individuality' Romantic attitudes towards, and aestheticization of, sickness and death where sickness is perceived as 'a way of making people "interesting"' and 'a test of moral character' (1991: 31, 42). Peter Brooks, too, cites Romanticism as a determining factor; 'confession … has become in Western culture a crucial mode of self-examination; from the time of the early Romantics to the present day, confession has become a dominant mode of self-expression'. Although as he also concedes in a warning which shadows each of the essays collected in this volume, confession, while 'the vehicle of the most authentic truth' is still 'capable of the most damaging, sometimes self-destructive, untruth' (2001: 9).

Given this long history, how do we explain what seems to be the sudden resurgence or re-emergence of confessional writing in the West in the second half of the twentieth century? Theodor Reik's 1961 *The Compulsion to Confess* exemplifies an increasing anxiety in this period to comprehend powerful unconscious forces, such as the 'urge for expression', which threatened to 'shape the destiny of us all' (195; xi). Christopher Lasch, writing in 1979, ascribed the rise of confessionalism, or of narcissism (a condition to which it is often likened), to a widespread cultural, political, moral, spiritual and personal malaise. This rise is allied, in the case of the United States, to 'defeat in Vietnam, economic stagnation, and the impending exhaustion of natural resources' and, in the case of Europe, to 'the growing strength of communist parties, the revival of fascist movements, and a wave of terrorism' (1979: xiii). These, he suggests, generate a loss of faith in authority and society, and a retreat to the inner self. For Deborah Nelson, it is not possible to consider modern confessional writing without also contemplating the cold war culture into which it emerged, a culture in which what had once seemed to be a reliable binary division between public and private life was, in pervasive and often contradictory ways, policed, challenged and subverted. Nelson points to the significance of changing attitudes towards gender in this new ideology: 'there is no more potent or longer-lasting critique of public and private in American culture than that which began with the feminist movement' (2002: 22). Other critics, too, have suggested a connection between the identity politics of the second wave feminist movement of this period and the rise of confession, some even defining confession as a predominantly female genre (Gammel 1999: 1). A number of the essays collected below implicitly or otherwise address this contention, seeing confession as part of a broader discourse of gender and sexuality, and indeed identity. Diane Middlebrook, in 'What was Confessional Poetry?', mentioned earlier, sees the rise of confessional writing in the late twentieth century as coincident with the pervasiveness of psychology in popular culture, and as the product of a period in which television became 'a solvent of boundaries between public and domestic life' (1993: 633). Of late, the emergence of the confessional television talk show has been seen as both source and product of contemporary confessional culture (Shattuc 1997).

The modern confessional writing discussed in this collection, and the theoretical approaches used in its delineation seem already to be worlds apart from the writing, and the perspective, displayed in Robert Phillips' influential study *The Confessional Poets* (1973) – itself exemplary of widespread critical tendencies in the first part of the period covered by this book. Where conventional readings of confessional writing identify a determinate 'I' speaking directly and colloquially to the reader (Phillips 1973: 17; Rosenthal 1959: 154), the 'I' of modern confessional writing is more complex, mutable and fluid. A distinctive and perhaps unexpected characteristic of the examples discussed here is the elision, or fragmentation, or dispersal of the authentic, self-identical, authoritative self who was apparently – and perhaps hitherto – at the heart of the confessional endeavour. Where Phillips describes such writing as 'an expression of personality, not an escape from it', as 'therapeutic and/or purgative', suggests that 'there are no barriers of subject matter' and 'no barriers between the reader and poet' and insists finally that it displays 'moral courage' (Phillips 1973: 16–17), the essays included below indicate that the opposite is the case. Time and again we come across strategies of evasion, displacement and obfuscation in the confessional writing discussed here; the possibilities of non-disclosure or of self-invention are as important as, if not more important than, 'expressions of personality'. There are multiple 'barriers' in this writing, and primary among these is the barrier of language. How might one represent 'personality' in a language which, after structuralism, we recognize to be elusive, non-referential and slippery, and which, post-Holocaust, as Susannah Radstone and Ann Keniston argue, we find to be wholly inadequate?

Phillips' assertion that confessional writing is 'therapeutic and/or purgative' is still a commonly held view; Erica Wagner describes Dave Eggers's *A Heartbreaking Work of Staggering Genius* as 'heart healing', for example (cited in Moss 2001) and Suzette Henke, here discussing contemporary life writing, or 'life-testimony', terms it 'scriptotherapy' (2000: xiii) – a term which implies the need, and delivery, of a cure. The continuing dominance of this view of confession as therapeutic, or cathartic, or as a form of 'healing' notwithstanding, it is striking that none of the essays below claim this as an effect of the confessions they discuss. Fragmentation, diffusion and attenuation are as likely as coherence, wholeness and closure. And modern confessional writing's acute awareness of the volatility of its (necessary) audience generates a profound scepticism about the likelihood of forgiveness or reintegration.

Laurence Lerner has suggested that the 'characteristics of confession' are 'factual accuracy of remembering, self-centeredness, self-abasement expressed in clichés' (1987: 52). It is precisely in its refutation of such assertions, I would counter, that modern confessional writing is distinctive. It is precisely in its confession of its inability to remember (see Gill's chapter on Ted Hughes's *Birthday Letters*), in its ironical parody of 'self-abasement expressed in clichés' (see Guenther's chapter on *Bridget Jones's Diary* or Nicol's chapter on *A Heartbreaking Work of Staggering Genius*), in its de-centring of the subject (Heddon's chapter on Bobby Baker, for example) that modern confession distinguishes itself.

One of the characteristics which all of the confessions discussed here share is this profound knowingness about the conventions and expectations of the form with which they play. In every case, it is these as much as the subjective experience ostensibly to be confessed, which are at stake. In this respect, this modern confessional writing both emulates and diverges from its precedents. If we look back to Rousseau, for example, we find a similar self-consciousness about the nature and limitations of his chosen form. However, what is distinctive about the work under discussion below is the flamboyant and persistent foregrounding of such knowledge. William Boyd's 1987 novel *The New Confessions*, a fictionalized account of one film-maker's life-long and frustrated involvement with Rousseau's text, exemplifies this tendency in its double self-reflexivity; it is self-declaredly knowing about the knowingness of its model. Eggers's *A Heartbreaking Work* works in a similar way, announcing in section C.2. of the acknowledgements that 'while the author is self-conscious about being self-referential, he is also knowing about that self-conscious self-referentiality' (Eggers 2000: np).

Where one-time cornerstones of confession (subjectivity, truth, authority, representation) are under question, as they are today, where does confessional writing and its study turn? How does it proceed and how are we to read it, in the light of a wide-scale scepticism about the desirability and reliability and accessibility of these cornerstones? The answer, often, is that what it turns to is its own failure to confess, and this is no longer or only because of a sense of the confessant's personal failing, or individual unworthiness, but because the practice itself, as conventionally perceived, seems inadequate and in need of radical revision. We might note in this context the persistent unease with which commentators and practitioners alike approach confession. I have identified elsewhere a rhetoric of natural disasters (volcanoes, hurricanes, tidal waves, earthquakes) which accompanies early analyses of confessional poetry (Gill 2004: 429). A similar anxiety informs the metaphors of disease and contagion which have characterized recent discussions of the mode. Geoffrey Hartman suggests that confession 'invade[s] both fictional and nonfictional space' (2002: 58) while Mary McCabe indicts it for stimulating an 'unhealthy curiosity' in the reader (1998: 28).

Many of the texts examined in this book share a similar ambivalence about, and a sense of the difficulties of, their own task. The studies of *Modern Confessional Writing* collected here offer strategies for understanding and overcoming these misgivings and for recasting the possibilities of the practice.

Bibliography

Augustine (1961) *Confessions*, trans. R.S. Pine-Coffin, Harmondsworth: Penguin.

Bossy, J. (1985) *Christianity in the West 1400–1700*, Oxford: Oxford University Press.

Boyd, W. (1987) *The New Confessions*, London: Hamish Hamilton.

Brooks, P. (2001) *Troubling Confessions: Speaking Guilt in Law and Literature*, Chicago and London: Chicago University Press.

Caldwell, P. (1983) *The Puritan Conversion Narrative: The Beginnings of American Expression*, Cambridge: Cambridge University Press.

Coetzee, J.M. (1992) *Doubling the Point: Essays and Interviews*, ed. D. Attwell, Cambridge: Harvard University Press.

Egan, S. (1999) *Mirror Talk: Genres of Crisis in Contemporary Autobiography*, Chapel Hill and London: University of North Carolina Press.

Eggers, D. (2000) *A Heartbreaking Work of Staggering Genius*, London: Picador.

Foucault, M. (1981) *The History of Sexuality. Volume One: An Introduction*, trans. R. Hurley, Harmondsworth: Penguin.

—— (1986) 'Truth and Power', in P. Rabinow (ed.) *The Foucault Reader: An Introduction to Foucault's Thought*, Harmondsworth: Penguin.

—— (1988) 'Technologies of the Self', in L.H. Martin *et al.* (eds) *Technologies of the Self: A Seminar with Michel Foucault*, London: Tavistock.

Gammel, I. (ed.) (1999) *Confessional Politics: Women's Sexual Self-Representations in Life Writing and Popular Media*, Carbondale: Southern Illinois University Press.

Gill, J. (2004) 'Anne Sexton and Confessional Poetics', *Review of English Studies* 55 (220): 425–45.

Gilmore, L. (1994) *Autobiographics: A Feminist Theory of Women's Self-Representation*, Ithaca and London: Cornell University Press.

Hartman, G. (2002) *Scars of the Spirit: The Struggle against Inauthenticity*, Basingstoke: Palgrave Macmillan.

Henke, S.A. (2000) *Shattered Subjects: Trauma and Testimony in Women's Life-Writing*, Basingstoke: Macmillan.

Lasch, C. (1979) *The Culture of Narcissism: American Life in an Age of Diminishing Expectations*, New York and London: W.W. Norton.

Lerner, L. (1987) 'What is Confessional Poetry?', *Critical Quarterly* 29 (2): 46–66.

McCabe, M. (1998) 'Laughing in its Face', *Times Literary Supplement*, 6 November: 28.

Middlebrook, D.W. (1993) 'What was Confessional Poetry?', in J. Parini (ed.) *The Columbia History of American Poetry*, New York: Columbia University Press.

Moss, S. (2001) 'A Staggeringly Post-Modern Work of Literary Trickery', *Guardian*, 9 August. Available online at: www.guardian.co.uk/Archive/Article/0,4273,4049704,00.html (accessed 2 May 2001).

Nelson, D. (2002) *Pursuing Privacy in Cold War America*, New York: Columbia University Press.

Phillips, R. (1973) *The Confessional Poets*, Carbondale: Southern Illinois University Press.

Reik, T. (1961) *The Compulsion to Confess: On the Psychoanalysis of Crime and of Punishment*, New York: Grove Press.

Rosenthal, M.L. (1959) 'Poetry as Confession', *The Nation* 189: 154–5.

Rousseau, J.-J. (1953) [1781] *The Confessions of Jean-Jacques Rousseau*, trans. J.M. Cohen, Harmondsworth: Penguin.

Shattuc, J.M. (1997) *The Talking Cure: TV Talk Shows and Women*, New York and London: Routledge.

Sontag, S. (1991) *Illness as Metaphor and Aids and its Metaphors*, Harmondsworth: Penguin.

Stone, L. (1990) *The Family, Sex and Marriage in England 1500–1800*, Harmondsworth: Penguin.

Tambling, J. (1990) *Confession: Sexuality, Sin, the Subject*, Manchester: Manchester University Press.

Watt, I. (2000) *The Rise of the Novel: Studies in Defoe, Richardson and Fielding*, London: Pimlico.

1 Dangerous confessions

The problem of reading Sylvia Plath biographically

Tracy Brain

Few writers have been more famous for being confessional – that is, for using their poetry and prose to tell their own stories – than Sylvia Plath. Biographies of Plath, which take many different forms, have done much to promote her as a confessional writer. But as John Sutherland writes, 'Every biography, even the most exhaustively researched, will be partial and, in crucial matters, irredeemably ignorant' (2004). I want to demonstrate the limits and dangers of reading Plath as a confessional writer by revealing the fundamental flaws in the biographical material on which such readings are based. The material I will focus on will include conventional biographies, Plath's own letters and journals, fictional and cinematic treatments of Plath's life, and recent comments by Plath's daughter, Frieda Hughes, about her mother's life and work. My position is not that Plath never wrote about herself, but that we can seldom know when she did, because so little of her life and thoughts, like anyone's, can be reliably documented. Moreover, to apply biographical material – whether it is trustworthy or not – to Plath's writing can result in a distorted view of what is in that writing, or even a failure to see what its other interests are.

It is not surprising that non-specialist readers assume that Plath uses her writing to talk about the events of her own life. Not many novelists or poets have their own photographic images placed on their front dust jackets, but most editions of *The Bell Jar* and *The Collected Poems* put Plath's picture on their covers. Such a practice suggests, before the book is even opened, that the contents are not fiction or poetry, but memoir or autobiography: the authoritative tale of Sylvia Plath by Sylvia Plath.[1] What may appear more surprising is that the premise of Plath's confessionality is so prevalent among literary critics and biographers, a constituency from whom we might expect more sophistication as readers.

The crudest of these critiques have discussed Plath's life and work as if they were exactly the same thing. Janice Markey tells us, 'Some of her poems ... were merely based on real events' (1993: 8). Plath's life (or more precisely, her death) is extrapolated from her work. Elisabeth Bronfen writes, 'Sylvia Plath's drive towards death was not only enmeshed with the radical change in poetic voice exhibited in the last poems', but also 'in her autobiographical novel *The Bell Jar* (1998: 10). Other critics, in an odd, methodologically unsound form of amateur psychology, have assumed that Plath's writing can be used as a reliable source for diagnosing her mental condition. In this light, David Holbrook reads her 1962 poem 'Elm' as evidence that Plath was 'schizoid', and as proof of her 'anguish' and 'deep lack of satisfaction' (1976: 121). Others see Plath's writing as a place where she revenges herself against those who have crossed her. Plath's 1962 poem 'Fever 103°' has been read by Michael Kirkham as her 'retaliation against her husband for his infidelity' (1988: 290).

Critics can slip, almost with no awareness that they are doing it, into discussing Plath's narrators as if they were Plath herself. Jacqueline Rose writes, 'As Plath puts it in "Blackberrying" ... "they must love me"' (1991: 133). Rosemarie Rowley concludes that 'Plath writes of *her* betrayal by the woman figure' (1998: 94, my emphasis) in the 1958 story 'Johnny Panic and the Bible of Dreams'. Others have been more self-conscious in their claim that Plath is writing about herself. Anne Stevenson's reading of 'Lady Lazarus' is typical. She sees it as one of three poems whose central personae are 'merciless self-projections of Sylvia', while in the last line the 'Sylvia figure' is 'very dangerous indeed' (1989: 269, 270).

Yet not all critics use such blunt instruments to equate Plath with her poetic voices and fictional characters. While arguing for a relationship between Plath's life and work, Susan R. Van Dyne is unusual in that she at least acknowledges the complexity of the mediation between Plath's lived existence and writing. 'Plath's habits of self-representation suggest she regarded her life as if it were a text that she could invent and rewrite' (1993: 1). Van Dyne's stance is that there is no one stable, truthful version of 'life', but different versions that are fictionalised and revised. Similarly, Linda Wagner-Martin talks about the 'various disguised personas' [*sic*] (1999: 54) Plath wrote in, rather than assuming that there is one Plath whose work can be read as straightforward autobiography (if there is such a thing). In an early essay on Plath, Margaret Dickie Uroff pointed out 'the techniques of caricature, hyperbole, and parody that serve both to distance the speaker from the poet and at the same time to project onto the speaker a subversive variety of the poet's own strategies' (1977).

David Yezzi observes that no good poem can be made entirely of personal confession: 'for the best poets of the late Fifties and early Sixties ... a poem could not subsist on biography alone – it still can't' (1998). Plath's poems certainly do not 'subsist on biography alone'. What is more, it is difficult to identify those moments that are biographical. Yezzi provides a useful working definition of what most critics mean when they use the term confessional poetry:

> What distinguishes confessional poetry's management of autobiography ... is the rawness of its address and the incorporation of guilty personal detail for emotional effect ... The 'I' of the poem is meant as a direct

representation of the flesh-and-blood poet ... What makes a poem confessional is not only its subject matter – e.g., family, sex, alcoholism,
madness – or the emphasis on self, but also the directness with which
such things are handled. Unflinching and generally extreme in their
diction and address ... what sets them apart from other poems that
incorporate details from life, is their sense of worn-on-the-sleeve self-
revelation and their artful simulation of sincerity. By relying on facts,
on 'real' situations and relationships, for a poem's emotional authenticity, the poet makes an artifice of honesty.

(1998)

What Yezzi describes here is a style – 'rawness' and 'honesty' – that can be
deliberately, even cynically, assumed.

Moreover, how do we trust 'facts'? How do we know what 'guilty personal material' really belongs to the writer? This is a problem whether our
knowledge of that material comes from a biographer and is therefore once or
twice, or three or more, times removed from the writer's direct experience,
or the writer herself, who may be lying or misremembering or using a
journal or letter to play with future writing material. Who provides the
'details from life' of a supposedly confessional writer that we then base our
reading of their poems upon? How do we know what 'situations' were
'"real"'? How can we ever hope to distinguish the 'extreme' 'diction and
address' that is prompted by lived events from a vividly imagined drama
that is the result of an expertly assumed style? In Plath's case, critics have on
occasion been so blinded by biography and the assumption that any narrator
at the height of emotional extremity must be Plath herself that they haven't
noticed she sometimes creates speakers and characters who don't share her
sex, or whose sexes are at least uncertain.[2]

Lucretia Stewart writes, 'now that we live in an increasingly confessional
age there are perhaps fewer secrets and lies. There are, however, surely more
half-truths and many more opportunities to present things as you want to
rather than as they actually are or were' (1999). Those readers who assume
they can 'know' Plath through her fiction or poetry often base this assumption on the evidence of biographical material. So and so says in their biography that Plath did or thought this, therefore it must be clear that such and
such a poem or story replicates that incident or thought. I often meet this
response from students, but such a way of reading is seriously flawed.
Stewart's assertion of 'half-truths' and the desire to present things 'as you
want' rather than 'as they actually are or were' is at the root of the problem.

Janet Malcolm, in one of the best books written on Plath and on biography as a genre, observes how hard it is for biographers to get their material:
'Some of the secrets are difficult to bring away, and some, jealously guarded
by relatives, are even impossible' (1994: 10). Malcolm's argument is that
readers trust biographers to tell them the 'truth' about how it was, but biographers have their own agendas, seldom have access to dependable

evidence, and are not always objective about how they present that evidence – that is, when literary estates even allow them to do so. First-hand witnesses to the same event often give contradictory information about what they saw and heard. We shall see that even the evidence which is assumed to be the most reliable, such as Plath's own journals or letters, can mislead us.

Pick any instance from Plath's life, trace what each of her numerous biographers says about that instance, and you will find quite differing accounts. I want to examine the contradictory accounts of Plath and her husband Ted Hughes's encounter with a bear while camping in Yellowstone Park during the summer of 1959.[3] The incident is worth pausing over, because most critics and biographers agree that it led directly to Plath's 1959 short story, 'The Fifty-Ninth Bear' (1979: 94–105). First I will set out the different accounts. I will then go on to examine the instances in them that Janet Malcolm describes as 'the sound of the crack opening in the wall of the biographer's self-assurance' (1994: 9).

This is what Anne Stevenson has to say about the bear encounter:

> They were woken by a shuffling noise outside their tent. They peered out to see a bear rip out the window ... of the car, lift out everything edible, and eat it. Outraged but not particularly alarmed – they were used to seeing tourists feed the bears – they watched for some hours. The first thing next morning, however, a terrified Sylvia dashed back from the washroom ... a man who'd tried to shoo a bear away from his stores had been killed in one blow that very night. 'We've got to get out of here!' cried Sylvia. 'The bears are killing people!' She was so upset that they left that morning.
>
> (1989: 160)

Stevenson does not tell us in her sources and notes on what she bases this account of the bear incident. Paul Alexander's version of the plundering bear goes like this:

> Unable to do anything, Sylvia and Ted glared at the animal from their tent. Finally, they tried – unsuccessfully – to fall back to sleep ... During the day, they reported the attack to other campers, prompting one to tell them about a woman in a nearby camp who had been mauled to death by a bear. That night, Sylvia and Ted covered both their car-window frames and their tent with kerosene and red-pepper flakes, the two substances known to ward off bears.
>
> (1991: 234–5)

Alexander, like Stevenson, does not tell us in his notes what sources he used for this material.

Plath's own long account of their skirmish with the bear in Yellowstone, in a letter to her mother written on 29 July 1959, is much more vivid ('the bear bowled a tin past our tent') and even humorous ('We lay there ... wondering if the bear would eat us, since it found our crackers so interesting') than anything her biographers can produce (1976: 349). Plath goes on to say:

> I mentioned the incident to a woman up early in the lavatory ... she had just moved from ... another camp, where a woman had been killed by a bear ... That woman, hearing the bear at her food at night, had gone out with a flashlight to shoo it away, and it turned on her and downed her with one vicious cuff ... Well, this story put proper concern into us, too. By twilight we had the car kerosened, flung red pepper everywhere, sprayed Fly-Ded all about, drank Ovaltine and took a tranquilizer each.
>
> (1976: 350)

Though first-hand, Plath's account of the incident is not necessarily accurate. Plath may be dramatising the events in a writerly way, perhaps for later use. Often, she wrote her letters over carbon paper, to keep copies for future reference, and future writing, and she may have done so in this case. She knew her mother kept all of her letters, and that she could always send for them or read them over if she wanted to use their contents for a poem or story or novel at a later date. In a postcard or personal letter of any type we can exaggerate or omit or alter facts or even not remember events perfectly. In a discussion of autobiography, Brian McHale warns that the 'appearance of self-exposure is caught up in an ontological game, and we may well wonder whether what we have glimpsed is the "real"' (1987: 207). It is with this warning in mind that I state that Plath's account is nonetheless the least mediated and temporally the closest to the event that we have.

The bear encounter is not one of the most controversial of events from Plath's life. It is not on a par with, for instance, the infamous argument Plath had with Hughes's sister Olwyn while in Yorkshire in 1960,[4] or the visit Assia Wevill and her husband made to Plath and Hughes in Devon on the 18th and 19th of May, 1962. It is worth digressing from Yellowstone for a moment to look carefully at one of these notorious incidents and to compare different accounts, in which Hughes and Plath are alternately cast as villain and saint. Here is Paul Alexander, who gives us no sources for his account of the Wevills' visit. He depicts Assia as a marriage-wrecking seductress against whom few women would stand a chance:

> Assia ... had the reputation of having affairs, especially with poets ... Strong-willed and determined, Assia – apparently – made the first move with Ted ... Creeping up behind him, she lifted her nightgown to her chin, released it to flutter down over his face and torso, and trapped him inside the nightgown with her.
>
> (1991: 276–7)

Contrast this with Stevenson, where Plath is blamed for the weekend going wrong, as well as for her husband's subsequent infidelity:

> Assia confided to Suzette Macedo that Sylvia had picked up 'a current of attraction' between Assia and Ted and had reacted badly. Suzette is sure there was nothing of a more romantic nature that weekend ... Assia might well have told her if there had been. Assia ... doubted whether the attraction between Ted and herself would ever have developed into an affair, as it later did, had Sylvia behaved differently.
>
> (1989: 243–4)

Note Stevenson's 'might well have told her', as if she is uncertain of the evidence she is presenting, and doesn't want to be too definite about its status, or her version of the story. Alexander's bracketed use of the word 'apparently' works in a similar way. Stevenson's sources and notes tell us that her account of the weekend is based on interviews with Assia's husband David Wevill, Assia's friend Suzette Macedo and Ted's sister Olwyn.

Linda Wagner-Martin tells us that to thank Sylvia for the weekend, Assia sent her 'a piece of needlepoint, the rose at its center already finished. Sylvia carefully worked the rest of the piece, until her own intuition about the nature of Assia and Ted's relationship made such activity impossible' (1987: 206). Wagner-Martin also tells us that 'The day after they left, Sylvia wrote two angry, revealing poems, "The Rabbit Catcher" and "Event"' (1987: 205). Stevenson also sees these two poems as a direct response to the Wevills' visit: 'For the first time ... Sylvia was using her own husband and offspring for material in a confessional way' (1989: 244). Both poems are certainly about the strains and difficulty of relationships. Yet biographical readings, which see the poems as a direct response to Plath's sense of threat by Assia, are distorted by what they think they 'know' of the life, and miss one of the most important points about 'The Rabbit Catcher' and 'Event'. In neither poem does the female speaker see herself as a lone victim who is tormented by a man. Rather, both poems look at the shared responsibility of the man and woman for the chasms that develop as the result of constant intimacy, and the price that both of them pay.

The female speaker of 'The Rabbit Catcher' uses the first person singular in the poem's first four stanzas. In the fifth stanza, she mentions a man for the first time, and conveys her sense of her separateness from him by referring to him in the third person singular. In the sixth and last stanza the speaker suddenly adopts the first person plural ('And we, too, had a relationship – / Tight wires between us'), which could encompass the speaker and the rabbits, or, as is more likely the case, the speaker and the man. If it is the latter, then the poem's last line ('The constriction killing me also') makes it clear that the man is being stifled as well as the woman. In fact, syntactically, his slow death is made the central point of the stanza, and hers, conveyed through the poem's last word, 'also', is expressed secondarily to his (Plath 1981: 193). 'Event' ends, 'Who has dismembered us? / The dark is melting. We touch like cripples'; the couple reconnect when 'The moonlight, that chalk cliff / In whose rift we lie / back to back' dissipates. 'Event' captures one of those nights where it seems impossible to touch in bed, but the breach begins to be mended the next morning, though not perfectly, still with the wounds and awkwardness and damage conveyed by the word 'cripples' (Plath 1981: 194). Both poems demonstrate sympathy for the plight of the man as well as the woman. It is debatable, even unknowable, whether Plath was already suspicious of Assia by the time the Wevills left Devon, and when, two days later, Plath sat down to write these poems.

Diane Middlebrook's biography of Hughes, *Her Husband*, recognises the complexity of any relationship these poems might have to biographical details: 'These were not poems about Hughes's infidelity, which Plath had apparently not yet detected' (2003: 167). Unlike most biographers, Middlebrook provides a nuanced, balanced and, when necessary, tentative, picture of what the weekend with the Wevills might have been like. She draws on numerous sources that are carefully referenced, whose contradictions are acknowledged, and which are treated with circumspection ('If these events actually occurred in the manner Hughes describes them' is a typically cautious phrase (166)). To read these poems as mere confessional responses to the weekend is to avoid the more important story they are telling: a story that Plath makes bigger than herself, and which contradicts any confessional narrative of the woman as a lone victim. If the marriage hadn't gone wrong and ended, biographers wouldn't present the Wevills' visit as they primarily do, with a distorting hindsight, and then squeeze 'The Rabbit Catcher' and 'Event' into a mould they do not fit: of a wife decrying her adulterous husband.

While the fifty-ninth bear incident doesn't excite the lurid interest of the possible moment where the Plath/Hughes marriage became doomed, there are nonetheless telling differences between the accounts of Plath and Hughes's experience in the national park. The biographers cannot agree on the sex of the person the bear killed. Stevenson has the bear kill 'a man ... in one blow' (1989: 160). For Alexander it is 'a woman' who is 'mauled to death' (1991: 234). Plath's own epistolary account – though not necessarily accurate – would appear to confirm Alexander's version of the victim's sex. Nor do the accounts agree on when the bear's fatal attack actually occurred. For Stevenson, it was 'that very night' (160). Alexander, presumably taking his cue from Plath's letter, is not so specific. He implies the fatality happened recently, but does not actually say when.

Stevenson's version is noteworthy for several reasons, not least of which is the anti-Plath bias that permeates her whole book and has been much remarked upon.[5] One of the more extraordinary things about it is the fact that she gives Plath the sort of made-up dialogue we would normally expect to find in a work of fiction but not in a biography. Punctuated by too many adjectives, overwrought verbs and exclamation marks, it is crude, unconvincing dialogue, as is so often the case with writers who attempt to make characters out of Plath and Hughes: 'We've got to get out of here!' cried Sylvia. 'The bears are killing people!' This depicts an hysterical Plath, and comes after the 'terrified Sylvia dashed back from the washroom' (1989: 160).

Plath's behaviour is made to seem all the more absurd, coming as it does after the information that Plath and Hughes weren't alarmed, were used to bears, and had watched this one for some hours in the night. From the moment Stevenson actively dramatises her, Plath is made to act alone, in a third person singular that wrecks the third person plural that until then had encompassed herself and Hughes. We are told, 'She was so upset that they left that morning' (1989: 160). Plath, Stevenson's narrative implicitly suggests, is skittish and changeable. Yet, assuming that Stevenson did not personally witness Plath and Hughes's journey across America during the summer of 1959, it is difficult to know why she uses biography – with its pretence of impartial research and authority and factual truth – to put words in Plath's mouth. Arguably, Stevenson does this because in the case of Sylvia Plath, the boundaries between biography and fiction are increasingly unclear.

Stevenson and Alexander differ about what happened once the bear had left and Plath and Hughes were able to leave their tent. Stevenson has Plath spoiling the trip single-handedly as the couple are forced to give in to her out-of-control emotions and to leave the park (1989: 160). Alexander, seemingly staying close to Plath's own epistolary account in this instance, has them remaining in Yellowstone the following night, when they sprinkle their tent with kerosene and red pepper. Stevenson has Plath visiting the washroom on her own, discovering that a bear had actually killed someone in the night, and bringing the information back to her husband. Alexander has Plath and Hughes reporting the news of their bear encounter to the other campers together, and learning together that there was a fatal bear attack. In this case, Stevenson's version is closer to the story Plath tells her mother in the letter, yet it is written, again, to establish the reader's view of an overdramatic Plath who must take all responsibility for reacting inappropriately. Alexander depicts the couple acting and reacting together, with no hint of estrangement. What is interesting about this is that although Stevenson's account might in this instance be closer to the primary source – Plath's letter and its revelation that she brought back the news of the real killing – it is further from the source than Alexander's in terms of Plath's portrayal of herself and Hughes responding to the incident together. Recall Plath's first person plural account: '*we* had the car kerosened ... and took a tranquilizer each ... *We* slept' (1976: 350, my emphases).

One of the most extraordinary things about these different accounts is that, even when there seems to be an obvious need to do so, the biographers do not allow their research to go beyond Plath and Hughes. When there is an external point that seems important, they do not allow it to disrupt the line of argument in which they are engaged. Neither biographer bothered to discover that there was no human fatality from any bear in Yellowstone Park in 1959. 'Five known bear-caused human fatalities and 1 possible fatality have occurred' in Yellowstone plus one 'in the Gallatin National Forest outside of the park' between 1907 and 1986: in 1907 (of questionable validity), 1916, 1942, 1972, 1983 (in Gallatin), 1984 and 1986. Only one of these fatalities even occurred in Plath's lifetime, when she was ten years old and long before she travelled to the national park with Hughes (Gunther 2003).

It seems plausible that the Yellowstone campers were prone to passing along these legends, and enjoyed scaring themselves and each other. It is possible that Plath genuinely believed that someone died the night the bear rummaged through their car. It is also possible that Plath knew no one had actually died, and made the fatality up in order to show her mother what an exciting time she and Hughes were having, just as she made up the husband's death in 'The Fifty-Ninth Bear'. The fact that she doesn't state when the fatal attack actually occurred might suggest that Plath realised the death was a sort of wilderness legend based on incidents that had happened, but only very infrequently. Plath does actually use the word 'story' in her letter to her mother: 'this story put proper concern into us' (1976: 350). Whether she does so to signal that the bear fatality might not have really taken place and might be an invented incident, or to mean a true account of something that actually happened, we will never know.

Whatever the case, biographers are united in their assumption that 'The Fifty-Ninth Bear' is a confessional story based on real events. Lucas Myers writes, 'I was surprised she made a story of the killing of a husband for her husband and their friends to see' (cited in Stevenson 1989: 317–18). Stevenson believes 'The Fifty-Ninth Bear' 'seemed to reveal' Plath's 'ill will against her husband', whose 'family and friends were appalled when it appeared' (161). Hayman calls 'The Fifty-Ninth Bear' the 'resultant story' from the bear encounter (1991: 137). Alexander tells us that 'Plath would use this episode as the basis for the short story' (1991: 235).

Yet if biographers dealing with this incident cannot check the most basic of facts; if they cannot agree on the concrete details of what actually happened; if they place differing emphases on Plath's behaviour and response to the event, then how can they know the extent to which Plath's short story is based on the real occurrence, or identify which aspects and emotions actually made their way into the fiction? Of course Plath observed bears in Yellowstone, and their behaviour around food and tents at night. Of course she gave a short story this setting. But isn't that the most we can say about the biographical elements of the story? More importantly, blinkered by our knowledge of Plath and Hughes's visit to Yellowstone, and the game they played with bears, we are in danger of missing the other things that are happening in 'The Fifty-Ninth Bear'. It is easy to overlook the fact that the story is a complicated exploration of sexual politics and the commercialisation of nature that turns wilderness into theme parks.[6]

It is not merely biographical accounts of Plath's life that are necessarily unreliable. It can be dangerous to view even Plath's own epistolary and journalistic words as 'true confessions', as definitive keys to her poetic or fictional writing. To do so can cause us to misread that writing, or blind us to the other things that are happening in it. We can follow this through if we begin with an excerpt from an unpublished letter Plath wrote to her mother in late November 1962, in which Plath accuses various women in Hughes's circle – friends and family – of being 'barren, either because of abortions or choice. This is the "smart" way with them, utter devotion to self. I despise this sort of life' (Plath 1962a). One week later, on 1 December 1962, Plath wrote 'Childless Woman'.

In this poem, the speaker's experience is far from Plath's own at the time of writing, when Plath was the mother of two children (though she suffered a miscarriage in early 1961 (Plath 1976: 408) and worried about her fertility in the months before she became pregnant with her daughter Frieda (Plath 2000: 500–1)). Despite the experiential distance between poet and narrator, biography has still shaped the expectations of readers. Anne Stevenson believes that 'Childless Woman' 'speaks scornfully of the barren woman's life-denying narcissism' (1989: 288). Ronald Hayman names it as part of the 'vindictive poetry [Plath] wrote ... to cheer herself up by commenting on her rival's sterility' (1991: 196). Certainly the preoccupation with childlessness that Plath expressed in her letter to her mother makes its way into the poem, but without the rancour that Stevenson and Hayman, guided perhaps by what they think they know of Plath's own life at the time, see there. And the rancour is all that these two see, as the 'real life' anger in the letter appears to blind them to what is actually happening in the poem – the most unfortunate effect of the assumption that a writer is confessional.

'Childless Woman' is measured and careful and cool. The poem builds up a conceit of the female body as a landscape. Plath develops a detailed analogy of the speaker's reproductive organs as parts of this landscape, and even offers medical reasons for the woman's infertility and consequent childlessness. The ovum or egg is a 'moon' which leaves the ovary or 'tree' with 'nowhere to go'. This could be because the fallopian tubes are kinked and twisted; the tubes are 'roads bunched to a knot', so the egg drops away, lost, with no route to any sperm. The woman has assimilated the cruel notion that to be childless is a sort of death; she envisions her landscape/body as 'a hand with no lines', believing she has no story to tell, no lifeline, no future.

Somewhere between writing to her mother and writing 'Childless Woman', Plath's thoughts move from the personal rage of the moment to a carefully considered meditation on what it might mean to be childless. The 'Childless Woman' who is Plath's speaker is not a monster. The reader is invited not to scorn her or hate her, but to pity her, to share her vantage point and, through it, to understand the pain of childlessness. The poem reflects a progression in Plath's thought not just in the short space of time between her letter to her mother and 'Childless Woman', but in the space of the nearly two years that passed since Plath wrote an earlier poem, 'Barren Woman', on 21 February 1961. To describe a woman as 'barren' is to use a cruel word, one that suggests she is defective and cannot fulfil her 'natural' womanliness. To describe her as 'childless' is to focus on what she lacks, on what she wants but cannot have.

The speaker of 'Childless Woman' can speak 'nothing but blood' and commands, 'Taste it, dark red!' (Plath 1981: 259). Tim Kendall cites this command in a list of examples he gives where Plath 'exploit[s] associations between Christ and eating', suggesting that the speaker of 'Childless Woman' makes an 'offer' of her 'menstrual blood' as a sort of religious sacrament (2001: 119, 120). Kendall's larger argument is interesting, but the single line he quotes from 'Childless Woman', accompanied by little explanation, is underdeveloped. The speaker of the poem wants to be pregnant, and month after month does not became so. In the poem, which is a dramatic monologue in which she seems mostly to be addressing herself (though she may be speaking to her husband or a friend and/or the reader) she attests to the sadness, sometimes even despair, she feels when her period comes, the way that her childlessness seems to take up all the space of her life and thoughts, and her body seems to be all there is. The blood means no baby. In a moment of highly compressed drama, when she says, 'Taste it, dark red!', she may be engaging in a kind of mock Eucharist, where the blood is like wine, but what is surely the case is that she is lamenting the blood, chiding herself for its presence. Momentarily unbalanced by her distress at its appearance, perhaps she touches herself and sees the blood on her fingers or underwear, then exhibits the evidence of her despair and renewed failure.

The dramatic gestures of the woman's body continue to the poem's end, when she tells us she will never breastfeed; her body will not give life, and therefore will never support life. '[T]his hill and this', her two breasts, will only entertain 'the mouths of corpses' (Plath 1981: 259). Here, the earlier reference to tasting blood becomes an ironic alternative to tasting milk. It is the only fluid associated with her reproductive cycle that her body can produce. Again, as with the blood, she seems to be motioning towards her own body, pointing to her breasts, first one, then the other, or touching them. No babies will suck there. Her body's inability to produce a child is a sort of death. The poem has moved far beyond the accusation of 'utter devotion to self' spiked by Plath's momentary rage at the 'barren' women in Hughes's circle (Plath 1962a), to a sympathetic look at the childless woman who is made to feel that she has no choice, and that with no child, all there can ever be is 'myself' (Plath 1981: 259).

Biographies have long been a staple in the world of Plath studies, and have played a central role in establishing the idea that Plath is a confessional writer. Janet Malcolm rightly notes that readers possess for biographies 'amazing tolerance' which they 'would extend to no novel written half as badly' (1994: 9). In recent years, biographies have been joined by novelistic and cinematic attempts to fictionalise Plath's life. As we saw in Stevenson's attempt to write dialogue for Plath as if she were a character in a novel, the distinction between biography and fiction is increasingly being eroded. As much as fiction, biographies present versions of Sylvia Plath who might be more accurately described as fictional characters than a real person. Similarly, novels and films about Plath might be more precisely called biographical novels and films. This blurring of genres might, if the device is foregrounded, result in a less naïve readership, but the cumulative effect of biographies, novels and films about Plath's life is nonetheless one in which readers and viewers don't always remember *where* they saw or read or heard what Plath is alleged to have thought or said. In many cases, by the time they read her poems or stories or her novel, the biographical interpretation has solidified into an absolute truth through which that text can be understood.

Sandra Gilbert addresses the question of just what these novels about real people actually are, and what readers should do with them. She asks, 'Should Emma Tennant's *Sylvia and Ted* and Kate Moses' *Wintering: A Novel of Sylvia Plath* be scrutinized for their biographical accuracy, or at any rate their psychological insight? Should they be read as themselves "readings" of Plath's *oeuvre*?' (2003). Moses's subtitle, '*A Novel of Sylvia Plath*', adds to the confusion of just what kind of a book she is offering, and whether its status is closer to that of a biography or a novel. Books such as Moses's and Tennant's are a type of historical fiction, in that they are set in the past and feature real historical events and people. Brian McHale argues that in postmodernist revisionist historical fiction 'history and fiction exchange places, history becoming fictional and fiction becoming "true" history – and the real world seems to get lost in the shuffle' (1987: 96). The same can be said of the novelistic accounts of Plath's life, and the 'biopic' *Sylvia*, though it is only in rare instances that the novels and film about Plath *intentionally* and *self-consciously* raise the question that postmodernist revisionists foreground as central: 'real, compared to what?' (McHale 1987: 96). Because of this generic confusion, I want to look further at some of these attempts to represent Plath as a character.

The author's note that Emma Tennant provides in *The Ballad of Sylvia and Ted*, possibly written to ward off any legal challenges, is an inversion of the customary disclaimer that swears and affirms that the work is purely fictitious, and any resemblance to real people or events is entirely coincidental. McHale describes the standard form of the disclaimer as a statement that presumes that art can be unproblematically mimetic. Such disclaimers are 'an obvious target for postmodernist parody' (1987: 54). The disclaimers we find in fictionalised versions of Plath's life are deviations from this standard form; their strange ambiguity inadvertently calls into question the truth and accuracy of narrative representation. They swear and affirm that their contents are both true and false.

Tennant's disclaimer is the only occasion in *The Ballad of Sylvia and Ted* where there is any self-conscious foregrounding of the book's uncertain status or any awareness 'that history itself may be a form of fiction' (McHale 1987: 96). Hers reads: 'Events described in the book are based on fact, and in the case of the story of Assia Wevill, Sylvia's rival, who also committed suicide, many of the facts were previously concealed or unknown. *The Ballad of Sylvia and Ted* is, nevertheless, a work of the imagination' (Tennant 2001: 7). Fact or fiction? Biography or novel? Tennant wants it both ways. The book is biographical ('based on fact'). The book is fictional ('nevertheless, a work of imagination'). Sandwiched between these two contradictory claims is the promise of more titillating revelation – the sort of promise biographies make to sell themselves: secrets will be uncovered, Assia's 'previously concealed or unknown' story will be revealed. Yet much of Tennant's material about Assia is tired and speculative, and has been the stuff of biography for some time.[7]

A central question we might ask of a novel about real people – or what we might even call a biographical novel – is one that should be asked of any novel: what is its quality and coherence as a serious work of art? If, momentarily at least, we suspend any questions about whether the story that *The Ballad of Sylvia and Ted* tells is 'accurate', we can judge the book instead in terms of its aesthetic and moral qualities. If we treat *The Ballad of Sylvia and Ted* in this way, it can only be described as bad (the narrative is unclear and confusing, full of messily choreographed scenes), portentous ('the oracle doesn't speak; the forest where she lives provides the answers' (112)), overwritten ('He sees the hare he ran over and killed, as its blood turns to flowers and the bouquet blossoms in his lover's hand' (146)) and littered with tabloid sensationalism ('Ted knows ... that this baby will kill Sylvia' (146)). An unsigned reviewer succinctly described the problem with the novel's dialogue by titling his or her review 'Real Poets Don't Gush'. *The Ballad of Sylvia and Ted* dwells on histrionic banalities of human behaviour with little depth.

If we open up these questions about the quality of Tennant's novel to include criteria about its representation of real events and people, as her disclaimer invites us to do, the judgements are even more damning. Tennant's book has Plath visit Hughes and Assia the night before she kills herself, and, during that visit, learn that Assia is pregnant. Here, as throughout the book, the scene is garbled, the writing melodramatic and clichéd. At the same time, the scene is based on conjecture and hearsay: 'Her composure melts in the heat of her humiliation. For surely, as all three stand there silent ... the knowledge must come to her of Assia's condition, her shame and guilt and joy' (149). In the end, it is difficult to say whether *The Ballad of Sylvia and Ted* is a poor novel, a bad biography, or both: it fails as fiction; it fails as information.

Like *The Ballad of Sylvia and Ted*, Kate Moses's 2003 novel, *Wintering*, begins with a disclaimer.[8] Like Tennant's disclaimer, Moses's renders the genre of her book uncertain, and intentionally obfuscates any distinctions the reader could make between what is made up and what might be true (unlike Tennant's book, Moses's does not try to seduce its readers with promises of tabloid revelations).[9] The disclaimer is one of the few things the two writers have in common. While the interests of *The Ballad of Sylvia and Ted* are trivial, the same cannot be said of *Wintering*. Unlike most of the attempts to fictionalise Plath, Moses's novel through its very structure is attentive to the poetry and emphasises its importance.

Moses frames the narrative of Plath's last winter through chapters that take their titles from the poems of Plath's *Ariel*, arranged in the sequence Plath intended for them. Moses's knowledge of Plath's work and life is original and scholarly, especially her insight into the place food and baking held in Plath's life,[10] and the use she makes of Plath's daily calendars, which are full of the details of Plath's shopping and cooking.[11] Moses deploys impressive research skills and provides a scrupulous account of her sources at the end of her book. While Tennant's disclaimer is the only place in her book where she appears, however crudely, to recognise some of the problems of representation, the structure of Moses's novel – compounded by her long list of critical, theoretical and biographical reading – emphasises her awareness of the mimetic challenges her book presents. While classic historical fiction 'camouflag[es] the seam between historical reality and fiction', *Wintering* 'seeks to foreground this seam' (McHale 1987: 90) through the juxtaposition of Plath's poetry titles with Moses's fiction and through the hefty scholarly apparatus Moses provides. This scholarship further blurs the boundaries between biography and novel, and contributes to the difficulty of being able to say just what sort of book *Wintering* is.

John Brownlow, who wrote the screenplay for the 2003 film *Sylvia*, remarks that when Plath and Hughes 'were doing the washing up, they didn't speak in verse'. Of course he is right and, conscious of the difficulty of 'put[ting] words into the mouths of two literary giants' (Brownlow 2003: 130), took his own advice to 'cut dialogue' 'wherever possible' in his script (vii). The challenge, though, for anybody who turns Plath and Hughes into characters, is to balance everyday banality with those moments when they would have had interesting conversations, and it is the latter that few writers manage to accomplish. Partly this is because to do so is so difficult. Partly it is because it is the soap opera story of the romance and breakdown that interests readers, as it did Brownlow, for whom 'the story was blindingly clear … It was a love story between two giants … But it was a marriage only one of them could survive' (vi). Here, with a spurious sense of inevitability, and sounding as if he is rehearsing what he wants the film's poster to say, Brownlow reduces the beginning of Plath's marriage to a tabloid headline.

Alison Owen, *Sylvia*'s producer, says, 'You do have a duty to get things as right as possible … I don't think you should be obsessive about detail, but I do think you need to remain sensitive to it' (cited in Brownlow 2003: 133–4). Certainly, in terms of the few facts that are absolutely knowable and verifiable, there are inaccuracies in *Sylvia*. For instance, the film has Hughes winning the prize for *The Hawk in the Rain* before his wedding to Plath rather than after, and the couple's arrival in America is misdated.[12] In her week-by-week calendar for 1962, Plath made a detailed note of what she planned to serve on Friday 18th May to her weekend guests: 'gingerbread' and 'beef stew' to the Wevills, possibly with some of the 'corn chowder' she noted the previous day (Plath 1962b). Should it be classed as an inaccuracy that the Plath character in the film is shown serving the Wevills soup and a pastry-topped meat pie instead, when information exists about what she planned to do? The answer is probably not. Nobody's sense of Plath and Hughes is going to be drastically distorted by the errors I have just cited; nor is their reading of the work. Yet if the biographer or film maker or novelist cannot get the small number of things that are verifiable right, readers and viewers must be careful not to build any reading of Plath's work as confessional on already shaky biographical foundations.

There is a serious level of misrepresentation that concerns me, though. One example of this occurs in the film *Sylvia* when Plath is shown expertly testing the temperature of a bottle of formula on her forearm. We can't be certain that this did not occasionally happen. Plath mentions in a letter that she organised a ' "relief bottle" ' for her baby daughter so she could attend a literary dinner at the home of T.S. Eliot (1976: 379, 380). However, to show Plath only feeding her baby in this way elides something that is central to her writing and her sexual politics, where there are frequent references to her pride in breastfeeding and her knowledge of what she was doing: 'she sucked at me … like a little expert and got a few drops of colostrum' (1976: 374). Plath thought breastfeeding was an important subject for poetry. In 'Morning Song', written on 19 February 1961, a breastfeeding mother addresses her baby: 'One cry, and I stumble from bed, cow-heavy and floral / In my Victorian nightgown./ Your mouth opens clean as a cat's' (1981: 157). My point is not that the failure to show the fictional Plath breastfeeding deprives the viewer of biographical information that they can then bring to her poem. The speaker of 'Morning Song' is much more than a mere version of Sylvia Plath, breastfeeding. Rather, my point is that the omission deprives the film's audience of important knowledge about Plath's interest in women's roles as mothers and in the female body.

A consequence of depicting the life as a soap opera – the narrative of a life that never dies, that comes to us in an unending series of instalments, disclosed decades after her death in lurid titles and sensationalist newspaper stories[13] – is the failure to say anything serious or important about the poetry. One way of not being serious about the poetry is to concentrate instead, as the film (in common with some novelistic and journalistic accounts) does, on the marital problems and suicide, but to do this misses what is important about Plath and Hughes's writing. *Sylvia* ends predictably, by perpetuating what is perhaps the most oft-repeated and fallacious link between Plath and her work. Tom Payne titles a 2003 newspaper article about Plath, 'Her Words Prophesy Her Own Suffering', while Philip Hensher writes, 'However good she became – and those late poems are brilliant, no doubt – she worked great damage. They are not poems to live with' (2004). Payne and Hensher typify the idea that Plath's ultimate confession was her death, and in particular that *Ariel*, the finished manuscript she left when she died, prefigured and caused that death. Look in *Ariel*, this most-common of biographical criticisms goes, and you will see the story of her despair, you will see what drove her to the end, and how she plots her route to get there.

Such a way of thinking was established with the first publication of *Ariel* in 1965, two years after Plath's suicide, and has continued ever since. For Robert Lowell, 'These poems are playing Russian roulette with six cartridges in the cylinder'. George Steiner believes that the poems 'take tremendous risks ... She could not return from them'. It strikes Alvarez that, 'In a curious way, the poems read as though they were written posthumously ... Poetry of this order is a murderous art'.[14] Some forty years later, the film *Sylvia* gives us the visual equivalent of such criticism. We are shown the snowy white manuscript of *Ariel*, and when Hughes bends to kiss it, the page blends into the whiteness of Plath's dead face, as if the first caused the second, as if Plath and *Ariel* were the same.

In November 2004 a new edition of Plath's *Ariel* was published, which reinstates Plath's selection and ordering of the poems.[15] Frieda Hughes writes the 'Foreword' to the restored *Ariel*. It is likely that because she is Hughes and Plath's daughter, readers, biographers and critics will turn eagerly to whatever material she provides. This is already the case, if an early review of the restored *Ariel*, written by Peter Steinberg and published on the very active internet website *The Sylvia Plath Forum*, is anything to judge by:

> The introduction by Ms. Hughes is phenomenal. Although she was only two years old when her mother's 'Ariel' voice emerged, Frieda was perhaps one of the only witnesses to their genesis. She also lived through the demise of her parents' marriage, and remembers the 'encouragement' of Aurelia Plath to boot Ted out of the house for his adultery.
>
> There are moments of brilliance throughout the Foreword ... Ms. Hughes discusses the very taboo subject of her father's infidelity. She does so with grace and candor.
>
> (Steinberg 2004)

Already we see the assumption that Frieda Hughes is necessarily authoritative about her mother's life and work. Her foreword is 'phenomenal'. As 'one of the only witnesses' to the writing of *Ariel*, what she has to say is welcomed with no caveats. There is a presumption that what Frieda Hughes 'lived through' and 'remembers' about the end of her parents' marriage, her grandmother Aurelia Plath's role in their separation, and Hughes's infidelity, must be true. It is inevitable that this new Frieda Hughes material will be used as further ammunition for reading Plath as a confessional writer. For this reason, I want to point out the limits of this material, and the inconsistencies of Frieda Hughes's published position with respect to her mother's life and writing.

Frieda Hughes's foreword objects strongly to cinematic and novelistic attempts to represent Plath:

> My mother's poems cannot be crammed into the mouths of actors in any filmic reinvention of her story in the expectation that they can breathe life into her again, any more than literary fictionalisation of my mother's life – as if writing straight fiction would not get the writer enough notice (or any notice at all) – achieves any purpose other than to parody the life she actually lived. Since she died my mother has been dissected, analysed, reinterpreted, reinvented, fictionalised, and in some cases completely fabricated.
>
> (Hughes 2004: 6)

Jacqueline Rose correctly asserts 'the right of every reader of Sylvia Plath to form her or his own view of the meanings and significance of her work' (1991: xi). It is clear from the present essay that there are views I am not in accordance with, but it is only through considering sometimes oppositional views that one can develop one's own. Frieda Hughes has every right to disagree with the ideas of the 'people' who attempt to 'reconstruct' Plath 'through their own interpretations' (Hughes 2002), but such interpretations are what writers open themselves up to when they put their work in the public domain. Interpretation is what writers seek, even if they, and those who know them, are sometimes made uncomfortable by it.

Interpretation depends on access to the writer's work. It is reported that the producers of *Sylvia* were unable to secure permission from the Plath estate to reproduce her poetry in the film (Brooks and Elliott 2003: 7; Alvarez 2004).[16] Ironically, such actions may be counterproductive, because when novelists or film makers cannot quote from the work, they have an even greater tendency to concentrate on the life and neglect the writing. Quotations from the work would, surely, allow the reader or audience to form their own judgements about what the writer is saying, and why the writer's or film's subject is worthy of a life study?

Frieda Hughes's new foreword to *Ariel* seems to read Plath as a confessional writer who hangs her poems on real events. For instance, the foreword tells us that 'Berck-Plage' is 'about the funeral … of a neighbour, Percy Key', while 'the couple so wickedly depicted in ["Lesbos"] lived in Cornwall'. 'Stopped Dead', we are told, 'refer[s] to my father's uncle Walter' (Hughes 2004: 5). Yet Frieda Hughes is critical of others for proceeding from a similar methodology: 'I saw poems such as "Lady Lazarus" and "Daddy" dissected over and over, the moment that my mother wrote them being applied to her whole life … as if they were the sum total of her experience' (6). It is untenable to assert categorically that certain poems are confessional, but dismiss other critics, readers and writers for making the same assertion. We need to take what we can from Frieda Hughes's work on her mother's writing, and the publication of the restored *Ariel*. But we need to treat Frieda Hughes's versions of 'real' events with as much circumspection as any others, and avoid unleashing an entirely new set of fallacious biographical assumptions that can then be brought to Plath's work.

In one sense, my argument has been underpinned by an assumption that readers of biographies or viewers of biopics trust them to provide reliable facts. Possibly, readers are not so naïve, and have a more postmodern sense of biographies as partial. They may read biographies or 'fictionalised' versions of 'the life' for entertainment and the sort of narrative excitement novels offer. If I have been unfair to the majority of Plath readers, it is probably because so many published critics continue to see her work in the crudest of biographical terms. The journalist, critic and novelist Philip Hensher is typical. He writes, 'Plath's story has been told so many times, and it is so horrible a story … The repulsive fact is that she was the first person to tell it, and she told it from beginning to end, culminating in a poem about a dead, "perfected" woman, written very shortly before she committed suicide'. In a drastically reductive and misogynistic assertion he goes on to say that 'like many women writers, she preferred to write about the outside world through the filter of her own emotions' (2004). The problem with the case of Sylvia Plath and biography is that the story of her life is such a force field, a nucleus of power that attracts everything, and prevents her poems and fiction from being read for their more important content.[17]

What are we missing in Plath's work by dwelling on the life? This is the question I have addressed at length in *The Other Sylvia Plath* (2001), but it seems worthwhile to list some of what has been overlooked. Before doing so, it is important to point out that to treat Plath's writing as invariably self-dramatising is to belittle it. The implication of such an exercise is that the ever-confessional Sylvia Plath was too unimaginative to make anything up, or too self-obsessed to consider anything of larger historical or cultural importance. For Hensher, while Hughes was a 'great poet' because he 'was quite simply interested in the outside world', Plath was not (2004). Yet Plath's writing is much more than personal. She uses her poems and fiction to look at a world that extends far beyond her own skin, and invites us to look with her. This is the case with her sustained response to environmental issues. She is preoccupied with the instabilities of language and national identity that result from living in two different countries. Her evaluation of the sexual politics of motherhood and women's reproductive bodies is sustained; as is her interest in the work of other writers, and the presence of other writers' texts within her own. One way forward might be to ask biographical treatments of Sylvia Plath to be more self-consciously postmodern by foregrounding their own relativity, by not allowing the reader to mistake what they offer for the truth. The best biographies – which are quite rare –

do this, as we see in Diane Middlebrook's *Her Husband*, and Janet Malcolm's *The Silent Woman*.

My biggest concern is that narratives of Plath's life draw attention from where it should be: her writing. Yet there is a paradox in this. Plath holds a prominent place in the public domain because people are fascinated by her life. Feminists have taken her up as a cause. Arguments have raged about her marriage to Hughes. She is a celebrity, and even the most scrupulous of Plath scholars can never be entirely free of taking advantage of the notoriety of her story. If Plath did not have the sort of fame that she does, students, and people interested in poetry, would still read her work; she would still occupy a place in the canon, but it would be a quieter place. The question that arises from this, is: should Plath studies be grateful for the way that the 'soap opera' life story generates public interest, or sorry for the way such interest shapes and distorts the interpretation of the work?

For me, the answer is yes and no: yes to the public interest, and no to the way interpretation of her work has been limited and skewed. If the books and films that perpetuated this interest shifted their emphasis away from soap opera and were self-conscious about the limitations of their material, critical interpretation would shift too.

Notes

1 On the use of Plath's image on the covers of her books, see Brain (2001).
2 See Brain (2001), for a discussion of the instability of gender identities in 'The Applicant', 'The Surgeon at 2 a.m.', 'Cut', and 'Leaving Early'.
3 I have looked elsewhere at the different accounts of her attendance at the protest march against the Aldermaston nuclear plant in 1960. See Brain (2001: 12–14). John Sutherland has looked at variant versions of the literary dinner party Plath attended at the home of T.S. Eliot (Sutherland 2004).
4 The contrast between Alexander in *Rough Magic* (1991: 252) and Stevenson in *Bitter Fame* (1989: 203–4) is startling.
5 See for instance, Rose (1991).
6 For a full discussion of sexuality and environmentalism in 'The Fifty-Ninth Bear', see Brain (2001: 97–105).
7 See Alexander (1991); and Hayman (1991), both published ten years before Tennant's novel.
8 Here is Moses's disclaimer: 'Although *Wintering* portrays real people and is inspired by actual events, it is a work of fiction. With some exceptions, the events, broadly defined, and situations portrayed here actually took place, but the author's rendering of those events and their particulars is invented. The characters' thoughts, conversations, and actions are a work of imagination' (2003b: copyright page).
9 The film *Sylvia*'s disclaimer does this too, though it comes at the end of the final credits, when most of the audience have left the cinema: 'While this motion picture is based on a true story certain characters have been changed, some main characters have been composited or invented and a number of incidents fiction-alised'. *Sylvia*, directed by Christine Jeffs (2003).
10 See for instance Moses (2003a).
11 The calendars are held in Smith College's Mortimer Rare Book Room.

12 These errors do not occur in the screenplay. See Brownlow (2003: 43–5).
13 See for instance, Neill (1998) 'The Fire That Still Burns After Sylvia'; Carey (1998) 'Fatal Attraction' and Hensher (2004) 'Ted or Sylvia: Who Was Better?'
14 All comments are reproduced on the inside front cover of the first English edition of *Ariel* (Plath 1965).
15 For full discussion of Plath's original *Ariel* and the effects of the alterations to her selection and ordering see Bundtzen (2001), Van Dyne (1993) and Perloff (1984).
16 Paradoxically, Frieda Hughes herself exercises the right to quote from and appropriate Plath's work as, for instance, in her poem, 'My Mother' (cited in Brooks and Elliott 2003: 7).
17 Recent critics such as Linda K. Bundtzen (2001) and Robin Peel (2002) are fighting this through thorough attention to Plath's manuscripts and her politics.

Bibliography

Alexander, P. (1991) *Rough Magic: A Biography of Sylvia Plath*, New York: Viking.
Alvarez, A. (2004) 'Ted, Sylvia and Me', *Observer* (Review Section), 4 January: 1–2.
Brain, T. (2001) *The Other Sylvia Plath*, Harlow & London: Pearson Education (Longman).
Bronfen, E. (1998) *Sylvia Plath*, Plymouth: Northcote House.
Brooks, R. and Elliott, J. (2003) 'Plath's Daughter Hits at BBC Drama', *Sunday Times*, 2 February: 7.
Brownlow, J. (2003) *Sylvia: The Shooting Script*, New York: Newmarket Press.
Bundtzen, L.K. (2001) *The Other Ariel*, Amherst: University of Massachusetts Press.
Carey, J. (1998) 'Fatal Attraction' (review of *Birthday Letters*), *Sunday Times* (Section 8), 25 January: 1–2.
Curtis, V. (2003) 'Wintering', *Scotland on Sunday*, 16 February. Available online at: http://entertainment.scotsman.com/home/text_only.cfm?id=8208& type=review (accessed 20 November 2004).
Gilbert, S. (2003) 'Dead Poet's Society' (review of *Wintering* and *The Ballad of Sylvia and Ted*), *The Women's Review of Books*, March 2003. Available online at: http://www.wellesley.edu/womensreview/archive/2003/03/highlt.html (accessed 21 November 2004).
Gunther, K. A. (2003) Bear Management Wildlife Biologist. Yell 701. Information Paper No. BMO-1. Yellowstone National Park, March 2003. Yellowstone National Park Official Website. Available online at: http://www.nps.gov/yell/nature/animals/bear/infopaper/info1.html (accessed 18 November 2004).
Hayman, R. (1991) *The Death and Life of Sylvia Plath*, New York: Birch Lane.
Hensher, P. (2004) 'Ted or Sylvia: Who was better?', *Telegraph*, 20 January. Available online at: http://www.telegraph.co.uk/arts/main.jhtml;sessionid=5HQWGEZOAS2GBQFIQMGSM5WAVCBQWJVC?xml=/arts/2004/01/20/boplat20.xml&secureRefresh=true&_requestid=33497 (accessed 4 November 2004).
Holbrook, D. (1976) *Sylvia Plath: Poetry and Existence*, London: Athlone Press.
Hughes, F. (2002) 'Father Dear Father', *Telegraph*, 29 October. Available online at: http://www.telegraph.co.uk/arts/main.jhtml;sessionid=CZ3INB4VU4 FWJQ FIQMGSM5WAVCBQWJVC?xml=/arts/2002/10/29/bohugh29.xml&secureRefresh=true&_requestid=20808 (accessed 14 November 2004).
——— (2004) 'Ariel Takes Flight', *Guardian* (Review Section), 13 November: 4–6.

(This is an edited version of Frieda Hughes's 'Foreword' to Sylvia Plath's *Ariel: The Restored Edition* [2004].)

Kendall, T. (2001) *Sylvia Plath: A Critical Study*, London: Faber and Faber.

Kenner, H. (1989) 'Sincerity Kills', in H. Bloom (ed.) *Sylvia Plath*, New York: Chelsea House Publishers.

Kirkham, M. (1988) 'Sylvia Plath', in L.Wagner-Martin (ed.) *Sylvia Plath: The Critical Heritage*, London: Routledge.

Malcolm, J. (1994) *The Silent Woman: Sylvia Plath and Ted Hughes*, New York: Alfred A. Knopf. First published in *The New Yorker*, 23 and 30 August 1993: 94–159.

Markey, J. (1993) *A Journey Into the Red Eye: The Poetry of Sylvia Plath – A Critique*, London: The Women's Press.

MacNab, G. (2003) 'Private property?', *Independent*, 10 October. Available online at: http://enjoyment.independent.co.uk/film/features/story.jsp?story= 451644 (accessed 6 November 2004).

McHale, B. (1987) *Postmodernist Fiction*, London: Routledge.

Middlebrook, D. (2003) *Her Husband: Hughes and Plath – A Marriage*, London: Little Brown.

Moses, K. (2003a) 'Baking with Sylvia', *Guardian* (Weekend Magazine Section), 15 February: 42–6, 105.

—— (2003b) *Wintering*, London: Sceptre.

Neill, H. (1998) 'The Fire That Still Burns After Sylvia' (review of *Birthday Letters*), *Times Educational Supplement*, 30 January: 12.

Payne, T. (2003) 'Her words prophesy her own suffering', *Telegraph*, 22 January. Available online at: http://www.telegraph.co.uk/arts/main.jhtml?xml =/arts/2003/ 11/01/bfplath01.xml (accessed 4 November 2004).

Peel, R. (2002) *Writing Back: Sylvia Plath and Cold War Politics*, London: Associated University Presses.

Perloff, M. (1984) 'The Two Ariels: The (Re)making of the Sylvia Plath Canon', *American Poetry Review* 13: 10–18.

Plath, S. (1962a) Letter from Sylvia Plath to Aurelia Plath, 22 November. Lilly Library, Indiana University.

—— (1962b) Sylvia Plath Calendar Entry, 18 May. Mortimer Rare Book Room, Smith College Library.

—— (1965) *Ariel*, London: Faber and Faber (First English Edition).

—— (1976) *Letters Home*, ed. A.S. Plath, London: Faber and Faber.

—— (1979) *Johnny Panic and the Bible of Dreams*, London: Faber and Faber.

—— (1981) *The Collected Poems*, ed. T. Hughes, London: Faber and Faber.

—— (2000) *The Journals of Sylvia Plath: 1950–1962*, ed. K.V. Kukil, London: Faber and Faber.

—— (2004) *Ariel: The Restored Edition*, foreword F. Hughes, London: Faber and Faber.

'Real Poets Don't Gush' (2001) Unsigned review of *The Ballad of Sylvia and Ted*, *Daily Telegraph*, 2 June. Available online at: http://www.telegraph. co.uk/arts/ main.jhtml?xml=/arts/2001/06/02/bobal2.xml (accessed 19 November 2004).

Rose, J. (1991) *The Haunting of Sylvia Plath*, London: Virago.

Rowley, R. (1998) 'Electro-Convulsive Treatment in Sylvia Plath's Life and Work', *Thumbscrew* 10: 87–99.

Steinberg, P. (2004) 'They Taste the Spring: Review of *Ariel* (The Restored Edition)', 8 October. Available online at: http://www.sylviaplathforum. com/ reviews/ariel-restored.html (accessed 20 November 2004).

Stevenson, A. (1989) *Bitter Fame: A Life of Sylvia Plath*, London: Viking.

Stewart, L. (1999) 'Verse Confessions', *Guardian*, 25 November. Available online at: http://books.guardian.co.uk/departments/poetry/story/0,6000,   107687,00.html (accessed 5 November 2004).

Sylvia, DVD, directed by Christine Jeffs, copyright Ariel Films and UK Film Council, 2003. Distributed by MGM Home Entertainment (Europe), 2004. Programme content copyright Icon Distribution, 2004.

Sutherland, J. (2004) 'When Stephen Met Sylvia', *Guardian*, 24 April. Available online at: http://books.guardian.co.uk/review/story/0,,1201328,00.html (accessed 4 November 2004).

Tennant, E. (2001) *The Ballad of Sylvia and Ted*, Edinburgh: Mainstream Publishing.

Uroff, M.D. (2004) 'Sylvia Plath and Confessional Poetry: A Reconsideration', *Iowa Review* 8 (1) (1977): 104–15. Reproduced. Available online at: http://www.sylviaplath.de/plath/uroff.html (accessed 7 November 2004).

Van Dyne, S.R. (1993) *Revising Life: Sylvia Plath's Ariel Poems*, Chapel Hill and London: University of North Carolina Press.

Wagner-Martin, L. (1987) *Sylvia Plath: A Biography*, London: Cardinal.

—— (1999) *Sylvia Plath: A Literary Life*, London: Macmillan.

Yezzi, D. (1998) 'Confessional Poetry and the Artifice of Honesty', *The New Criterion* 16 (10). Available online at: http://www.newcriterion.com/archive/16/jun98/confess.html (accessed 6 November 2004).

2   Confessing the body

Plath, Sexton, Berryman, Lowell, Ginsberg and the gendered poetics of the 'real'

Elizabeth Gregory

I do it so it feels real.

> Sylvia Plath, 'Lady Lazurus'

For the rats
have moved in, mostly, and this is for real.

> John Berryman, 'Dream Song #7'

Confessional poetry came to prominence in the 1950s and 1960s in the work of Robert Lowell, Anne Sexton, Sylvia Plath, John Berryman and Allen Ginsberg, and continues a force today in the work of such poets as Sharon Olds and Mark Doty. The mode transforms and comments upon the 'impersonal' poetics of the modernists who immediately preceded the confessionals. In developing their contrastingly 'personal' approach, the 1950s confessional poets utilized the methods of psychoanalysis and psychotherapy, which had only recently gained wide acceptance in the US and with which they all had direct experience. Their work has deeply influenced much poetry since, opening up the possibility of moments of personal 'sharing' in the work of poets in every mode. At the same time it has been looked down upon, for being too 'real' – as an outpouring of unedited data from the world of experience (a view indicated in the frequent linkage of the adjective 'mere' with the noun 'confessionalism'). And it has been disparaged as too feminine. Though the mode first appeared in the work of male poets,[1] it is often associated with its female practitioners, and condemned as trivial and self-indulgent (see Gammel, Travisano and Perkins for a range of readings of this association).[2] The two criticisms are not unrelated. This essay explores the connections between the work's 'reality' claims, its gendering and its depictions of the body – a nexus of concerns that I will argue are linked in a way that clarifies the operation of the mode overall.

   The five poets I discuss here employ the confessional mode variously, but all in ways that challenge dominant ideas about the operation of poetic authority. All challenge the basis of such authority in exclusionary hierarchies that link, and mark as secondary, the categories of the 'feminine', the 'real' and the 'body'. By laying claim to and affirming value in these 'secondary' terms, these poets move toward introducing alternative authority patterns that can admit new speakers talking about new material. All employ reference to their gender presentation in the world outside the poem to authorize their speech within it. These references are not synonymous with direct representation of their sexuality or their biography. But they do refer us to the ways in which gender positioning informs reception of work, while at the same time offering a means of engaging the historical gendering of the poetic family romance. And by pointing to the parallels between poetic representations of gender and those active in the world outside the poem, and to the ways in which the two realms have always interacted, they suggest new ways in which poetry can effect change in the way the world imagines authority.

Though the term confessional poetry has been current since M.L. Rosenthal introduced it in a review of Lowell's *Life Studies* in 1959, its definition and its usefulness have been much debated. Nevertheless the name has stuck, because it seems to capture something important about the poetry. To begin with a brief definition: confessional poetry draws on the poet's autobiography and is usually set in the first person. It makes a claim to forego personae and to represent an account of the poet's own feelings and circumstances, often by reference to names and scenarios linked to the poet. The work dwells on experiences generally prohibited expression by social convention: mental illness, intra-familial conflicts and resentments, childhood traumas, sexual transgressions and intimate feelings about one's body are its frequent concerns. The transgression involved in naming the forbidden gives rise to the term 'confession', which, via its religious, psychoanalytic and legal associations, summons up ideas of sin, mental breakdown and criminality.

The shock value inherent in such links plays an important part in the operation of this poetry, but defenders of the work have objected that the term focuses attention on these elements and obscures the poets' artistry and more subtle effects. Objections have also been made to the term's suggestion of an identity between poet and speaker – its perceived implication that the poet 'confesses' in the poems as s/he might to a priest or doctor. Clearly, though based on elements of the poet's life, such work cannot be restricted to literal retellings of events or 'true' emotions. As recent studies in autobiography confirm, some transformation must occur in the process of rendering any set of facts into narrative, poetic or not. Indeed, confession's reality claim is an extremely artful manipulation of the materials of poetry, not a departure from them. But it has confused some readers, who endorse the claim for a special confessional 'truth'.

Thomas Travisano has made a case against the term, deeming it reductive and prejudicial (1999: 32–70). He builds on complaints made by some of the poets themselves. For instance, Berryman responded to being called confessional 'with rage and contempt' and later found it necessary to insist that the *Dream Songs* were 'essentially about an imaginary character (not the poet, not me), named Henry' (Travisano 1999: 32). Not all poets objected – Sexton spoke proudly of herself as the '*only* confessional poet' (Middlebrook 1991: 382). But to avoid the unwelcome associations, alternative names have developed, including 'personal', 'autobiographical' and 'self-exploratory' poetry. While acknowledging the difficulties raised by the term confessional poetry, I employ it here to explore those elements of the work, often transgressive, that the term illuminates.

Principal among the transgressions at issue in confessional work, I suggest, is its exploration of shifting gender scripts. Gender roles (and the intimately linked issue of sexual orientation) are among the few behaviours subject to discipline in all three of confession's pre-poetic domains: the church, the clinic and the court. Confession to homosexuality or to lack of interest in mothering a newborn, for instance, might be taken and judged in any of these venues. But focus on gender develops not only because the poets want to talk about their personal experience with it. The confessional stance importantly allows its poets to rework their relation to the poetic tradition. The dynamics of this tradition have been patterned on a gendered, familial model – the poetic family romance described by Bloom (1973), which historically has followed a patriarchal model in which authority circulates among fathers and sons, and from which mothers and daughters are pointedly excluded. Confession to departures from received gender and family models offers a means to transform those dynamics or to explore what transformation might involve.

In one form or another, all of the poets named in the title challenge the established tradition by confessing themselves 'feminine'. Clearly such a claim will have different valences for self-presenting male and female poets, as well as for self-presenting heterosexuals and homosexuals (and I refer here to the way in which gender and sex are employed within the work as part of the authority claim of the poet). But all of these poets operate in tension with the long-operative Western view of femininity as a kind of sin in itself, calling forth shame. This view underlies the historical representation of femininity in poetry as a silent, sanitized body that serves as the topic of discussion by and among masculine speakers. For these speakers, femininity arouses both excitement and shame (quickly displaced onto the 'source' of the excitement) at the need the excitement reveals.

In invoking religious, legal and psychoanalytic frameworks, the term confessional poetry raises a question about the work: does it disclose secrets in order to repent of them, thus reinforcing the initial negative judgement that kept them secret (the religious or legal dynamic), or to decathect that judgement (the psychoanalytic dynamic)? In part, these poets' confessions to the 'sin' of femininity mean to redefine it positively; but their attempts, as will become clear below, meet with various results.

Along with its gender focus, confessional work puts into play a *reality trope* – the blurring of the border between reality and fiction such that it seems as though poet and speaker are one. This trope is a variation on the sincerity claims that poets have long employed to convince readers that their work deserves attention. Inevitably both tropes involve much artful manoeuvring within the framework of speech presentations with which readers are familiar and comfortable. And inevitably this framework is gendered. In claiming to speak from the 'real' rather than just the sincere, confessional poets push against the boundaries of the poetic, claiming access to something more primal from which they claim authority. Julia Kristeva's concept of the 'True-Real' assists here in pointing to the nostalgic gesture implicit in references to 'reality' as if it were a place outside language and interpretation, when instead it is always informed by the linguistically based understanding of the perceiver. Kristeva links the 'True-Real' to the idea of the archaic mother, who inhabits a mythical extra-linguistic space (1986: 235). In calling on the reality trope, confessional poets call upon the authority of such a mother, located in a space outside language, though within the paradoxical situation of the poet, whose material is the very language the archaic mother or the 'feminine' would seem to escape.

In addition, the reality trope, which contravenes the more standard poetic claim to an authority of imagination, raises questions about the role of reputation in poetic authority claims. Though it *is* a trope, this device points up the way that facts about poets (their 'characters' and whatever is known about their social positions) have long been part of the active penumbra of poetry, throwing shadows around the work that inform its reception. From Dylan Thomas and Marianne Moore to Sir Philip Sidney, John Milton and even Homer and Sappho, the public personae and frequently the celebrity of poets have shaped the way readers approach and absorb their work. Exactly how this happens, and how it changes over time as reputations evolve, varies and lies open to dispute. But confessional work brings the issue to the fore.

The mode remains popular with poets and readers, as the careers of Lucile Clifton, Mark Doty, Rita Dove, Tony Hoagland, Marilyn Hacker, Sharon Olds and C.K. Williams, among many others, attest. Confession may draw readers not only through its invocation of a pre-linguistic real, but also because it reveals the constructedness of life-scripts generally. The arbitrariness of our 'selves' presages the possibility that the 'real' world might be remade otherwise and that its claims to permanence and stability are themselves fictional. Alternatively, it may attract because it allows us to connect with 'selves' we recognize as similar. Whatever its appeal, the mode has power and over the past fifty years has demonstrated a robust adaptability.

Initial evidence of this adaptability came early, when male and female poets employed the confessional mode to quite different effect from the start. But both began from a shared premise, which linked 'femininity' with 'reality', via the traditional and still active gender division that links men to the world of imagination and ideas and women to the world of the body and, by analogy, I argue, the 'merely' factual – that which is apparently untransformed by imagination.[3] Confessional poetry developed as a transformative adoption of this view of feminine creativity – defined as realistic, literal, physical or untranscendent. Masculine creativity, by contrast, in this model includes imaginative, literary, mental or innovative work.

For female poets, the move into confessionalism involves finessing the literalism to which they had been confined into a position of poetic strength. Confessional poetry crosses the line from literal into literary: moving biographical material formerly associated with nonliterary prose into the poetic realm and claiming for it a new 'feminine' authority of the 'real'. Sexton and Plath figure this transition in their images of female physicality and literal (pro)creativity within the new context of literary creation. More than a third of Plath's mature poems involve some baby imagery, and nearly a quarter take babies or pregnancy as a major subject or principal metaphor. Sexton too employs the female body and its productivity as a consistent emblem in her negotiation of her status as poet. These images are linked to confessions to illness, which also involve a gendered confession of embodiedness, and in the case of mental illness, a pointed blurring of mind/body distinctions. When writing about such material is demonstrated to take nerve and imagination, it develops a new affect. The segue of 'feminine' material into the 'masculine' poetic realm offered these female poets a pass into the formerly forbidden zone.

For male poets of the 1950s, this 'feminine' position served as a figure for their sense of their 'secondary' position as heirs of the dauntingly successful modernists. Confession's ordinarily unauthoritative personal pose paradoxically offered authority, in its differentiation of confessional work from that of the 'impersonal' modernists. The originality of the new work gave it new value. By embracing the 'feminine' confessional position, these poets aimed to revalue the secondariness associated with it and by analogy the secondariness of their own post-modern position. The effort was to win authority for themselves, but the process threatened the hierarchies out of which authority and status have long sprung. Hence the work of some confessionals betrays ambivalence about the full embrace of the signifiers of secondariness. This dynamic carries forward an inheritance from the modernists (who themselves struggled against feelings of secondariness, to the Romantics, which they too addressed through gendered structural innovation).[4] As we will see, I read Berryman's first-person rendering of childbirth in 'Homage to Mistress Bradstreet' as an engagement with the authority questions at stake for male poets who take up the 'feminine' confessional mode.

The process of poetic positioning is differently inflected for self-presenting homosexual poets of both sexes, since they challenge received definitions of 'feminine' and 'masculine'. The transgressive confession to femininity that animates the work of all the confessionals is represented in the work of poets who 'confess' homosexuality in scandalous demonstrations of love and respect for the body, which comes to mean differently outside the traditional gender hierarchy of the mind/body binary. In these poems, men admit to having bodies and to loving them, and women see their bodies as valuable outside their service to men.[5] These poets' wrenching round of attitudes toward traditional gender assumptions is aided by the confessional mode and its troping of the literal world of the body through references to literal facts.

In moving to admit 'feminine' speech to the poetic realm, male and female confessional poets of all orientations engage the realm of the 'real', and particularly the body – the clearest emblem thereof. In the course of confessing to having bodies, these poets reflect upon how those bodies define their writing. In this work the body begins to speak about its own experience and to refuse the mind/body distinction, revealing the two to be mutually constitutive. While ostensibly the site in which firm identity (the 'truth' about oneself) is asserted, confession turns out to be a place in which received definitions of gender, of family roles, of the mind/body relation, and of poetry are submitted to scrutiny and become blurred.

Plath and Sexton

Both Sylvia Plath and Anne Sexton draw particular attention in their poetry to female bodies and to the physical aspects of womanhood, conventionally considered inappropriate not only to poetry but to public discourse generally. In so doing, both invite readers to notice that they, the poets, are women. They write poems about childbirth, pregnancy, miscarriages, abortions and menstruation. These have been read as experience narratives, not unlike other biographical details included in confessional poetry. But these particular details are pivotal metaphors for the operation of confessional poetry overall, which dares to speak of the nexus of physical, emotional and personal relations that has long been understood as woman's province. As Steven Gould Axelrod notes of Plath, 'whereas female as well as male tradition has generally opposed motherhood to literary creation, [she] sought to associate them' (1990: 146). The same may be said of Sexton. In flaunting the daily elements of women's ordinary physical lives, these poets trouble the boundaries of the poetic gender map. Such troubling revalues the active (as opposed to the objectified) female body positively; it demonstrates that women have minds; and it implies that men have bodies.

While at one level their poems call upon the authority of an archaic mother in invoking the 'real' world of the pre-linguistic body, the call is complicated by awareness of the fact that historical bias against women speakers largely precludes appeal to such alternative authority. The evidence of the linguistic canniness of all the speakers (female and male) who employ this trope further tangles the story. While no more insincere than any other poetic authority claim, this work ironizes its authority claims even as it plays upon them, raising questions about the operation of authority overall. The work also points up the ways in which the bodies of the speakers are constructed through their place in the social/cultural nexus (since, for example, women are not any more embodied than men, though the culture interprets them as though they were).

Sexton's poem 'Those Times' tells of a girl-child reduced to and blamed for her body, who imagines and accomplishes a transformation of her relation to that body. In the poem, antecedent to much of Sharon Olds's work, the speaker's mother humiliates her with nightly bodily inspections (a 'bedtime ritual / where, on the cold bathroom tiles, I was spread out daily'). The daughter spends the days in a closet, 'avoiding myself, / my body, the suspect' and 'silently' waiting to grow up and away. The mother, co-opted by her oppressors, betrays her own femininity in punishing the daughter's. But the daughter imagines things otherwise, laying 'such plans of flight, / believing I would take my body into the sky, / dragging it with me like a large bed'. At the close she redefines her femininity positively, expressing awe at her own creative capacity (her monthly periods are likened to the blooming of 'an exotic flower'), and astonishment that:

> ...children,
> two monuments,
> would break from between my legs,
> two cramped girls breathing carelessly

Where the speaker had been confined to a closet, these children break free from a cramped space – not just the womb, we can infer, but the limitations that their mother faced in childhood. The speaker breaks free too, achieving the transcendence she'd dreamed of – not a transcendence of the body (she will drag the body into the sky), but a transcendence of the choice between body and mind. The poem closes with an assertion of insight and of the speaker's capacity, acquired as a child, to 'hear / the unsaid more clearly' that is the prelude to this poem (1981: 118–21). The speaker's childhood experience teaches her to recognize and redefine the power dynamics of the world she grows into, though not to escape them entirely. The poem concerns itself with the body and its productions, but in itself it offers evidence of the speaker's ability to produce in other realms as well.

The allusions to the speaker's authorship of the poem suggest that the poet and the speaker are one and bring us back to the issue of confession's reality claims. This is re-enforced by references to the speaker's two daughters (a biographical fact) and a problematic 'Mother', familiar from earlier biographically-based poems. The poem that immediately follows in *Live or Die*, 'Two Sons', treats similar material (maternal/child relations and the physical production of children, this time through food and lessons) but in a pointedly non-biographical context. Though the lonely bitterness portrayed here as the emotions of a mother whose children have married and moved on might apply to the mothers of daughters as well, or to one who imagines such a departure, the apposition reminds us not to assume an exact coincidence between Sexton's work and her life. 'In poetry', Sexton was fond of saying, 'truth is a lie is a truth' – a fine synopsis of the reality trope.[6]

Plath's poems frequently link literary and physical creativity. 'Morning

Song', the opening poem of *Ariel*, celebrates the arrival of a baby in terms that analogize the infant and the volume she appears in: 'Love set you going like a fat gold watch. / The midwife slapped your footsoles, and your bald cry / Took its place among the elements' (1981: 156). The poem's bald cry and the baby's enter in tandem, calling the reader's attention to the poet's ability to operate in both realms. Likewise, the poem's conclusion links the child's cry with the poems that follow: 'And now you try / Your handful of notes; / The clear vowels rise like balloons' (1981: 157). Sexton creates a like linkage in 'In Celebration of My Uterus'.

But the lives on display in the poems are not portraits of pure physical contentment. Instead they tell tales of babies who bring just as much pain as they do joy, and of parents who terrorize their offspring eternally in memory. Sexton's poem 'The Death Baby' for example, asserts multiple links between the speaker's own childhood, her mothering, her poetry and her longing for an end. In Plath's 'Tulips', babies enter not as characters but as similes; the threatening flowers 'breathe / Lightly, though their white swaddlings, like an awful baby' (1981: 161). In her 'Stopped Dead' a metaphoric baby's cry ('a goddam baby screaming off somewhere') haunts the poisoned atmosphere around a couple on vacation: 'There's always a bloody baby in the air. / I'd call it a sunset, but / Whoever heard a sunset yowl like that?' (1981: 230). The baby takes a place like that of sunsets and natural description in the poet's palette. It is a new trope to be employed to various effect.

From before the time she became pregnant, Plath looked forward to the poetic material pregnancy would provide. In a journal entry she anticipates, 'Maybe some good pregnant poems, if I know I really am' (2000: 474). She seems to plan here to be her own muse, at the same time that she indicates that she assumes that reality (knowing she's pregnant) authenticates confessional work. But the fact that they were planned in advance complicates any view of them as ad hoc response to experience. Plath's 'You're', written two months before the birth of her first child, portrays a growing foetus, as does Sexton's 'Little Girl, My Stringbean, My Lovely Woman' written much after the birth. Both convey, arguably, no special mother's knowledge. They do bespeak, however, a special attentiveness to the experience of pregnancy that had rarely been paid in poetry – an attentiveness born both of experience and of the knowledge that this material could supply not just good images, but a powerful new field of poetry. 'Little Girl' works to imagine a better world for the daughter, a world in which the body does not shame.

Plath's and Sexton's poems about suicide and death also use the reality trope to claim the authority of documented bodily experience. Again the material has particularly feminine resonance. The poetry of suicide, especially failed suicide, engages the familiar poetic reduction of the female to the silent body (via the blazon, for example, which itemizes favourite parts of the beloved's body) or the 'merely' real. But this work refunctions the poetic female suicide, turning it from evidence of a feminine inability to speak into material female poets can speak about: think of 'Lady Lazurus', with its insistence that its artful suicides 'feel' real but are not, and its triumphant resurgence at the close (1981: 244–7). Its tale of repeated and ongoing attempts (a total of nine are predicted) promises a long progression of poems on the line between the real and the ficted. She foresees herself writing still at ninety, mining a rich vein of poetic material. Sexton's 'Suicide Note' similarly discusses multiple deaths.

Both figures are akin to those invoked in Sexton's anthem 'Her Kind': 'possessed witch[es]' who are 'not ashamed to die' (1981: 16). At the same time that it speaks of a willingness to consider suicide, Sexton's phrase also indicates a more general willingness to be public about things the culture usually shames its members into silence about. Their kind do not die of shame; instead they contest the rule of shame that has enforced the age-old silence about female experience and about the life of the body at the same time that they dispute their limitation to that subject. Rather than being possessed by special occult powers of femininity, both 'witches' might be said to be possessed of a special access to poetic authority in opening up the repressed (occulted) feminine to public view.

In the real world, of course, both poets did succeed at suicide eventually, further blurring the literary/literal line. And while their deaths have contributed to their renown, it is also arguable that these have distracted readerly and critical attention from the poetry's artfulness. The paradox is that in their examination of the 'real' as experienced by the gendered subject, Sexton and Plath lay themselves open to familiar judgements that reduce women to bodies, revel in evidence of their being unable to control those bodies, and at the same time condemn them for breaking out of the lockstep of marital chastity (evidenced in the poems both in descriptions of extramarital encounters and in the fact of describing the body publicly, arguably a form of unchastity). So while confession may offer a way out of old orders, that way also risks becoming a route back in.

Berryman and Lowell

In their confessional work, both John Berryman and Robert Lowell invoke the body through reference to mental illness and, in Berryman's case, suicide. But they are much less direct in their discussions of the body's functions than Plath and Sexton. In part, this is because the analogy to poetry works less well with the male body, which does not visibly bear; and in part, because both feel anxiety over strong identification with 'feminine' territory, which paradoxically includes the male body. Instead of presenting intimate details about male physical experience, both poets speak of the body by becoming ventriloquists – using the voices of others, variously and vicariously, and acknowledging their own 'femininity' at a remove.

Berryman does this most obviously in his 'Homage to Mistress Bradstreet' which he opens with a séance wherein his speaker 'self' invokes Bradstreet: 'Out of maize & air / your body's made, and moves. I summon, see', and then assumes her perspective 'I come to stay with you, / and the Governor, & Father, & Simon, & the huddled men' (1968: 11, 12). In the next line Bradstreet begins: 'By the week we landed we were, most, used up'. The ventriloquistic effect, in which Berryman seems to be possessed by Bradstreet, straddles the line between personal confession and the persona poem.

The effect reminds us that all poets working in the confessional mode, including Plath and Sexton, might be said to ventriloquize aspects of themselves in their work, since all confessional work involves creation of a persona, ficted for the purposes of the poem, though sharing the name and elements of the biography of the poet. Berryman's *Dream Songs* are generally viewed as confessional because they point to a connection between the poem's emotional dynamics and the poet's biography. But the songs employ a very complex speaker, who sometimes seems to represent the poet and at other times is very clearly a character named Henry, who speaks from aspects of the poet's experience within a minstrel show framework that marks him as a ventriloquist's dummy.[7] Lowell suggests the blurriness of the lines here: 'The poems are about Berryman, or rather they are about a person he calls *Henry*. Henry is Berryman seen as himself, as *poète maudit*, child and puppet' (1987: 108).

In 'Homage to Mistress Bradstreet', Berryman takes the opportunity to narrate a childbirth in the first person:

> So squeezed, wince you I scream? I love you & hate
> off with you. Ages! *Useless.* Below my waist
> he has me in Hell's vise
> [...]
> Monster you are killing me Be sure
> I'll have you later Women do endure
> I can *can* no longer
> and it passes the wretched trap whelming and I am me
>
> drencht & powerful, I did it with my body!
> (1968: 17)

This account emphasizes shame in physical function ('shame I am voiding oh behind it is too late'), but also includes pride in physical accomplishment ('I did it with my body!'). Though the poem does not fit the standard confessional model, Berryman described the process of writing the poem as a *couvade* (Simpson 1982: 226), and there are good reasons to view the poem as speaking to Berryman's own poetic concerns in a manner verging on the confessional. The poem may be seen as his transition into confession, since he began writing his confessional *Dream Songs* very shortly after.

For Berryman the contrast created by this adoption of a birth-giving female poetic persona opens up the door to reflection on the genderedness of poetry by men and the limitations that masculinity involves. But such reflection is not the only purpose, especially since it imports a substantial risk of loss of status. As noted earlier, male confessional poets of the 1950s utilize the mode to assist in the ongoing intergenerational struggle for poetic originality. Reviewing a collection of essays on Eliot in 1948, Berryman anticipated the preemption of Eliot's 'perverse and valuable doctrine' of poetic impersonality by the dynamic of his own future work: 'Perhaps in the end this poetry which the commentators are so eager to prove impersonal will prove to be personal, and will also appear then more terrible and more pitiful even than it does now' (Haffenden 1982: 206). Twenty years later, in his acceptance speech for the National Book Award, he spoke even more directly of the intergenerational antithesis:

> It is no good looking for models. We want anti-models. I set up the Bradstreet poem as an attack on *The Waste Land*: personality, and plot – no anthropology, no Tarot pack, no Wagner. I set up *The Dream Songs* as hostile to every visible tendency in both American and English poetry ... The aim was the same in both poems: the reproduction or invention of the motions of a human personality, free and determined, in one case feminine, in the other masculine.
>
> (Haffenden 1982: 352)

The Waste Land here stands in for modernist work generally. The takeover of Bradstreet's voice figures well the dream of postmodern priority, since Bradstreet is regarded, gender notwithstanding, as the first American poet.

But gender remains crucial: the choice of this foremother speaks also to the special concerns of Berryman's generation, who were troubled by both a perceived 'effeminization' of poetry in the wider cultural scene (a longstanding concern, itself the source of the militancy of the emphatically 'masculine' male moderns) and an effective effeminacy associated with the secondary status of being merely *post*modern. Bradstreet doubles Berryman, J.M. Linebarger notes, in that both wrote at times when poetry was deemed (by some) inappropriate to their gender (Benfey 1993: 164–5). In addition, like the female confessional poets, Berryman here claims access to poetic power via the analogy of literal (pro)creativity with that of literary creativity that the birth scene provides. The identification with Bradstreet is partial, though. To insist upon the finessing of the literal aspect of their link, Berryman makes a point of disparaging Bradstreet's literary efforts ('all this bald / abstract didactic rime I read appalled'; 'the proportioned, spiritless poems accumulate' (1968: 14, 24)). In so doing, he also affirms his continued masculinity through contrast of his 'better' poetry with hers, signalling his continued anxiety about identification with Bradstreet's gender and distinguishing himself from it at the same time that he puts it to use.

This reading of Berryman's portrait of Bradstreet is supported by reference to a later directly confessional Berryman poem, 'Two Organs'. The poem begins with a reminiscence about a college philosophy lesson taught by Irwin

Edman at Columbia: 'I remind myself at that time of Plato's uterus – / … an animal passionately longing for children' which wanders through the body if denied them. Berryman goes on to connect the two creativities: 'For "children" read: big fat fresh original & characteristic poems. // My longing yes was a woman's' (1970: 16). Upon this advice, the poet turns (almost) to his own body, which he 'undresses' through the mediation of an 'unworldly' European friend, whom he describes shouting as he pees while fishing, 'I wish my penis was big enough for this whole lake!' 'My phantasy precisely at twenty', the speaker affirms (1970: 17). Mention of a uterus (even Plato's) opens the way both to the male speaker's acknowledgement that he has a feminine ('a woman's') aspect and finally to his confession to having a body. Though virility is the topic of discussion, it is not reinforced in the description. The poem's contrast of wish and reality risks seeming ridiculous at the close, on purpose to examine the ways in which fantasy and the body, the imaginary and the real, masculinity and femininity are always interactive. The ridiculous effect is fallout from the unfamiliarity of looking at the male body outside the protective fantasies in which it is so often shrouded. Berryman, as confessional poet, risks seeming ridiculous, here and elsewhere, in order to establish an authority of the secondary of which he may partake. The operation of this authority through revaluation of the linked domains of the real, the feminine and the body, is neatly represented here.

Robert Lowell's 'Words for Hart Crane' takes a different approach to establishment of an authority of the secondary, but with correspondent effect. Lowell's *Life Studies* (1959) was his first volume to include confessional work, along with other material. The 'life studies' in this new book include numerous portraits of family members in moments of crisis, and 'confessions' of such personal difficulties as marital trouble and intermittent madness.

Among the confessionals Lowell holds a peculiar position. Because his prominent New England family tree includes the poets James Russell Lowell and Amy Lowell, his family stories might be understood already to be part of the public realm, as Elizabeth Bishop suggested in a 1957 letter to Lowell (1994: 351). As such, the status of the 'real' material he can reveal is particularly questionable because it is already ('really') poetic. Lowell's work blurs the line between the real and the artistic particularly thoroughly. He invokes this family history insistently, talking as much about other members of his family as about himself. In addition he talks much about and through other poets (speaking for them in the loose translations of *Imitations*) and about historical figures (in *History*).

'Words for Hart Crane' appears at the end of the third part of *Life Studies*, directly preceding the 'Life Studies' section, in which the poems for which Rosenthal would coin the term 'confessional' appear. It is a persona poem; but one particularly well situated to raise questions about the relation of confessional work and persona poetry generally. An unusual elegy, set in the first person and in quotation marks, it differs from the form of the other three elegies in Part Three, all of which, more traditionally, are spoken by a narrator about the individual there mourned, who is addressed in the second person. The punning title lets us know that these words are both written for Crane as an elegy, and written for his ghost to speak, as a kind of monologue.

The monologue he speaks is confessional in that the speaker, 'Crane', declares his homosexuality explicitly. He admits to 'stalking sailors' and links his poetic lineage to his sexuality: 'I, / *Catullus redivivus* [...] used to play my role / of homosexual' (1967: 55). This confessional effect is reinforced by the use of quotation marks at the start and end. While these may be read as dialogue markers, they also suggest a direct borrowing from the text of a personal statement, particularly coming so near to the poems that follow in Part Four. Lowell invokes a line of homosexual poets quite specifically in this poem – Whitman, Catullus and Crane. Shelley, of fluid sexuality, appears at the close, as part of an apparent invitation to the reader (explicitly male: 'Who asks for me, the Shelley of my age, / must lay his heart out for my bed and board' (1967: 55)) into a kind of sexual relation with the speaker. The tradition of the elegy, in which the present poet lauds a prior one and in the process demonstrates his own skill and lays claim to his predecessor's authority, sets Lowell at the end of this line. This move turns the poem into Lowell's own confession after all – not of literal homosexuality but of something akin to a literary homosexuality; that is, to speaking in the confessional poems that follow this one (as he follows Crane) from what might be called a feminized position, or at any rate a position that renders sexuality and gender role claims complex. By introducing the new work through a feminized speaker, Lowell points both to the situation in poetic history he feels himself to be in and to some ambivalence about his enterprise. Both the situation and the ambivalence are marked by a degree of blurriness in the gender identification of the poet (insofar as he is invoked as a character in the poem via the elegiac format), which may speak to a related blurriness about the status of the identity of the poet in the confessional poem. (We get more evidence of flexible sexuality in 'Skunk Hour', wherein the 'fairy decorator' thinks of giving up his unprofitable shop and marrying (1967: 89).) The use of quotation marks along with the first person pronoun in 'Words for Hart Crane' allows Lowell to at once identify himself with and separate himself from the Crane character he creates. As with Berryman's variously feminized heterosexual men, the gay man here stands in for the male American, postmodern poet who seeks to revalue his secondary position positively.

Ginsberg

Homosexuality as trope gets different but related inflection in the work of Allen Ginsberg, whose *Howl* (1956) may be said to be the first directly confessional poem.[8] Unlike Lowell, Ginsberg's claims to a blurred gender status within the poetic family romance are echoed in his biography. In *Howl* he talks about gay sex and about being crazy and writes of 'confessing out the soul ... with the absolute heart of the poem of life butchered out of their own bodies' (1988: 131). Ginsberg's presentations of the body and of his own 'feminine' status (as a man who offers himself as a love object to other men) trope and reinforce the reality claims that the poem makes via its coincidences with his biography.

But his biography itself already had a literary history, courtesy of William Carlos Williams, who had literarized Ginsberg's 'reality' in *Paterson*. There he quoted Ginsberg's letters and effectively claimed to be Ginsberg's 'true' (poetic) father, ousting his biographical father, another, less successful poet.[9] Though the confessionals define themselves through contrast with the modernists, the modernists were not as patently impersonal or monolithic as summary statements suggest. Williams had already attempted in *Paterson* a revolt against the insistently masculine authority claims of T.S. Eliot's *The Waste Land*, through a dynamic of feminization with proto-confessional elements. Williams begins by destabilizing the Father/Son dynamic of poetic inheritance that his poem's title invokes. In place of a male poetic heir, he chooses a female, the little-known Marcia Nardi, whose letters to him requesting mentorship and support he cites extensively in Books 1 and 2. In these letters, the ventriloquized Nardi 'confesses' herself a woman poet, struggling in unfair circumstances. In choosing a daughter, Williams embraces femininity and asserts value therein, to revalue the secondary ranking he perceives to accrue to American modernist poets (as opposed to 'European' poets like Eliot and Pound). As the poem progresses, however, the risks of association with a female heir become too great for Williams, and in Books 4 and 5 he introduces Ginsberg as safer substitute – feminized but still masculine too.[10] In speaking personally in his own poetry, Ginsberg continues the role Williams cast him in.

Ginsberg fills his work with celebrations of the male body and of sex ('whole mountains of homosexuality, Matterhorns of cock, Grand Canyons of asshole' (1988: 214)) in ways that hardly sound 'feminine', but that in the terms of the divisions discussed here are just that. He addresses this issue in *Kaddish*, an elegy for his mother which is not quite ventriloquistic but which does 'confess' both Naomi Ginsberg and himself and connects them intimately. Though she is portrayed in madness and extremity, the portrait does not condemn. Three lines in, Ginsberg refers us to 'Adonais' last triumphant stanzas', making Naomi the Keats to his Shelley. He recounts what he knows of her life – including a late night bus trip to a rest-home after a mental breakdown, told from the perspective of his twelve-year-old self accompanying her, and the story of her return to the family, years later, with many details of her difficulties. Through 'release of [these] particulars' (the facts of daily life) he aims to 'illuminate mankind'. In so doing he borrows from her, whose mad visions he recognizes as a source of his own poetics: '(mad as you) – (sanity a trick of agreement) –' (212). He reports her vision of meeting God at his 'cheap cabin in the country' (219), full of details and homely responses to crisis:

> I cooked supper for him. I made him a nice supper – lentil soup, vegetables, bread & butter – miltz – he sat down at the table and ate, he was sad.
>
> I told him, Look at all those fightings and killings down there, What's the matter? Why don't you put a stop to it?

Further on Ginsberg offers details of her ordinary body – which turns out to carry records of many ordinary dramas, presented within the framing drama of his own current Oedipal imaginings:

> One time I thought she was trying to make me come lay her – flirting to herself at sink – lay back on huge bed that filled most of the room, dress up around her hips, big slash of hair, scars of operations ... I was cold – later revolted a little, not much – seemed perhaps a good idea to try – know the Monster of the Beginning Womb – Perhaps – that way. Would she care? She needs a lover.
>
> (Ginsberg 1988: 219)

Naomi's ordinary body becomes monstrous in this description – not only in its details but in the undiscriminating desire her son attributes to it ('Would she care?'). The attribution being his creation, we can read the scene as reflective of his own highly ambivalent take on his 'feminine' role. Throughout this poem Ginsberg plays against gender expectations, tying himself to the 'feminine' body, and to the 'real' details of his mother's life, which he shapes to fit the literary frame and to employ as part of his own (Shelleyan) move to reform the networks of literary authority to admit him and a whole new range of ordinary material for which he claims significance. But, again following Williams, after first claiming the alternative authority of the 'feminine' – thickened here through its ties to the 'real' and the 'body' – Ginsberg goes on in the Monster passage to distance himself somewhat from the riskiness that linkage entails. But he remains at risk, nonetheless.

All five of the poets discussed here employ the confessional mode to open up discussion of the power dynamics of poetry and the society it reflects and addresses. Gender politics supply the entrée to a range of linked issues of power. While these poets do not resolve the issues, they illuminate them brilliantly and expand the available options for speech. The relation between the different poets' self-presentations itself offers important evidence of the discourse among them.

Notes

1 The mode extends the first-person lyric mode, long the domain of male speakers, who employ it to establish a 'sincerity' claim that paves the way for the 'reality' claim of the confessionals. See, for instance, Forbes (2004).
2 Although Gammel writes about prose and popular media, her analyses of the gendering of confession speak to the poetic experience as well. Travisano's work enacts the trivialization, and Perkins provides a historical framework for understanding it.
3 See Homans's (1986: 1–39) tracking of this division from *The Oresteia* through Lacan. Plath explores the topic in 'Magi'.
4 See Gregory (1996: 1–24).
5 Space limits prevent treatment of the work of a self-presenting lesbian poet here, but Bishop, Rich and Hacker offer rich and various examples.
6 See Middlebrook (1991: 258).
7 Lowell calls Henry 'John's love-child and ventriloquist's doll' (1987: 117).
8 Rosenthal coined the term in 1959 in reviewing Lowell's *Life Studies*, but Lowell's technique was influenced by W.D. Snodgrass, Sexton, Plath and others. Ginsberg's text preceded Lowell's and fits the description offered in the second paragraph of this essay. Phillips omits Ginsberg from his *Confessional Poets* not because he doesn't consider his work confessional, but because he does not find it sufficiently poetic.
9 While all biography is necessarily textual, Ginsberg's experience as the 'real' subject of another poet's work informs his expansion on this precedent in *Howl*.
10 See Gregory (1996: 73–127).

Bibliography

Axelrod, S.G. (1990) *Sylvia Plath: The Wound and the Cure of Words*, Baltimore: The Johns Hopkins University Press.
Benfey, C. (1993) 'The Woman in the Mirror: John Berryman and Randall Jarrell', in R. Kelly and A. Lathrop (eds) *Recovering Berryman: Essays on a Poet*, Ann Arbor: University of Michigan Press.
Berryman, J. (1968) *Homage to Mistress Bradstreet and Other Poems*, New York: Farrar, Straus & Giroux.
—— (1970) *Love & Fame*, New York: Farrar, Straus & Giroux.
Bishop, E. (1994) *One Art: Letters*, ed. R. Giroux, New York: Farrar, Straus & Giroux.
Bloom, H. (1973) *The Anxiety of Influence*, New York: Oxford University Press.
Forbes, D. (2004) *Sincerity's Shadow: Self-Consciousness in British Romantic and Mid-Twentieth-Century American Poetry*, Cambridge: Harvard University Press.
Gammel, I. (ed.) (1999) *Confessional Politics: Women's Sexual Self-Representations in Life Writing and Popular Media*, Carbondale: Southern Illinois University Press.
Ginsberg, A. (1988) *Collected Poems: 1947–1980*, New York: Harper & Row.
Gregory, E. (1996) *Quotation and Modern American Poetry: 'Imaginary Gardens with Real Toads'*, Houston: Rice University/Texas A&M University Press.
Haffenden, J. (1982) *The Life of John Berryman*, Boston: Routledge & Kegan Paul.
Homans, M. (1986) *Bearing the Word: Language and Female Experience in Nineteenth-Century Women's Writing*, Chicago: University Chicago Press.
Kristeva, J. (1986) *The Kristeva Reader*, ed. T. Moi, New York: Columbia University Press.

Lowell, R. (1967) *Life Studies & For the Union Dead*, New York: Farrar, Straus & Giroux.

—— (1987) *Collected Prose*, New York: Farrar, Straus & Giroux.

Middlebrook, D. (1991) *Anne Sexton: A Biography*, Boston: Houghton Mifflin.

Perkins, D. (1976) *A History of Modern Poetry*, Cambridge: Belknap.

Phillips, R. (1973) *The Confessional Poets*, Carbondale: Southern Illinois University Press.

Plath, S. (1981) *The Collected Poems*, ed. T. Hughes, New York: Harper & Row.

—— (2000) *The Journals of Sylvia Plath*, ed. K.V. Kukil, London: Faber & Faber.

Rosenthal, M.L. (1959) 'Poetry as Confession', *The Nation*, 19 September: 154–5.

Sexton, A. (1981) *The Complete Poems*, Boston: Houghton Mifflin.

Simpson, E. (1982) *Poets in Their Youth: A Memoir*, New York: Random House.

Travisano, T. (1999) *Midcentury Quartet: Bishop, Lowell, Jarrell, Berryman, and the Making of a Postmodern Aesthetic*, Charlottesville: University Press of Virginia.

3 'To feel with a human stranger'

Adrienne Rich's post-Holocaust confession and the limits of identification

Ann Keniston

In a 1992 essay, Shoshana Felman notes that Holocaust survivor Paul Celan's poem 'Death Fugue', perhaps the preeminent poem of the Holocaust, 'is contingent upon various forms of apostrophe and of address' (1992: 32). Yet Felman's emphasis is on the fragmentation of this address:

> The open wound is marked within the [poem's] language by the incapacity of '*we*' to *address*, precisely, in this poem of apostrophe and of address, the '*he*'. It is in this radical disruption of address between the '*we*' ... and the '*he*' ... that Celan locates the very essence of the violence, and the very essence of the Holocaust ... As an event directed toward the creation of a '*thou*', poetry becomes, precisely, the event of creating an address for the specificity of a historical experience which annihilated any possibility of address.
>
> (1992: 33, 38)

For Felman, Celan's adherence to address both dismantles address and marks the fact that the 'possibility of address' has already been lost. This paradox underlies Felman's implication that Celan's address – along, perhaps, with poetic structure, figure and form more generally – enacts the kinds of dislocations that are more often read in sociological, political or psychoanalytic terms. The apostrophe of 'Death Fugue', that is, not only conveys the Holocaust's violence but more crucially embodies that violence and thus the 'very essence' of the Holocaust itself.

Adrienne Rich's poems are radically different from Celan's. Her poems about the Holocaust were written decades after the end of World War II, in a country physically removed from the concentration camps, from the position of someone who did not experience their effects at first-hand. Yet Rich's poems do something similar to what Felman claims of Celan: they enact formally a series of contradictions and dislocations that are more often read as political. More exactly, as Celan 'radically disrupt[s] address' through address itself, Rich's recent poems, in particular in her 1995 volume *Dark Fields of the Republic*, ask through a series of scenes of incomplete or disrupted address whether the dialogue these scenes imply – in which one person listens to, judges and validates the utterances of another, a situation that I will argue below recalls a particular version of confession – is even possible. Such questions are rendered particularly acute by Rich's position as a non-witness, someone compelled to chronicle a series of events that she has not experienced, events that Rich often associates with the Holocaust. Like Felman, Rich locates the fracturing of her own address in the predicament of the post-Holocaust writer, someone writing about an experience that has 'annihilated' both its own historical reality and the means through which it can be represented.

Rich's emphasis on the conflicted, even untenable nature of poetic address and dialogue helps explain why I will be reading her poems and in particular *Dark Fields* in relation to the concept of confession, a notion distinct from, but for the post-Holocaust writer inflected by, the paradoxes associated by Felman and others with Holocaust testimony.[1] My definition of confession is quite different from that adopted by many literary scholars: it emphasizes not personal self-disclosure so much as a situation of speaking to a particular other and thus focuses on the relation, to adapt the common religious terms, between speaking confessant and listening confessor. Reading Rich in relation to this mode of confession both clarifies confession's connection to testimony and situates Holocaust testimony in a longer confessional tradition, one Rich's poems help renovate and broaden. Discussions of literary confession are often limited to the writing of a particular period and genre – American poetry of the 1950s, for example, or American memoir of the 1990s. Earlier readings of Rich's 'confessionalism' have tended to adhere to this narrow notion.[2] But the definition of confession I am putting forth by way of Rich's poems is broader: it emphasizes a discursive situation characterized by blockages of various kinds. At the same time, Rich's fragmented, resistant confession evokes distinctively post-Holocaust and postmodern preoccupations with the failure of conventional notions of subjectivity, language, memory and history.[3]

Rich's preoccupation with both the need to represent others and the problems this effort involves is cogently expressed in her essay 'Dearest Arturo'.[4] Here, in the course of a more general consideration of the relation of poetry to politics and more particularly of 'why poetry and politics aren't mutually exclusive' (1993: 22), Rich considers fiction, citing a statement by Arturo himself:

> You've said, *The great justification for the act of reading and writing fiction is that through it we can be disciplined and seduced into imagining other people's lives with understanding and compassion, even if we do not 'identify' with them.* Yes.
>
> (1993: 26)

Fiction, Arturo claims, enables us to locate a realm, if an 'imagin[ed]' one, in which we gain access to the experiences of others. Yet Arturo's words do not imply the simple imposition of ourselves into the lives of others. Rather, while fiction writers routinely 'imagine' others' lives, their acts of fictional invention do not always impel them as authors to 'identify' with these others.[5] Arturo seems partly to be distinguishing a desired 'imagination', a realm apparently internal, psychological and fictional, from something far riskier, an identification that while it may derive from 'understanding and compassion' seems to risk a kind of appropriation or erasure of such experience. Thus Arturo's formulation implies a tension about fiction itself. Reading and writing it need 'justification': the term suggests a kind of defensiveness. And fiction involves discipline and seduction, a dynamic that includes both coercion and pleasure.

The distinction implied if not fully elaborated by Arturo and Rich between imagining someone else's experience and identifying with that other is central to Rich's poetic effort to imagine or empathize with the experiences of people unlike herself without identifying with or appropriating these experiences. That effort also offers a way to understand her often inconsistent use of address, as enacted by the structure of 'Dearest Arturo'. As the title suggests, Rich's essay is written as a letter, with a salutation at the start and a signature at the close. This is a form Rich has often turned to, especially in her recent poems and essays. Rich is explicit about why she is writing to Arturo in the first sentence of the letter: 'I'm writing you tonight because I feel mired in the frustration of addressing that "someone" to whom I must explain why poetry and politics aren't mutually exclusive. Maybe I can begin if I think of myself as talking to you' (1993: 22). The perils for Rich on the night she is writing lie in the difficulty of imagining and addressing a disembodied, perhaps unfriendly, ' "someone" '. Arturo, or the fiction of addressing him, permits her to escape the 'frustration' of speaking impersonally. Imagining Arturo as her audience, that is, enables her to speak; the essay itself proceeds by means of the fiction of Arturo as reader. That Arturo himself is so different from Rich in ways on which she elaborates in the essay is irrelevant to this speech act: Rich's imaginative act does not require her to identify with – to insist on her similarity to – Arturo.

The idea that she is speaking to Arturo is itself a fiction, as Rich makes clear at the outset with the conditional 'if I can think of myself as talking to you'. But it is only at the essay's end that Rich reveals that Arturo will never receive this letter: he is dead, and has died while she was writing to him. Yet this fact does not prevent her continued address to him nor, it seems, his response: 'Well, our *conversation* goes on, as we promised each other. Tenderly and angrily and with laughter. "There is no death, only dying," you said' (1993: 26–7, my italics). This gesture, which ends the essay, emphatically affirms the possibilities of imagination or fiction articulated by Arturo: the letter embraces the radical fiction that Arturo is not really dead. Yet insofar as the 'conversation goes on', it is one to which Arturo's response remains, except to Rich, inaudible. Or to be more exact, his contributions are out of sequence: Rich has included his words, but they were spoken before the letter was begun. In this way, the essay exists only through the denial in which it originated. Writing requires an act of will and compassion predicated on a partial, imperfect erasure of difference, on, that is, the attempt to unmake difference not only interpersonally – between self and other – but chronologically, between the dead and the dying. The essay transforms something final into something continuous, something finite into something without end. For Rich, address itself permits something like Arturo's notion of fiction to be achieved. Yet if the essay ends by yielding to fiction's 'seduc[tion]', the fiction, because it is identified as such, also functions as a mode of 'discipline'.

In this context, it seems more than coincidental that the terms in which Arturo describes fiction – we are 'disciplined and seduced into imagining other people's lives' – are so similar to those used by Peter Brooks to define confession. Confession, Brooks claims, citing Thomas A. Tentler, is 'a "system of discipline and consolation" one by which the individual seeks and receives absolution and at [the] same time is subjected to a regimen of orthodoxy in behavior and belief' (2000: 91). The terms are not identical; Arturo's seduction is more immediate, more visceral than Tentler's consolation. Yet both emphasize an interplay originating in a relation between the self and the other that at once invites the possibility of intimacy and forbids it, setting in the place of or alongside that immediacy the possibility of removal, chastisement, 'a regimen of orthodoxy'. The analogy also suggests that confession, rather than being wholly accurate or true, cannot be anything but a constructed fiction.

The confession present in literary works is a relatively austere speech act in contrast to oral confession, one to which the possibility of actual response or dialogue remains imaginary. If authors are thought to be confessing to their readers, these readers remain absent from the scene of the confession: they cannot respond, ask for clarification, or grant absolution or punishment. Even when the confession occurs within a literary work, its privacy – an element central at least to religious confessions – is violated by the invisible presence of the reader. Literary confessions are meant to be overheard. Literary texts thus often intensify the interpersonal and other tensions present in spoken confession. Poems in particular tend to emphasize such tensions. In Northrop Frye's influential terms, lyric poetry often mimics address while turning away from its actual audience: 'the lyric poet normally pretends to be talking to himself or to someone else: a spirit of nature, a Muse ..., a personal friend, a lover, a god, a personified abstraction or a natural object' (1957: 249), although lyric 'does not address a reader directly' (1957: 4) and 'avoids [even] the mimesis of direct address' (1957: 25). And much lyric – including but not limited to the poems of the so-called 'Confessionals' – relies on address, employing, that is, a 'you' that seems central to the act of poetic utterance.[6]

The definition of confession as interpersonal interaction that I have begun to lay out differs significantly from most discussions of confessional poetry, which emphasize unrestrained personal disclosure.[7] The term has recently come under attack especially in relation to the so-called Confessionals (including Robert Lowell, Sylvia Plath and Anne Sexton) who, many readers now claim, were far more socially and politically conscious than has been acknowledged by the critics who identified them as confessional. Similarly, several recent attempts at defining a 'post-confessional' poetry emphasize a relation between the wider world and the self.[8] Yet these readers tend not to consider confession as a speech act, one that assumes a particular audience and occurs in particular circumstances.

Definitions that do take into account such issues tend to emphasize or at least draw evidence from nonliterary confessions. For Michel Foucault, confession involves the simultaneous presence of what seem almost to be two mutually exclusive models: in confession, the confessor who 'listens and says nothing' is 'not simply the interlocutor but the authority who requires the confession, prescribes and appreciates it, and intervenes in order to judge, punish, forgive, console, and reconcile'; the confessor therefore possesses 'the agency of domination'. Yet any relief granted the confessant comes not from the confessor but from 'the expression alone, independently of its external consequences', an expression that itself 'exonerates, redeems, and purifies [the confessant]; it unburdens him of his wrongs, liberates him, and promises him salvation' (1978: 61–2). Confession for Foucault emphasizes the tension between these two models.

While Foucault's model emphasizes the inconsistent role played by the confessor, Peter Brooks undermines the separateness of confessant and confessor. Claiming, like Foucault, that confession always 'implies a listener, however impersonal – an interlocutor to whom the confessional discourse is proffered', Brooks argues that confession ultimately breaks down identity, or something like what Arturo calls identification:

> the speaking *I* necessarily implies a listening *you* who can in turn become the *I* while the speaker becomes *you* ... the expression of subjectivity takes place in a context of intersubjectivity. Saying *I* implies and calls to a responsive *you*, and in this dialogic, transferential relation consolation and self-definition are to be found.
>
> (2000: 95, Brooks's emphases)

To confess thus leads not to an affirmation of self but to an erasure of the boundaries of self: the speaking subject becomes permeable, identical with the listener. Dori Laub, in the same volume as the essay by Felman with which I began, makes a similar point about Holocaust testimony, but even more strongly. The act of testimony, Laub claims, grants 'the interviewer-listener ... the *responsibility* for bearing witness that previously the narrator felt he bore alone, and therefore could not carry out'. This reciprocity leads to a chronological inversion: 'the listener (or the interviewer) becomes the Holocaust witness *before* the narrator does' (1992: 85, Laub's emphases).

Although Rich's *Dark Fields of the Republic* seldom refers directly to confession, it emphasizes a series of acts of partial or incomplete witnessing – a term that does recur. The incompleteness of these acts reveals Rich to be evoking, but more crucially interrogating, the possibility of a transparent or mutual relation between speaker and listener. The volume's affirmation of the simultaneous necessity and fictionality of intimate address is consistent with but more dramatic than the confessional situations evoked by Brooks or Foucault: often speaking directly to a 'you', these poems emphasize the inaccessibility, dispersal and multiplication of this 'you'.[9] Part of this dispersal comes about through a manipulation of temporal modes that recalls Rich's impossible, ongoing conversation with the dead Arturo, a mode central to much elegiac poetry as to much poetry in general. Rich's extreme version of confession, though, does more than emphasize the fictionality of its address. Rather, Rich locates this disruption of chronology in the situation of writing about and in the aftermath of the Holocaust, linking address to a belatedness that recalls the redemptive, impossible scene of witnessing described by Laub.[10]

That Rich's address affirms even as it attempts to unmake absence is cogently expressed in 'Sending Love', much of which catalogues a series of scenes in which characters send love across distances, usually but not always in written form (on 'pale green aerograms, ... a postcard', through 'e-mail', 'with a money order', 'on a memo', in 'braille'). The poem is not concerned with the reception of these love letters; what matters instead is 'sending it, sending it', an act of faith in presence that exists in a context of absence elaborated most directly by the poem's ending:

> Grace who always laughed is leaning
> her cheek against bullet-proof glass
>
> her tears enlarged
> like scars on a planet
> [...]
>
> Victor fixes his lens
> on disappearing faces
>
> – caught now or who will ever
> see them again?
>
> (1995: 33–9)

The glass against which Grace leans, like Victor's camera lens, is a barrier, marking the separation the rest of the poem has worked to deny, and its existence, it seems, is part of what has converted her laughter to tears. In one way, Victor's gesture inverts Rich's essay's insistence on turning a final act (death) into a continuous one (dying): he is engaged in fixing what is evanescent. But the effect is similar: by converting the 'disappearing faces' into fixed images, he attempts to prevent their vanishing. But the gesture – like that of the poem itself – is ultimately an inadequate effort to alter time and with it absence. It cannot unmake the fact of their 'disappearing'.

Other poems throughout the volume enact similar gestures of approach and withdrawal, invoking a range of characters who refuse to resemble the speaker (in 'Revolution in Permanence'), addressing others who never fully become 'you' but retain the third-person verb (in 'Edgelit'), and at times interrogating directly the impulse to identify with an addressed other:

> Little as I knew you I know you: little as you knew me you know me
> […]
>
> My testimony: yours: Trying to keep faith
> not with each other exactly yet it's the one known and unknown
> who stands for, imagines the other   with whom faith could be kept.
> (1995: 59, typography in the original)

In the first line, the tension is between syntactic parallelism – past and present knowledge are analogous, and the experiences of 'I' and 'you' seem analogous as well – and the direct assertion that these two figures know each other 'little'. The subsequent lines more dramatically exploit this tension. The testimony of I and you are not exactly analogous, as the ambiguous phrasing ('My testimony: yours') suggests; what is unknown as well as known 'stands for, imagines the other'. The impersonal construction of the final fragment-like sentence ends up affirming a paradox: faith itself is as strong as the actual characters who yearn toward each other. Or perhaps the problem lies in the apparent elision of 'stands for' and 'imagines'. Because identification and imagination here are not distinguished, the attempt to 'keep faith' becomes mere physical proximity: faith can be 'kept' with or beside some other being.

Such moments reveal the intensity of Rich's preoccupation with otherness but also the care with which she refuses to step precipitously into an identification she clearly recognizes to be fraught with problems. In the process, they reveal the limitation of readings that emphasize the way Rich's use of 'you' binds together distinct, even opposing, realms or her ability to synthesize the 'personal' with the 'political' or 'self' with 'other'.[11] A similar paradox is elaborated more directly in 'In Those Years' (1995: 4), the second poem in *Dark Fields*. The poem emphasizes the difficulties of personal disclosure and more crucially of the possibility of imagining other people's experiences; it emphasizes in this way the difficulties Foucault and Brooks argue inhere in confession, which both insists on unbridgeable distance and permits the reciprocity of 'I' and 'you', or at least the fiction of it. Perhaps more crucially, the poem locates this failure of identification in a failure of chronology. The poem's enactment of obstructed and disruptive temporality links history itself with the failure of collective vision and the identification that goes with it.

From the first line, 'In Those Years' establishes an impossible time frame, in which the present is imagined as past by means of the future:

> **In those years,** people **will say,** we **lost** track
> of the meaning of *we*, of *you*
> we found ourselves
> reduced to *I*
>   (1995: 4, boldface mine)

This opening seems a straightforward indictment of a discourse that is wholly limited to what is later called 'personal life'. The poem seems to condemn this loss of the collective realm:

> and the whole thing became
> silly, ironic, terrible:
> we were trying to live a personal life
> and, yes, that was the only life
> we could bear witness to
>   (1995: 4)

At the same time, the speaker maintains sympathy with the impulse to retain and accurately record or 'bear witness to' the private life: the poem identifies those who bear witness in this way as 'we' and their attempts are affirmed with 'yes'. Yet the poem's structure clearly affirms such a personal realm to be untenable. The narrative is interrupted by and ends with the violent and unexpected incursion of history:

> But the great dark birds of history screamed and plunged
> into our personal weather
> They were headed somewhere else but their beaks and pinions drove
> along the shore, through the rags of fog
> where we stood, saying *I*
>   (1995: 4)

Violating the attempt to define a wholly personal realm, characterized by 'saying *I*', the birds make a mockery of the remnants of selfhood.

The poem is powerful as polemic partly because of its impersonality: 'I' occurs only as a concept, and the speaker favours instead the 'we' of communal utterance or pronouncement. In this way, Rich enacts pronominally the point the poem seems to be making: it refuses merely to say 'I', enacting the possibility of an alternative to the singular pronoun and all that it represents. Yet using 'we' seems insufficient as a way to counter the personal.

'We', after all, refers to the group of people clinging to the personal ('we were trying to live a personal life'; the birds descend 'into our personal weather'; 'we stood, saying *I*') and so does not directly provide an alternative to the 'silly, ironic, terrible' predicament of 'I'. Any sense of inevitability is further hindered by the randomness of the birds' descent. 'Headed somewhere else', they are not harbingers of the future (evoked by the first line's 'people *will* say') but rather 'birds of history', marking a past impossible to change. The failure is even more radical with the pronoun 'you': after the second line, the speaker, or perhaps the format of the poem, fails to find a place for 'you', for some plural or singular entity who cannot be easily included with the 'I'. The poem thus implies a desire (that we recover the meaning of *we* and *you*) that it does not fulfil. In some ways it remains a chronicle of loss and impossibility. The title's combination of distance (whole years are evoked) and particularity (they are not any years but 'those') seems nearly nostalgic, and the poem seems in the end more a lament than a call to action.

In this way, although 'In Those Years' argues for the importance of using 'you' as well as 'I', the poem refuses or is unable to do so. Rather, its attempt to 'bear witness' seems to preclude not only what Arturo called identification but also imagination; indeed, the poem is stringent in its refusal to equate self with others. The impulse underlying confession – to be absolved by speaking to 'you' – seems central to this poem. Yet the poem refuses both its speaker and its readers this absolution. In the most literal sense, the characters are unchanged at the poem's end: they continue saying 'I', seemingly ignorant of the uselessness of their words.

I noted above the ways that the poem's first line scrambles chronology, looking forward ('we will say') to something currently unrecognized ('we lost sight'). Through this situation, as through her continuing conversation with the dead Arturo, Rich examines the workings of memory by disrupting chronology. History enters the poem in abstract, partly personified form. Yet by definition, history is past; it has already occurred. This paradox is crucial to the poem: history here, as in other poems in the volume, is wrested from its position in the past, yet it nonetheless fails to alter anything.

History, then, functions as a kind of ghost or spectre, part of whose function seems to be to disrupt notions of chronology or history itself, a notion that recalls the passage from Felman with which I began. For Felman, Celan's address involves a chronological conundrum: seeking to 'creat[e] an address for the specificity of a historical experience that annihilated any possibility of address', it is caught in its own belatedness; address has already been annihilated, so Celan's effort to invent it is impossible. In Laub's stronger terms, Holocaust testimony involves an inversion of chronology so radical that the listener to the testimony precedes the testifier to whom he listens, 'becom[ing] the Holocaust witness *before* the narrator does' (1992: 85).

Rich's poem involves a similar problem, enacted if anything through a more drastic curtailment of the possibilities of bearing witness or confession marked partly by 'you'. That Rich is thinking of the kinds of disruptions associated by Felman with the Holocaust is suggested by the image of the birds of history, which strongly evokes Walter Benjamin's reference to the angel of history. This angel, Benjamin claims, is condemned helplessly to witness a past he cannot repair, 'one single catastrophe which keeps piling wreckage upon wreckage and hurls it in front of his feet', even as he is 'propel[led] into the future to which his back is turned' (1955: 259–60). Just as Benjamin's angel is thwarted in his desire to act, to 'make whole what is smashed', the humans in Rich's poem are defined by a desire – 'to live a personal life' – rendered ridiculous by the incursion of the birds. Both the humans and the disruptive birds of 'In Those Years' participate in what Benjamin suggests is the tragedy of history, whose lessons can be neither corrected nor applied to the future. Benjamin's antichronological image of the angel, though, is historically specific: it was a response, as Benjamin elsewhere explained, to 'the war [World War II] and the constellation it brought with it' (1940). Rich's allusion to Benjamin is also an allusion to the way that World War II redefined the relation between past and future, and to what Benjamin called 'the problem of memory (and that of forgetting)' (1940).

The Holocaust's disruptions of history and memory are enacted in 'In Those Years', as in other Rich poems, through disruptions of the kind of address central to both confession and testimony. In this context, Felman's notion of the 'incapacity of "*we*" to *address*, precisely in [Celan's] poem of apostrophe and address, the "*he*"' (1992: 33) accurately characterizes Rich's obliteration of a 'you' the speaker has implied is a necessary means of escaping the limits of 'I'. 'In Those Years' emphasizes the importance of what Laub, like Rich, calls 'bearing witness'. But while Laub keeps open the possibility of a 'repossession of the act of witnessing' through the subsequent shared act of testimony, Rich's post-Holocaust vision prohibits it. Rich evokes the interpersonal act of witnessing identified by Laub, yet Rich's characters are in the end caught in the solipsistic act of bearing witness to their own lives for themselves alone. The 'you', retained in fragmented and inconsistent form by Celan, is for Rich a mode of speech that, while desired, cannot be sustained.

The failure of address in 'In Those Years' marks a loss and distance different from those chronicled by Celan and other Holocaust survivors. Rich, unlike Celan, is not a survivor; her witnessing of the Holocaust, as other poems make clear, has involved distances both cultural and geographical. Such distances may explain Rich's emphasis not so much on the need to remember the Holocaust as on the obstructions deriving from her speakers' passionate yet belated position.

In this context, the sequence 'Then or Now' is particularly revealing: it considers the relation of the Holocaust to memory while emphasizing questions of guilt and innocence central to confessional discourse partly, as in 'In Those Years', by enacting the difficulty of address.[12] The sequence, like several other poems in the volume, considers directly the relation between two historical moments, one of them explicitly connected to the Holocaust. Unlike Rich's earlier poems on the Holocaust, most notably 'Eastern War Time' and '1948: Jews' in the 1991 *Atlas of the Difficult World*, 'Then or Now' refuses directly to connect now with then.[13] The first-person speaker enters only in the present moment of the poem, and past events, in which the speaker does not participate, are chronicled in all their otherness. These scenes remain, like the snapshots taken by Victor in 'Sending Love', distinct and disconnected. In the sequence's third poem, 'Sunset, December, 1993', though, Rich considers directly the conflicting impulses involved in linking past with present:

> Dangerous of course to draw
> parallels   Yet more dangerous to write
>
> as if there were a steady course, we and our poems
> protected: the individual life, protected
>
> poems, ideas, gliding
> in mid-air, innocent
> [...]
> Dangerous not to think
>
> how the earth still was   in places
> while the chimneys shuddered with the first dischargements.
>   (1995: 29)

The passage recalls the depersonalized tone of 'In Those Years' and considers similar issues related to the 'individual life, protected', yet it asserts far more directly that this private, shielded, innocent life is 'more dangerous' than the risks of analogy or identification. The difficulty of choosing among 'dangerous' alternatives is evident in the final image of the concentration camp chimneys discharging the smoke and ash of murdered bodies. The awkward term 'dischargements' marks the difficulty of attempting to convey what, although the poet struggles to 'think' of them, remains nearly impossible to represent. Moreover, the earth's continuance is represented as past ('the earth still was in places') even as the poem seems to take place in the present moment of 1993. The dischargements seem in this context both unforgettable and impossible to set into the normative structures of chronology or history.

'And Now' is the sequence's final poem, and one like 'In Those Years' that has sometimes been read as a direct statement of principle or ars poetica.[14] Like 'In Those Years', though, the poem does not so much

embrace as question models of confession or testimony that require an identification of speaker with listener. Beginning with address to a 'you' who
seems to be both lover and reader, the poem moves away from intimate
address in a way that recalls the abandonment of 'you' in 'In Those Years'.
But where 'In Those Years' considers the dangers of a wholly 'personal'
realm, 'And Now' focuses more directly on the difficulties of identification
itself. The poem considers the impossibility of finding kinship with others
even as it insists on the importance of recording and chronicling what
occurs. While the speaker begins with and seems to long for the possibility
of sympathetic and accurate witnessing, this desire seems, in the end, unob-
tainable.

The opening lines of the poem present a passionate confusion of lover and
reader, of intimate and more universal modes of love:

> And now as you read these poems
> – you whose eyes and hands I love
> – you whose mouth and eyes I love
> – you whose words and minds I love –
> (1995: 31)

The addressee is at once singular (possessing a 'mouth') and multiple (possessing 'minds'), and the speaker addresses her/them with certainty and
immediacy. In its address to and imagining of the situation of the reader,
the opening line strongly recalls 'Dedications', a similarly positioned poem
in Rich's previous volume, which ends the title sequence 'An Atlas of the
Difficult World'. All of the lines in 'Dedications' begin with the assertion 'I
know you are reading this poem', followed by a range of scenes and situations. This epistemological certainty in the earlier poem at one point
permits a statement about the possibilities of sympathetic identification that
seem to transcend what Arturo articulates about imagination: 'I know you
are reading this poem in a waiting-room / of eyes met and unmeeting, of
identity with strangers' (1991: 25, my emphasis). Here it is possible to
identify, even in silence and discomfort, with those unlike oneself, a situation the poem itself both mimics and facilitates.

Yet while 'And Now' begins similarly to that earlier poem, it seems at
least partly a reconsideration of that poem, as the title suggests. One of the
most striking echoes comes in the last lines of the poem, in which the
notion of 'identity with strangers' in 'Dedications' is inverted. Rather than
confirming the possibility of identification, the poem emphasizes its impossibility. Here is the remainder of the poem:

> don't think I was trying to state a case
> or construct a scenery:
> I tried to listen to
> the public voice of our time

tried to survey our public space
as best I could
– tried to remember and stay
faithful to details, note
precisely how the air moved
and where the clock's hands stood
and who was in charge of definitions
and who stood by receiving them
when the name of compassion
was changed to the name of guilt
when to feel with a human stranger
was declared obsolete.

(1995: 31)

The poem ends with the possibility of 'feel[ing] with a … stranger', an act of empathy that seems, as in 'Dedications', to verge on identification. Yet here, the point is opposite to that of the earlier poem: this impulse has become 'obsolete' – associated with an earlier and now-untenable moment – or at least has been 'declared' as such. This difference is echoed by others in the poems. 'Dedications' gains power from its Whitmanian anaphora: the poem's repeated phrase resists narrative development or change. Instead, the poem is a celebration of a variety of modes of reading and of the variety of people who receive the poem. But 'And Now' contains far more syntactic and tonal variations and implies a more complex scenario of removal or loss over time. Perhaps most strikingly, in a way that recalls 'In Those Years', the pronoun 'you' in 'And Now' is removed from the poem. 'You' recurs in each of the poem's first four lines, partly recedes in the negative imperative 'don't think' of the fifth line, and after that does not return. At the same time, the first-person voice of the opening recedes: the second half of the poem contains no personal pronouns at all. Not surprisingly, this removal of the personal leads to a change in diction. The poem moves away from the physical immediacy of the 'details' which the speaker 'tried to remember and stay/faithful [to]' a far more abstract and passive mode. Beginning with an identification between speaker and addressee as well as poet and reader, the poem ends up turning away from both addressee and speaker. If there is another human presence at the end of the poem, it is that of the disembodied, antithetical voices who have 'declared obsolete' the idea of compassion.

Yet, as in 'In Those Years', the loss is not absolute. The speaker persists in her attempt to 'listen / to the public voice of our time' and 'survey our public space'. And even as it turns away from address, the poem insists through its parallel structure ('don't think I was trying', I tried to listen', 'tried to remember') on a speaker attempting to justify her poetic choices to a listener. In this way, even as Rich challenges the possibility of a simple 'I'/'you' relation, she marks the importance of address, identification and empathy. Perhaps most striking among these strategies is the way the poem affirms a highly qualified analogy between the poet and the reader by repeatedly representing the speaker as a receiver of information rather than a maker of poems: her role is 'to listen', 'to survey', and 'to remember and stay / faithful to details'. From this position as recipient, she can chronicle what has occurred, albeit impersonally, detachedly, with all the 'precis[ion]' of an inanimate object or camera. That the poem forsakes the 'steady course' described in the sequence's third poem is part of the point: this radically curtailed position permits Rich to achieve something like a post-Holocaust mode of witness.

Paradoxically, the poem affirms, in a present moment defined by its position after the Holocaust, a kinship engendered by passivity and stillness, an identification deriving not from the attempt to set oneself into someone else's life nor even to speak directly to someone else but from the near-deanimation of the witness. This mode of witnessing derives from the refusal of the entire sequence to insert now into then or even, more modestly, to elaborate an analogy between the two realms. By rupturing the I/you bond, by attempting to witness not the past but merely 'now', the poet can establish a kinship, an identification not with the victims or perpetrators of the Holocaust but with the actual reader. Such an evasion is possible only in written rather than spoken confessions, since only written confessions distinguish addressee from audience. Rich derives from the artificiality of the lyric 'you' – the other who is never actually present, who cannot respond to whatever the poem is confessing – a kinship that transcends the 'imaginary' realm of lyric address to a more solid mode of identification. Rich's explicitly post-Holocaust poetry permits something different from the aesthetics of limitation in the models of confession and testimony set forth by Foucault, Felman and Laub. 'And Now' affirms a mode of confession that assumes the limitations of the self–other dynamic. Within this confined and belated space, the poem opens up the possibility of a mode of communication that partly recalls the I/you fusion of Brooks's confession. The poem, after all, really has a reader, as both 'Dedications' and 'And Now' directly assert. By shifting from apostrophe – address to the absent, the inanimate or the dead – to reader address, Rich evokes something closer to actual conversation, albeit one that must surmount obstacles of space and time: the reciprocated speech for which confession yearns.

Acknowledgement

I am grateful to Jane Detweiler for help at a crucial stage in the revision process.

Notes

1 For more on Holocaust testimony, see Laub (1992), Caruth (1995) and Ostriker (2001), whose essay 'Beyond Confession: The Poetics of Postmodern Witness'

suggests an analogy between confession, the compulsion to bear witness and the Holocaust.

2 The characteristics of the 'confessional' school of poetry are outlined by Rosenthal (1967) and Middlebrook (1993). Although most critics stop short of calling Rich herself a confessional poet, several associate the shift in her work to a more autobiographical and also politically informed poetic aesthetic with the 'influence' of 'the confessional mode' (Martin 1984: 179).

3 The analogy I am proposing between post-Holocaust and postmodern writing is partly chronological: the origin of the postmodern is sometimes located just after World War II. Yet I also mean to suggest that much of the fragmentation of speech and temporality generally associated with postmodern writing can be located in the disruptions effected by the Holocaust. Lyotard is among the critics who have argued most directly that the Holocaust marked the breakdown of modern paradigms of progress, narrative and emancipation.

4 Rich's essay does not identify Arturo except by his first name, although early in the essay she compares him with herself: 'We're different generations, cultures, genders; we're both gay, both disabled, both writers' (1993: 22).

5 I am, I should make clear, making more systematic a distinction at which Rich's essay only hints. In fact, the passage I cited from the essay is followed by an amplification in which Rich seems to espouse something like identification, a situation in which 'our own questions' meet the world's 'questions, [in which we] recognize how we are in the world and world is in us –' (1993: 26).

6 For more detailed discussions of poetic address see Culler (1981), Waters (2003) and Keniston (2001).

7 Confessional poetry was famously defined by M.L. Rosenthal in terms of its relation to a wholly personal realm: such poems emphasize 'private humiliations, sufferings, and psychological problems' (1967: 26), although they do so in a way that makes the poet's 'psychological vulnerability and shame an embodiment of his [*sic*] civilization' (79). A recent essay collection, *After Confession: Poetry as Autobiography* (Sontag and Graham 2001), emphasizes the continued pertinence of this notion, as its title suggests.

8 See, for example, Orr (1993) and Ostriker (2001). Dickie explicitly redefines Rich's confessional status, arguing that she espouses a 'poetry that is a public confession and cleansing, poetry that sounds like a prayer of contrition' (1997: 165).

9 Approximately three-quarters of the poems in the volume contain an addressee, although the identity of this addressee is not consistent.

10 For a discussion of belatedness and the Holocaust, see Caruth (1995: 4–5, 11).

11 Hogue, for example, argues something nearly opposite to what I claim: for Hogue, Rich's poems 'transport the reader into the testimonial position from which the poem speaks' (1998: 413–14). Rich's inconsistent 'you' permits a kind of triple identification of speaker, addressee and reader (1998: 422). The risks of such readings in relation to Rich were most explicitly elaborated by Charles Altieri twenty years ago. Altieri claims that such readings expose Rich's writing to two distinct but linked charges: that of a wholly polemical poetry, one defined by the subservience of the personal to the political agenda, or one that valorizes an unthinking aesthetic of fusion (1984: 173). Rich's essays make it clear that she is acutely aware of such risks (1993: 47). More moderate is Erkkila's claim that while Rich once espoused a poetics of fusion, she has more recently questioned the notion.

12 In a note to 'Then or Now', Rich describes the origin of the poem in her 'reflect[ion] on concepts of "guilt" and "innocence" among artists and intellectuals like myself in the United States' (1995: 78). For a detailed reading of these concepts see Hollenberg (1998).

13 These earlier poems emphasize the contrast between someone resembling Rich

herself – an assimilated Jewish girl living in the US during World War II – and the actual occurrences of the Holocaust. The juxtaposition of time and place reveals the discontinuity between the two realms. Yet the processes of memory are in these earlier poems unhindered: the scenes described seem real. 'Deportations', the only poem in the sequence directly to compare them and us, then and now, does so within a space explicitly characterized as dreamed.

14 Hogue, for example, claims the poem 'seems written in the spirit of an ars poetica' although she notes that the poem emphasizes not the 'witness[ing of ... an observable event, but the process by which the speaker has tried ethically to bear witness' (1998: 418).

Bibliography

Altieri, C. (1984) *Self and Sensibility in Contemporary American Poetry*, New York: Cambridge University Press.

Benjamin, W. (1955) *Illuminations*, ed. Hannah Arendt, New York: Harcourt.

——— (1940) Letter to Gretel Adorno, 7 May 1940, Qtd. in Lloyd Spencer, 'On Certain Difficulties with the Translation of "On The Concept Of History"'. Available online at: http://www.tasc.ac.uk/depart/media/staff/ls/WBenjamin/TranslWB.html (accessed 5 June 2004).

Brooks, P. (2000) *Troubling Confessions: Speaking Guilt in Law and Literature*, Chicago: University of Chicago Press.

Caruth, C. (1995) 'Introduction', in C. Caruth (ed.) *Trauma: Explorations in Memory*, Baltimore: Johns Hopkins University Press.

Culler, J. (1981) *The Pursuit of Signs*, Ithaca: Cornell University Press.

Dickie, M. (1997) *Stein, Bishop and Rich: Lyrics of Love, War and Place*, Chapel Hill: University of North Carolina Press.

Felman, S. (1992) 'Education and Crisis, or the Vicissitudes of Teaching', in S. Felman and D. Laub (1992) *Testimony: Crises of Witnessing in Literature, Psychoanalysis, and History*, New York: Routledge.

Erkkila, B. (1992) 'Adrienne Rich, Emily Dickinson, and the Limits of Sisterhood', *The Wicked Sisters: Women Poets, Literary History, and Discord*, New York: Oxford University Press.

Felman, S. and Laub, D. (1992) *Testimony: Crises of Witnessing in Literature, Psychoanalysis, and History*, New York: Routledge.

Foucault, M. (1978) *History of Sexuality. Volume One: An Introduction*, trans. R. Hurley, New York: Vintage.

Frye, N. (1957) *Anatomy of Criticism*, Princeton: Princeton University Press.

Hogue, C. (1998) 'Adrienne Rich's Political, Ecstatic Subject', *Women's Studies* 27: 413–29.

Hollenberg, D.K. (1998) 'Holocaust Consciousness in the 1990s: Adrienne Rich's "Then or Now"', *Women's Studies* 27: 377–87.

Keniston, A. (2001) '"The Fluidity of Damaged Form": Apostrophe and Desire in Nineties Poetry', *Contemporary Literature* 42: 294–324.

Laub, D. (1992) 'An Event Without a Witness: Truth, Testimony and Survival', in S. Felman and D. Laub (1992) *Testimony: Crises of Witnessing in Literature, Psychoanalysis, and History*, New York: Routledge.

Lyotard, J.-F. (1998) *The Differend: Phrases in Dispute*, trans. G. Van Den Abbeele, Minneapolis: University of Minnesota Press.

Martin, W. (1984) *An American Triptych: Anne Bradstreet, Emily Dickinson, Adrienne Rich*, Chapel Hill: University of North Carolina Press.

Middlebrook, D. (1993) 'What was Confessional Poetry?', in J. Parini and B. Millier (eds) *The Columbia History of American Poetry: From the Puritans to Our Time*, New York: Columbia University Press.

Orr, G. (1993) 'The Postconfessional Lyric', in J. Parini and B. Millier (eds) *The Columbia History of American Poetry: From the Puritans to Our Time*, New York: Columbia University Press.

Ostriker, A. (2001) 'Beyond Confession: The Poetics of Postmodern Witness', in K. Sontag and D. Graham (eds) (2001) *After Confession: Poetry and Autobiography*, Saint Paul: Graywolf.

Parini, J. and Millier, B. (eds) (1993) *The Columbia History of American Poetry: From the Puritans to Our Time*, New York: Columbia University Press.

Rich, A. (1991) An *Atlas of the Difficult World: Poems 1988–1991*, New York: Norton.

—— (1993) *What Is Found There: Notebooks on Poetry and Politics*, New York: Norton.

—— (1995) *Dark Fields of the Republic: Poems 1991–1995*, New York: Norton.

Rosenthal, M.L. (1967) *The New Poets*, New York: Oxford University Press.

Sontag, K. and Graham, D. (eds) (2001) *After Confession: Poetry and Autobiography*, Saint Paul: Graywolf.

Waters, W. (2003) *Poetry's Touch: On Lyric Address*, Ithaca: Cornell University Press.

4 'Your story. My story'

Confessional writing and the case of *Birthday Letters*

Jo Gill

> The real mystery is this strange need. Why can't we just hide it and shut up? Why do we have to blab? Why do human beings need to confess? Maybe, if you don't have that secret confession, you don't have a poem – don't even have a story. Don't have a writer.
>
> (Hughes 1995: 75)

Ted Hughes's *Birthday Letters* was published unexpectedly in 1998.[1] As surprising as the emergence of the collection was its markedly personal, even confessional, tone – a tone which Hughes had largely eschewed in his previous work. Here, it seemed, was Ted Hughes doing what nobody had thought he would ever do, telling what he had hitherto refused to tell, giving for the first and only time his 'version' (Alvarez 1999: 210) of his personal and literary relationship with his wife, Sylvia Plath. This was a story which had been told many times by other people on or beyond its peripheries but which, when told in the first person, acquired the apparent authority and authenticity of lived experience. Here at last, it seemed, was Ted Hughes's 'secret confession'.

There are grounds for thinking about *Birthday Letters* as confessional poetry and numerous commentators have explicitly or otherwise chosen to read it within such a framework (Wagner 2000; Graham and Sontag 2001). Certainly the collection seems to invite such a reading. It shares many of the received characteristics of the 'confessional mode' which dominated American poetry in the 1950s and 1960s and which was hugely influential both elsewhere (see A. Alvarez's introduction to his anthology *The New Poetry* (1962) which advocated a similar turn towards 'extremism' in British verse) and since. Hughes and Plath were acquainted with Lowell, Sexton and other leading poets in the nascent confessional movement in Boston in the late 1950s (Davison 1994; Middlebrook 2003). The persistent linking of Plath's name with this group may, over the years, have given grounds for associating Hughes with some of the movement's key figures and moments, although his work had, until *Birthday Letters*, seemed to maintain a cautious distance. This, his final collection of poems, emerged in 1998 into what has been characterised as a late twentieth century 'culture of confession' (Eakin 2004: 1). Leigh Gilmore's observation that 'Suddenly, it would seem, memoir has become *the* genre in the skittish period around the turn of the millennium' (2001: 1) neatly contextualises its appearance.

This background notwithstanding, it is the argument of the present essay that *Birthday Letters* may more productively be read in terms of its self-conscious resistance to any straightforward identification with confessionalism. What is striking in *Birthday Letters*, I will argue, is the urgency and thoroughness with which it critiques the received attributes and parameters of the mode. This is not, however, to posit a wholesale rejection of the form, but rather to suggest that the collection reappraises it and renegotiates its own place in it. Most importantly, as I will show, it re-envisions and recuperates some of its potential. *Birthday Letters* bridges, or more properly embodies, the tension between divergent ways of approaching the mode. And although it acknowledges that confession is artful and that it produces rather than reflects truth and subjectivity, it also finally recognises, and claims, some kind of cathartic release. In this way, *Birthday Letters* is a deeply challenging book – to subject and addressee, to confession and its criticism alike.

Although it is tempting to read *Birthday Letters* in terms of its revelation of the other side of the stories previously related by Plath or by a succession of biographers (each of whom, according to Jacqueline Rose, insists 'that she or he has a greater claim to the truth than the one who went before' (2003: 51)) the poems themselves make no claim to any privileged access or insight. Instead, they emphasise by the repeated use of questions and negative constructions the unreliability of their representations.[2] The poems show us a subject uncertain of his own history, his own past, for example in '18 Rugby Street' where the initial clarity and detail of the description soon gives way to the hesitant 'I guess', and 'I had no idea', and 'Blank', and finally 'I cannot remember' (1998: 20–4). This is a subject testing the nature and limits of self-knowledge (in 'Fidelity': 'I still puzzle over it – doubtful, now, / Whether to envy myself or pity' (29)) and the nature and limits of personal responsibility (in 'The Rabbit Catcher', 'What had I done? I had / somehow misunderstood' (144)). The poems are concerned primarily with confessing not what, but how little, they know and we should note the frequency with which the poems admit, and seek exculpation for, their own ignorance. In 'Trophies', the speaker concedes 'little did I know' (18), in 'Robbing Myself', 'I did not know ... / You never knew' (166), and in 'Visit' 'she did not know' and 'I did not know he was wrong / Nor did I know ...' (7).

Such a reading runs contrary to orthodox perceptions of the mode, exemplified by M.L. Rosenthal who first delineated it in his review of Robert Lowell's *Life Studies* (1959: 154). Confessional poetry is said to feature an autobiographical voice which speaks with 'uncompromising honesty' about taboo subjects including the author's 'private humiliations and sufferings'

(Rosenthal 1959: 154). According to early commentators, it is 'highly subjective', 'most often narrative', 'written in the open language of ordinary speech', and displays 'moral courage' (Phillips 1973: 16–17).[3] It holds out the promise of personal catharsis and therapeutic gain; the speaker (confessant) is subject to an irrepressible and spontaneous 'compulsion to confess' (Cox and Jones 1964: 108) – the 'need' which Hughes in the comment quoted above is so anxious to understand – and it is only by confessing that he or she will achieve relief.

Although on a first reading *Birthday Letters* seems confessional in the sense outlined above (it features the revelation of previously hidden truths, the exploration of taboo areas, an authenticity of voice and is cathartic or therapeutic), what is of real note is the way in which it undermines or disrupts these practices and values. If it is a confession it is a confession which, as the words of Ted Hughes used as my epigraph suggest, raises more questions than it answers, more problems than it resolves. Most importantly, if *Birthday Letters* is to be thought of as a confession, it should be understood as a confession which is as preoccupied with its own status, with its own discursive processes and with the nature and limitations of the mode as it is with the true story or 'secret' ostensibly at its heart. It is a form of meta-confession, motivated not simply by the need to tell all (Hughes's to 'blab' (1995: 75)) but by the desire to understand, confess and defend its own dynamics.[4]

If for Hughes, to return to the epigraph with which I opened this essay, there is no story, no poem, no writer without there first being a 'secret confession', it is also apparent that there is none of these without an audience. *Birthday Letters* is a confession which is profoundly aware of its audience, and which is structured in such a way as to guarantee, and to make visible, that audience's role in the production of its truths. A conventional reading of confessional poetry (as exemplified by Rosenthal, Phillips *et al.*, outlined above) emphasises the primacy of the confessing subject as the conduit for some pre-textual truth. A more radical Foucauldian reading, however, recognises the importance of the auditor to the realisation of the confession and argues that its meaning can only emerge as the product of a complex, dynamic and symbiotic, although not necessarily or always equal, relationship. For Foucault 'one does not confess without the presence (or virtual presence) of a partner who is not simply the interlocutor but the authority who requires the confession, prescribes and appreciates it, and intervenes in order to judge, punish, forgive, console, and reconcile' (1981: 61).

The self-conscious strategies of address employed throughout the book with the insistent 'I' apostrophising an explicit or implied 'you' (who is first and foremost the poems' primary addressee, Plath, but also a wider, indeterminate readership; the readers of the poem) help to consolidate and confirm the importance of this discursive bond. The carefully structured narrative framework of the collection, with its chronological sweep and its accretion of incidents and experiences invite and reward the readers' (confessors') attention. The intimate first-person narrative voice which interpellates and confides in us seems to offer privileged access to hitherto 'secret' details (the colour of Plath's wedding outfit, the story behind the well-known photograph of Plath sitting among the daffodils with her children (34, 143)), thereby seducing us into offering both our commitment and our blessing.[5] In examples such as these, the poems anticipate and manipulate our own prior knowledge as readers of Plath's life (in biographical accounts, the *Journals* and *Letters Home*) and work (the poems and stories). They ask us to corroborate the stories they tell us, ask us to bring our experience to bear – experience which, in places seems more reliable, certainly more accessible, than that of his primary addressee. Internally, too, the reader's evaluative or hermeneutic powers, consideration and assent are sought and expected. The repeated staccato questions of '18 Rugby Street', for example, 'How did you enter? What came next? / How did Lucas delete himself, for instance? / Did we even sit?' (22), place the reader in the situation of witness or more properly as judge. Our given role is to assess the available evidence and to assuage the speaker's doubts.

In his *Paris Review* interview, speculating about confessional writing, Hughes suggests that poetry may be 'a revealing of something that the writer doesn't actually want to say, but desperately needs to communicate, to be delivered of' (1995: 75). We should note the epistolary metaphor and the implication that in 'delivering' himself of his secret, he displaces the responsibility for it on to its recipient. The structure of *Birthday Letters* is important in consolidating the speaker/reader (confessant/confessor) relationship. The notional transmission of letters explicit in the title, and implicit throughout, makes the 'I'/'you' bond which is always at the heart of confessional discourse visible and functional.

Hughes's choice of the letter in this context is not unprecedented, nor is it disinterested. Foucault describes the use of letters as an 'ancient' confessional technique: 'the examination of conscience begins with this letter writing' (1988: 27, 30). More recently, Plath's own *Letters Home* (1976) is an obvious, and in its frequently noted equivocalness a provocative, subtext. Contemporaries Robert Lowell, Anne Sexton and William Carlos Williams used letters as the bases of poetry collections of their own. Lowell notoriously modelled his collection *The Dolphin* on correspondence from his estranged wife (and garnered much criticism, for example from Elizabeth Bishop, for so doing).[6] William Carlos Williams attracted approbation for his use of letters from Allen Ginsberg and Marcia Nardi in *Paterson* while Anne Sexton's posthumous *Words for Dr. Y.* (1978) contains a sequence of 'Letters to Dr. Y', her lover and one-time therapist. The addressee in such cases stands in the place of a muse – an absent or lost other who is responsible both for inspiring the poems and for receiving them, who is their origin *and* their destination. Given these precedents, Hughes's choice of the trope of the letter signals not only a desire to enter into dialogue with the personal past, but also a willingness to risk engagement with a confessional tradition which he had hitherto shunned. The self-conscious use of the epistolary framework also works to foreground the potentially unsettling nature of confessional discourse. The letters function as a metonym for confessional writing more generally; they represent something private and indeterminate (Hughes's 'secret confession' (1995: 75)) made concrete and offered for public scrutiny. It is here that the complex ethics of confessionalism are writ large and that we are forced into a recognition of our part, our complicity even, in the confessional circuit of exchange. We become guilty by association. We are made party to unwelcome insights and unexpected truths, and as readers we are forced to admit at the very least to our own voyeurism, our scopophilia.

Leigh Gilmore develops Foucault's point about the importance to the realisation of the confession of the relationship between the confessant and confessor by identifying a third party in that exchange – the confessional text itself (the 'tale' or, as in this collection, the 'letter'): 'In order to catalyze the dynamics of what we recognize as confession, the stage must be set with a penitent/teller, a listener, and a tale' (1994: 121). In the lines from Hughes's 'Visit' which I have taken as my title ('It's only a story. / Your story. My story' (9)) the speaker concedes the validity of this model and of the kind of triangulation which Gilmore posits: Hughes's 'It's only a story' signifies Gilmore's 'tale', while his 'Your story. My story' connotes her 'listener' and 'penitent/teller' respectively (Gilmore 1994: 121). Nevertheless, Hughes's speaker seems unwilling to accept the implied parity of the three functions. The syntax of these lines with the emphatic closing 'my story' represents a last, desperate insistence on the importance of subjective experience. It is '*my* story' (my emphasis) which insists on having the last word (9).

The recognition in *Birthday Letters* of the importance of the audience is accompanied by an equal and opposite sense of its inherent problems. Other confessional poets have conceded the same difficulties. Plath's 'Lady Lazarus' famously decries the 'peanut-crunching crowd' (1981: 244). Anne Sexton's 'Making a Living' offers a sustained critique of the exploitative relationship between suffering subject and intrusive reader. Sexton's speaker, Jonah, makes a living from retelling 'each detail' of his traumatic experience and declares 'it will profit me to understand it' (1981: 350). Hughes's poem 'Daffodils' uses the same idiom: 'Mainly we were hungry / To convert everything to profit' (1998: 127). Both poems display a deep ambivalence about the ethics of this kind of self-exploitation and specifically about the reification and commodification of the confession.

Hughes's 'Chaucer' examines the dynamics of such an exchange. The poem's addressee is pictured atop a stile shouting lines of Chaucer's *Canterbury Tales* to an audience of cows. The confessing subject is locked into a difficult and demanding relationship with her audience – an audience which is at first desired (she strives to 'hold the reins of [the cows'] straining attention') but soon becomes threatening, overwhelming: 'they shoved and jostled shoulders'.[7] The balance of power shifts such that it is the audience which requires and demands the confession, and the subject who struggles to deliver, to sustain the performance. 'Chaucer', like Plath's 'Lady Lazarus', recognises that the confession, once initiated, comes under its audience's control; it asks about the repercussions 'If you were to stop? Would they attack you, / Scared by the shock of silence, or wanting more – ?' (1998: 51–2). Arguably, there is a self-reflexive element to Hughes's question and a suggestion that this poem, like the larger collection, may have arisen precisely in response to these kinds of demands from a hostile audience.

The conflict with the audience in some of these poems, particularly the later ones 'Costly Speech' and 'The Dogs Are Eating Your Mother', masks a reluctant recognition of their equal prerogative over the elusive truth, their hermeneutic power. As Foucault insists of the model of confession which has historically pertained: 'The truth did not reside solely in the subject who, by confessing, would reveal it wholly formed ... it could only reach completion in the one who assimilated and recorded it' (1981: 66). What the subject concedes is that he cannot know or recover the truth that he seeks. Such a truth, it transpires, is generated only in the process of being spoken and, crucially, audited. In such a context, who owns the story? In a well-known letter of 1989, written during a particularly fraught series of exchanges with Plath critics and biographers, Hughes insisted 'I hope each of us owns the facts of his or her own life' (cited in Rose 1991: 65). In many ways, *Birthday Letters* is a reflection on, and perhaps a rethinking of, that assumption – a concession of the misguided 'hope' of his original assertion. What it shows is Hughes's gradual, painful discovery that there are no determinate 'facts' to be controlled, only unanswerable, rhetorical questions and memories which although constantly seeking corroboration, cannot be guaranteed. If the 'life' is constructed in the process of retelling it (to recap Hughes, 'if you don't have that secret confession, you don't have a poem – don't even have a story. Don't have a writer'), it is not possible to separate the 'life' from its textualisation – from its production and its reception, its writing and its reading.

Again and again *Birthday Letters* points to the disjunction between memory and its representation, truth and confession: in 'Visit' 'suddenly I read all this – / Your actual words, as they floated / Out through your throat and tongue and onto your page' (8). 'The 59th Bear' rages against its addressee's attempt to 'turn ... life to paper / ... our dud scenario into a fiction' (9) in her short story of the same title (Plath 1979), while ironically, of course, committing exactly the same sin itself. The collection is forced to accept that truth is only ever textual. As Linda Hutcheon puts it 'the past is only known to us today through its textualized traces (which, like all texts, are always open to interpretation)' (1989: 81). We read the past, hence the endless allusions to decipherment, signs, and forms of reading in *Birthday Letters*, hence 'letters' (these poems and, metonymically, language in general) which must be read in order to be meaningful. And we create multiple new truths for the reading in our own writing.

Hughes's speaker cannot remember what really happened hence the cease-less questions and expressions of doubt throughout the volume. More importantly, he cannot access the elusive truth of his own experience other than by a process of reading and interpreting disparate signs from the past. In the opening poem of the collection, 'Fulbright Scholars', he has no direct access to the object of his search. Rather, his contact must be mediated by a text; in that poem by a captioned photo which he may or may not have really seen but which figures in his memory as first evidence of her existence. In other poems, the root to the lost 'real' is represented in and by his addressee's journals ('Visit', '18 Rugby Street', 'The Gypsy'), letters ('The Hands'), drawings ('Drawing'), stories ('The 59th Bear'), and poems ('Cary-atids (1)', 'The Earthenware Head' and numerous others). Each source is meaningless without readerly interpretation, without the 'hermeneutic func-tion' which Foucault ascribes to the confessor (1981: 67, 66). In 'Visit', the speaker's epiphany, like ours as the audience, comes from reading. In his case, his reading of his addressee's journals – which here assume the status of a kind of *ur*-confession – and in our case through our reading of this very poem. The speaker meets the truth 'on a page of your journal as never before' while we meet the truth on a page of this poetry collection as never before (8). If we function as the speaker's confessor (if, in Foucault's terms, we receive and judge the confession) then he performs the same role for his addressee.

Hughes's speaker is also, of course, reading himself (Candace Lang describes autobiography as a process of reading one's own past 'as one would a book' (1982: 11)). He is both subject and object of his own confession. The form of the letter is instrumental in confirming this split. It plays with notions of absence and presence, addressing an 'other' who is both 'here' in the sense that they are being addressed, and not 'here' precisely in the sense that they can only thus be addressed. Janet Altman characterises letter writing thus: 'It is truly a communication with specters, not only with the specter of the addressee but also with one's own phantom, which evolves underneath one's own hand in the very letter one is writing' (1982: 2). The speaker works, then, as his own confessor in an act of self-witnessing pro-pelled by his construction of himself (the Ted Hughes of the poems) as a dramatic participant or persona in the poems. Lynda K. Bundtzen (2001: 14–15) and Diane Middlebrook (2003: 260) have noted Hughes's tendency to speak of himself in the third person when commenting on Plath's literary affairs as though to dissociate himself from his actions. In *Birthday Letters*, too, he steps back from his self and from his past and watches, witnesses, judges, himself from the outside.

The position which the speaker/confessant adopts in many of these poems of watching and reading himself in the process of watching and reading his addressee confirms the symbiotic nature of the confessional relationship – a relationship which is closed, hermetic and finally paralysing. Anne Sexton's loosely epistolary poem, 'For John, Who Begs Me not to Enquire Further', depicts its subject and addressee bonded by their shared gaze: 'and some-times in private / my kitchen, your kitchen, / my face, your face' (1981: 35). Hughes's 'The Beach' traces a sequence of personal, cultural and geographical schisms (self vs. other, deprivation vs. plenty, England vs. America) but closes with the utterly divergent parties caught in each other's gaze: 'here, at my feet, in the suds, / The other face, the real, staring upwards' (156). Each face (the real and the reflected, the self and the other) is locked into, paralysed by, and finally indistinguishable from the other. Yet what seems hermetic and private and sealed is finally liberated by being offered for public display. What we have, in the end, is a doubling or multiplication of confessions, a confessional dialogue not simply in the sense that each party speaks to the other and functions as both confessant to and confessor of the other, but in the sense that both parties combine, speak with one voice, and position the reader as the outsider playing the necessary and functional role of *their* ultimate confessor.

One of the primary concerns of *Birthday Letters* is with the nature of the language which it has at its disposal. A conventional reading of confession depends on a trust (a 'fidelity') in language, in its referentiality, its instrumentality and its ability to translate experience onto the page. *Birthday Letters* cannot accept these as givens. If the root of confession – its *raison d'être* for subject and reader alike – is its ability to represent experience in language, then this book is deeply disturbed by its own possible failure to achieve this. The book raises huge questions – about knowledge, and responsibility and memory, and truth, and identity – but fundamental to its broaching of these is the problem of language, and language here is a barrier not a conduit. It is slippery and evasive and intransitive and it leaves the speaker/confessant in the impossible situation of being unable to speak, being unable to render account. From this, we might conclude two things: first, as I've already suggested, that what *Birthday Letters* is confessing is its realisation of the impossibility of its own project and, second, that the confession resides as much in what it does not say, in its secrets and silences, as in what it does manage to voice.

Throughout the collection we find repeated allusions to the slipperiness or indeterminacy of language; to 'signs' and 'a code' ripe for misreading, to 'conjectural, hopelessly wrong meanings' (39, 139, 37). These signal a larger anxiety about the practicalities and the ethics of turning experience to account, of turning 'life to paper', as 'The 59th Bear' has it (94). Robert Lowell's 'Letter' from the sequence 'Marriage' makes a similar point, complaining 'I despair of letters', but closing with the plaintive 'I hope nothing is mis-said in this letter' (1973: 58). How can one render the past in a language which so often in these poems proves fallible or opaque or incomprehensible? Although in an early and well-known essay 'Poetry in the Making' (1967), Hughes confidently asserts the malleability and instrumentality of language: 'Words are tools ... a word has its own definite meanings' (1994: 19), in these poems the relationship is acknowledged to be far less straightforward. Here language is the source not of clarity and insight ('definite meanings') but of confusion and misunderstanding. Hughes recognises the problem for the poet in modernity of the failure or unreliability or sheer impossibility of language. As he notes of the work of Hungarian poet, János Pilinszky, '"After Auschwitz" ... The mass of the human evidence of the camps, and of similar situations since, has raised the price of "truth" and "reality" and "understanding" beyond what common words seem able to pay' such that 'all words seem obsolete or inadequate' (1994: 232, 234).[8] A similar self-consciousness about the inadequacies of its own language and, relatedly, of the uncertainty of its own truths, coupled with a scepticism about authority, subjectivity and representation, are what mark *Birthday Letters* as an exemplary *modern* confession.

Hughes's poem 'Fidelity' traces the shift from a misplaced confidence in the reliability of language as a way of documenting experience to a recognition of its intransitive non-referentiality; the shift, perhaps, from a faithful (hence the title) language to one which cannot be trusted and must be carefully monitored. The main body of the poem is fluid and descriptive, clearly locating the speaker's experience in space ('Alexandra House' in 'a top room / Overlooking Petty Cury. A bare mattress') and time (in his 'twenty-fifth year') and in a personal context (in a relationship with 'a lovely girl, escaped freshly / from her husband'). Yet there is something dispassionate about this scene-setting as though the speaker were either witnessing a life other than his own, or providing only enough detail to satisfy external enquiries. In this context 'Fidelity' connotes faithfulness in law, the juridical requirement to provide just and accurate evidence. A note at the end of the poem undermines the confidence of these initial representations though, and gestures towards the real issue which is the speaker's concern about faithfully rendering his experience, about making language subordinate to his needs: 'You will never know what a battle / I fought to keep the meaning of my words / solid with the world we were making'. 'Fidelity', then, is about more than marital or legalistic unfaithfulness, it is about the awful risk of linguistic or textual bad faith (28–30).

'Your Paris' confirms the slipperiness of language, exemplifying the post-Saussurian split between signifier and signified. As the opening line explains: 'Your Paris, I thought, was American'. This is just the first in a series of misprisions, misunderstandings and mistranslations – of language and hence of experience. Previous textual representations of Paris ('the chestnut shades of Hemingway, / Fitzgerald, Henry Miller, Gertrude Stein') although meaningful to the poem's American addressee, bear little resemblance to the real, and signify nothing to the embattled English speaker. In this poem, which should see the English and American participants united in this foreign culture by their common language, it is precisely the differences within the language which split them apart. Language for the addressee functions not as a means of self-exposure but as a mask or defence mechanism, an 'emergency burn-off / To protect you from spontaneous combustion'. For the speaker, language is an overwhelming, incomprehensible flood which is no longer, if it ever was, the subject's 'tool' but a force which dominates him: 'Your gushy burblings – which I decoded / Into a language, utterly new to me / With conjectural, hopelessly wrong meanings' (36–8).

Paradoxically, the more the poem seems to say, the less it tells. The language of these poems plays what Foucault, in the context of the multiplying discourses of sex in the modern period, has called a 'defensive role'. The poems, by saying and revealing 'so much' conceal their object; they function as a form of 'screen-discourse, a dispersion-avoidance' (Foucault 1981: 53). Hughes suggests as much in 'The Earthenware Head' which alludes to Plath's use of language in her poem on the same theme: 'You ransacked thesaurus in your poem about it, / veiling its mirror, rhyming yourself into safety' (57–8). This is the effect of *Birthday Letters* which seems, on the surface at least – and this is an artful effect of the strong narrative thread, the unity of themes and metaphors, the apparent simplicity of diction and directness of address – to be telling all but leaves us finally knowing little, and uncertain about quite how much has been revealed. We are blinded by the glare of exposure, of revelation. The multiple images of fire, light, flames (in Platonic terms, metaphors for insight and illumination) dazzle us. The mirrors, windows and lenses promise clarity of perception but instead, in their fractured and distorted or clouded shape, merely mislead. If we take confession to be a technique for producing truth (for Foucault, truth is the 'system of ordered procedures for the production, regulation, distribution, circulation, and operation of statements' (1986: 74)) and self-knowledge (one of the 'specific techniques that human beings use to understand themselves' (1988: 18)), we must also recognise that these poems offer strategies for avoiding such knowledge.

The vivid surface notwithstanding, it is between the gaps, in the un- or under-stated that truth, perhaps, lies. In an essay on his play, 'Orghast', Hughes recalls an occasion when he interviewed two survivors of the traumatic World War I campaign at Gallipoli. He found one interviewee to be voluble and the other 'monosyllabic' but it was from the 'taciturn' survivor that he learned the true, unspoken, horror of the experience:

> Words and natural narrative, dramatic skill concealed everything in the one. While in the other, exclamations, hesitating vague words, I don't know what, just something about his half-movements and very dumbness released a world of shocking force and vividness. The same principle works in all sorts of situations.
>
> (1994: 123)

In the essay on the poetry of János Pilinszky, cited earlier, Hughes concedes, in a comment which I contend stands also for *Birthday Letters*, that 'silence can be a resonant form of speech' (1994: 232). This is a paradox or enigma which *Birthday Letters* is aware of and exploits. In his poem 'The Gypsy' (1998: 117) the speaker is horrified by hearing a gypsy's malevolent curse. What he finds even more traumatic though is his addressee's refusal to acknowledge it: 'you / never mentioned it. Never recorded it / In your diary'. Her silence is more ominous than any comment she might have made. Sarah Churchwell reads *Birthday Letters* as an 'open secret' (2001: 104) and suggests that 'its narrative told us little that we didn't already know' (121). I would argue that its silences tell us much more than this, that they tell us something about the impossibility of telling, that they confess the impossibility of confession.

'Error', which seems to announce itself as the ultimate confession, the revelation of the originary sin or Fall, the catastrophic misjudgement from which all other disasters have flowed, proves finally to be as preoccupied with what it cannot or will not tell us. It begins by envisioning Devon, the English county to which the speaker has brought his addressee, as 'my dreamland', 'my land of totems. Never-never land'. Its own certainties or clarities are thus undermined, exposed to be phantasmagorical. We are sharing somebody else's ongoing nightmare: 'I sleepwalked you' and can expect no accuracy of representation. Equally, like so many of these poems, 'Error' is full of questions, indicating again, the title of the poem notwithstanding, the speaker's uncertainty about or reluctance to disclose what, precisely, the 'error' is.

This is a world of darkness and gloom, realised in onomatopoeic and assonantal lines: 'a gloom orchard / Under drumming thatch' (this 'gloom orchard' is, of course the reverse of the garden of Eden but paradoxically, as a place of error, identical with it) and synaesthesia 'the murmur of rain, and staring at that sunken church, and the black / slate roofs'. It is a world of isolation and mutual incomprehension where the local villagers 'Jabbered hedge-bank judgements, a dark-age dialect'. Again language is a weapon which is wielded at the addressee, enforcing her alienation rather than encouraging communion. Curiously and crucially this dreadful, fateful scene is evoked both by the impermanence or transience of the metaphors (the 'bubble' of 'closed brilliance' suggests a fragile bell jar, the 'transparency' suggests a shiny, insubstantial film or negative) and by the resounding – I use the adjective advisedly – silence which underpins the whole: the 'blank sheet', the 'silent', the 'unseen' (122–3). Here, as throughout the collection (and arguably in confessional writing more generally), it is the unsaid or unseen, that which we hear 'crying soundlessly', that seems uncannily to speak.

Reflective, glassy, brilliantly mirroring surfaces such as these (conventionally metaphors for clarity of representation and faithful mimesis) are frequently shown to be fractured, shattered or otherwise distorted. In 'The Bird', for example, multiple images of glass accumulate from the 'glass dome' of the opening line (inevitably recalling Plath's *The Bell Jar* which shares many of these preoccupations) to the 'ice-caked ship', the 'chandelier of lacy crystals', and the glass tumbler at the climax of the poem which suddenly shatters into myriad pieces: 'Every crumb // was flawed into crystals infinitely tiny' (77–9). Each of these metaphors reminds us of the fragility of truth and its representation, the fallibility and multiplicity of what might at first appear to be direct insight.[9]

Given this, what is it, finally, that these 'letters' deliver? ('Why do human beings need to confess?'). Hughes has talked about, and demonstrated, the need for an audience. He has talked about and demonstrated the plangent force of silence, he has confirmed that what remains unsaid is as important as, and perhaps more important than, the ostensible story. He has conceded that the 'story' may be just that; a fictionalisation, certainly a dramatisation, of experience, the product of imagination not necessarily the symptom of actuality. But what these letters also suggest – and this is uncomfortable perhaps for the post-humanist reading of confession I've proposed above – is that for the confessing subject there is a form of catharsis or purgation within sight. This is realised in repeated allusions throughout the poems to fire, heat, burning, to the purifying effects of self-immersion in this inflammatory material.

Plath also uses burning and conflagration in her poems ('Witch Burning' in 'Poem for a Birthday', 'Burning the Letters', and 'Lady Lazarus' come to mind (1981: 135–6, 204–5, 244)) as a means to and metaphor for self-transformation and finally for self-destruction. Hughes's interest, as I have suggested, is in what this dreadful and painful process – metaphorically and self-referentially, the painful, burning, self-immolating process of writing and publishing these poems – generates. Many critics have noticed the preponderance of the colour red (images of blood or burning) throughout the volume and have puzzled over the emergence of the colour blue, used in connection with the volume's primary addressee, in the closing lines of the final poem, 'Red': 'In the pit of red / You hid from the bone-clinic whiteness. // But the jewel you lost was blue' (197–8).

The hell of immersing oneself in this 'pit' of memories and the burning, caustic, inferno of the experience is better, in the end, than the deathly sterility or cold numbness (the 'bone-clinic whiteness') of refusing so to do. In a 1998 letter to Keith Sagar, Hughes acknowledges that his early and longstanding refusal to address the material encapsulated in *Birthday Letters* was blocking and finally '"destroying" him "physically, literally"' (cited in Patterson 2001). Although in 'Red' the addressee is submerged among the burning (flame red, ash white) colours of the furnace, we finally see that it is only out of the burning and shameful purgation of confession that the spectre or spirit of his sought object can emerge, like the blue tongues of flame, from the red embers of a dying fire. The emergence of the colour blue at this point inescapably takes the reader back to Plath's 'Ariel' with its opening panorama of 'substanceless blue', confirming the circularity and intertextuality of confession.[10] Linda Wagner-Martin notes the use of the colours white, silver, gold and red in Plath's 'Burning the Letters' and suggests that these represent stages in the process of self-purification. She, too, notes a residual trace of ' "faint blue violet" ' in the poem which 'accrues from the process of turning ash into nothingness' (1999: 144).

Frazer in *The Golden Bough* (a text which was hugely formative for Hughes) traces the development of two distinct theories of fire: the purification theory sees it as 'a cleansing agent' (1950: 648), a 'fierce destructive power which blasts and consumes all the noxious elements' (642), the 'solar' theory sees fire as creative, productive, 'positive' (642). *Birthday Letters*, I contend, has it both ways (as Frazer notes, the two views are 'not wholly irreconcilable' (642)) and more. For it is also possible to see the flames of *Birthday Letters* as Pentecostal. The flames, at last, give Hughes the power of speech, endow him with a language with which he can finally communicate.

And although I have just suggested that this therapeutic or cathartic rationale seems contrary to the kind of reading I've been offering, I would like to qualify this by arguing that it is the absolute self-conscious centrality of this purgative process, and the questioning of it implicit in its repeated foregrounding in the text, which makes this paradoxically part and parcel of these poems' exemplary confessional status. *Birthday Letters* cannot accept that such a catharsis can come easily and thus it takes purgation alongside all of those other received characteristics of confessional writing – its referentiality, its truth value and so on – and tests its limits. What it finds is that the kind of purification by fire which underpins so many of the poems is a necessary part of the confessional process but not its chief justification or telos. Instead, the fires which burn throughout the collection extend or attenuate or displace the confession such that it never truly reaches completion.

Hughes's earlier poem 'The Accused', from his 1978 collection *Cave Birds*, uses fire imagery in its explicit representation of the trauma of confession. The accused here 'confesses his body', delivering his physical, spiritual and mental self for trial by fire: 'On a flame-horned mountain-stone, in the sun's disk, / He heaps them all up, for the judgement' (1993: 76). There is no complete consumption or immolation here though, instead the process leaves traces: 'there his atoms are annealed'. 'Annealed' may be defined as both 'to burn in colours upon glass, earthenware, or metal, to enamel' and 'to toughen after fusion by exposure to continuous and slowly diminished heat'. Surely both of these might be read as metaphors for confessional poetry and as foretelling the process of writing *Birthday Letters* – in each case delivering an aesthetically pleasing artefact and a transformed (here toughened) subject? Most importantly, the purgation delivers something of value to its audience, the confessors. In 'The Accused', the 'one' who was committed to the flames leaves a residue – the 'rainbowed clinker' – a residue which in its symbolic prolepsis and multiplicity is ripe for endless further interpretation. Foucault calls confession an 'infinite task' (1981: 59) and this registers the daunting ceaselessness of confession, its endless displacement of the truth such that there is always a further stage of revelation or corroboration or contradiction, always something else to read and interpret. As Peter Brooks puts it, there is 'no endpoint for confession' only an 'uncontrollable proliferation of narratives' (2001: 33, 48).

The answer which *Birthday Letters* offers, then, to Hughes's 'Why do human beings need to confess?' is to be found in his initial speculative responses to his own question ('without that secret confession, you don't have a poem – don't even have a story. Don't have a writer'). The need to confess is the need to create; the need to create stories, narratives, meaning and subjectivity (for Foucault, the need 'to constitute, positively, a new self' (1998: 49)). This is potentially a hugely liberating process. To be able to concede or confess that one does not know what really happened, although at first disorientating (one can sense the note of despair in some of the plaintive questions in the early poems in the collection) can prove finally purposive. To be able to abandon the reductive search for certainty, and the rhetoric of the law courts, and turn instead to imagination, speculation, indeterminacy offers a more satisfying, and paradoxically more faithful, representation of personal experience than strict adherence to verifiable evidence (in so far as this might be attained) could provide. The need to confess, as *Birthday Letters* learns, is the need to realise (in the sense both of 'to recognise' and 'to create') what is there. As Nancy Miller explains in her account of writing a memoir: 'For me as a writer, the answer to the question of what "really" happened is literary – or at least textual. I will know only when I write it' (2004: 157).

Confession does not reveal some pre-textual truth – *Birthday Letters* is not, then, documentary evidence – it constructs multiple and shared stories. The rainbowed clinker in 'The Accused' and the prismatic and enigmatic blue jewel which emerges, phoenix or Lazarus-like, from the flames in the final poem, 'Red', are ripe for ceaseless and divergent readings. And the visible but paradoxically 'lost' blue jewel which closes *Birthday Letters* stands as a metaphor for the promise and the impossibility of confession, which hides more than it tells, which veils its truths in enigmatic images, which makes demands of the reader's hermeneutic and creative powers, and which can finally only displace its secrets onto somewhere else, in ceaselessly circulating letters.

Acknowledgement

I would like to acknowledge the support of the British Academy whose offer of an Overseas Conference Grant enabled me to share an early version of this paper at a conference on 'Confessions', Université de Provence (March 2004).

Notes

1 See Wagner (2000) for an account of the publishing history of the volume.
2 *Birthday Letters*, according to its American publisher's rather hyperbolic

'Reader's Guide' is the 'untold portion of one of the great tragic love stories of our time' (Farrar *et al.* 2004).

3 Clare Tomalin says that Hughes is 'as formidable as he is brave' (1999: 153). The convention notwithstanding, recent confessional writers have resisted being labelled courageous. See Gill (2001: 85).

4 *Birthday Letters* is self-conscious about its own 'processes of production and reception'. It is, in Linda Hutcheon's terms, textually as much as biographically 'self-reflective, self-informing, self-reflexive, auto-referential, auto-representational' (1984: 1).

5 The photograph is reproduced in Erica Wagner's *Ariel's Gift* (2000) and Plath's *Journals* (2000).

6 Ted Hughes's sister, Olwyn, was at one time interested in publishing a small limited edition of Lowell's *The Dolphin*, testing the water with what was, from the outset, acknowledged to be a controversial collection (Hamilton 1983: 421). See Nelson (2002: 65) for more on the controversy surrounding Lowell's book, and Goldensohn (1992: 165) for more on Williams.

7 Blake Morrison and Robert McCrum have commented on the pressure of audience responses to their own confessional memoirs (Morrison 2004: 1–2; McCrum 1999: 227ff.).

8 The paradox, as Leigh Gilmore notes, is that 'at the same time language about trauma is theorized as an impossibility, language is pressed forward as that which can heal the survivor of trauma' (2001: 6).

9 See Gill (2004) for a discussion of the relationship between confession and narcissism.

10 I am grateful to one of my postgraduates, Russ Hayton, for reminding me of this.

Bibliography

Altman, J. (1982) *Epistolarity: Approaches to a Form*, Columbus: Ohio State University Press.

Alvarez, A. (1962) *The New Poetry*, Harmondsworth: Penguin.

—— (1999) 'Ted Hughes', in N. Gammage (ed.) *The Epic Poise: A Celebration of Ted Hughes*, London: Faber and Faber.

Brooks, P. (2001) *Troubling Confessions: Speaking Guilt in Law and Literature*, Chicago and London: Chicago University Press.

Bundtzen, L. (2001) *The Other Ariel*, Amherst: University of Massachusetts Press.

Churchwell, S. (2001) 'Secrets and Lies: Plath, Privacy, Publication and Ted Hughes's *Birthday Letters*', *Contemporary Literature* 42: 102–48.

Cox, C.B. and Jones, A.R. (1964) 'After the Tranquillized Fifties: Notes on Sylvia Plath and James Baldwin', *Critical Quarterly* 7: 11–30.

Davison, P. (1994) *The Fading Smile: Poets in Boston, 1955–1960*, New York: Knopf.

Eakin, P.J. (ed.) (2004) *The Ethics of Life Writing*, Ithaca and London: Cornell University Press.

Farrar, Strauss & Giroux (2004) *Birthday Letters: Reader's Guide*. Available online at: http://www.holtzbrinckpublishers.com/images/Books/ReadersGuides/0374525811 RG.pdf (accessed 9 December 2004).

Foucault, M. (1981) *The History of Sexuality. Volume One: An Introduction*, trans. R. Hurley, Harmondsworth: Penguin.

—— (1986) 'Truth and Power', in P. Rabinow (ed.) *The Foucault Reader: An Introduction to Foucault's Thought*, Harmondsworth: Penguin.

—— (1988) 'Technologies of the Self', in L.H. Martin, H. Gutman and P. Hutton (eds) *Technologies of the Self: A Seminar with Michel Foucault*, London: Tavistock.

Frazer, J.G. (1950) *The Golden Bough: A Study in Magic and Religion*, London: Macmillan.

Gill, J. (2001) 'Someone Else's Misfortune: The Vicarious Pleasures of the Confessional Text', *Journal of Popular Culture* 35 (1): 81–93.

—— (2004) 'Textual Confessions: Narcissism in Anne Sexton's Early Poetry', *Twentieth-Century Literature* 50: 59–87.

Gilmore, L. (1994) *Autobiographics: A Feminist Theory of Women's Self-Representation*, Ithaca and London: Cornell University Press.

—— (2001) *The Limits of Autobiography: Trauma and Testimony*, Ithaca and London: Cornell University Press.

Goldensohn, L. (1992) *Elizabeth Bishop: The Biography of a Poetry*, New York: Columbia University Press.

Graham, D. and Sontag, K. (eds) (2001) *After Confession: Poetry as Autobiography*, Saint Paul: Graywolf.

Hamilton, I. (1983) *Robert Lowell: A Biography*, London: Faber and Faber.

Hughes, T. (1993) *Three Books: Remains of Elmet, Cave Birds, River*, London: Faber and Faber.

—— (1994) *Winter Pollen: Occasional Prose*, London: Faber and Faber.

—— (1995) 'Ted Hughes: The Art of Poetry', *The Paris Review* 134: 54–94.

—— (1998) *Birthday Letters*, London: Faber and Faber.

Hutcheon, L. (1984) *Narcissistic Narrative: The Metafictional Paradox*, New York: Methuen.

—— (1989) *The Politics of Postmodernism*, London and New York: Routledge.

Lang, C. (1982) 'Autobiography in the Aftermath of Romanticism', *Diacritics* 12: 2–16.

Lowell, R. (1973) *The Dolphin*, London: Faber and Faber.

McCrum, R. (1999) *My Year Off: Rediscovering Life After a Stroke*, London: Picador.

Middlebrook, D.W. (2003) *Her Husband: Hughes and Plath – a Marriage*, London and New York: Viking.

Miller, N. (2004) 'The Ethics of Betrayal: Diary of a Memoirist', in P.J. Eakin (ed.) (2004) *The Ethics of Life Writing*, Ithaca and London: Cornell University Press.

Morrison, B. (2004) 'Secrets and Lies', *Observer* (Review Section), 3 October: 1–2.

Nelson, D. (2002) *Pursuing Privacy in Cold War America*, New York: Columbia University Press.

Patterson, C. (2001) 'Ted on Sylvia, for the Record'. Available online at: http://books.guardian.co.uk/print/0,3858,4240909-99936,00.html (accessed 5 July 2004).

Phillips, R. (1973) *The Confessional Poets*, Carbondale: Southern Illinois University Press.

Plath, S. (1966) *The Bell Jar*, London: Faber and Faber.

—— (1976) *Letters Home: Correspondence 1950–1963*, ed. A. Plath, London: Faber and Faber.

—— (1979) *Johnny Panic and the Bible of Dreams*, London: Faber and Faber.

—— (1981) *Collected Poems*, ed. T. Hughes, London: Faber and Faber.

—— (2000) *The Journals of Sylvia Plath: 1950–1962*, ed. K.V. Kukil, London: Faber and Faber.

Rose, J. (1991) *The Haunting of Sylvia Plath*, London: Virago.

—— (2003) *On Not Being Able to Sleep: Psychoanalysis and the Modern World*, London: Chatto & Windus.

Rosenthal, M.L. (1959) 'Poetry as Confession', *The Nation* 189: 154–5.

Rousseau, J.-J. (1953) *The Confessions of Jean-Jacques Rousseau*, trans. J.M. Cohen, Harmondsworth: Penguin.

Sexton, A. (1978) *Words for Dr Y.*, Boston: Houghton Mifflin.

—— (1981) *Anne Sexton: The Complete Poems*, ed. L. Ames and L.G. Sexton, Boston: Houghton Mifflin.

Tomalin, C. (1999) 'Daffodils', in N. Gammage (ed.) *The Epic Poise: A Celebration of Ted Hughes*, London: Faber and Faber.

Wagner, E. (2000) *Ariel's Gift: Ted Hughes, Sylvia Plath and the Story of Birthday Letters*, London: Faber and Faber.

Wagner-Martin, L. (1999) *Sylvia Plath: A Literary Life*, New York: St Martin's Press.

5   *Bridget Jones's Diary*
Confessing post-feminism

Leah Guenther

In 1995, the British newspaper the *Independent* ran a then-anonymous column entitled *Bridget Jones's Diary*. The column, in a freshly ironic and satirical manner, chronicled the daily vicissitudes of a thirty-something London 'singleton'. In 1996, Helen Fielding, the column's author, emerged with a novel by the same name, a novel that continued to document the title character's obsession with her vices: chocolate, cigarettes, Chardonnay and unsuitable suitors. After the novel's success, the columns were given a new home at the *Daily Telegraph* in 1997; the original novel was translated into thirty-three languages; and a successful sequel, *Bridget Jones: The Edge of Reason*, emerged in 1999. Both books were eventually translated into film as well, the original novel being adapted for release in 2001 and the sequel in 2004. The Bridget Jones phenomenon did not stop there, however. The success of Fielding's work is said to have spawned the genre of 'chick-lit' in both Britain and America: countless first-person novels penned by countless first-time female novelists began to hit the shelves.

Nevertheless, while Fielding's work has enjoyed much commercial success, Fielding's novel and its progeny have been criticized for reinforcing conventional gender roles while pretending to challenge them. Furthermore, detractors lambasted the novel for its adherence to traditional romantic plot devices, criticisms that were helped along by the fact that Fielding modelled the plot of the first novel on Jane Austen's *Pride and Prejudice* and its sequel on *Persuasion* – albeit in both cases with a sense of the latent complexity and ambivalence of Austen's women characters' experiences and desires.

The present essay seeks to challenge these frequently dismissive views of Fielding's work. While conceding the persuasiveness of some critiques of the book, it aims to recuperate *Bridget Jones's Diary* – and its heroine – by offering a new reading of the text as feminist confessional. The first part of the essay identifies and assesses the validity of typical criticisms of the work. It addresses Fielding's choice of the diary form, analysing Bridget's use of the diary as a device of self-monitoring and examining the ways in which the diary serves her as an in-house confessional. The second part of the essay considers the novel's relation to feminism – second and third wave feminism and what has been labelled 'post-feminism' – by inspecting its critics' responses as well as the way that feminism as a category is treated within the text. The final portion of the essay evaluates the effect of this new feminist confession. By moving away from the contentious term 'post-feminist' that has too often been applied to Fielding's work and its successors, the term 'new feminist confession', as used here, connotes some of the complexity of the field of feminism as well as *Bridget Jones's Diary*'s relationship to it.[1] To its credit, *Bridget Jones's Diary* addresses aspects of both second and third wave feminism, choosing, as will be argued, not to pit wave against wave but, instead, to merge elements from each in order to form a new brand of feminist confession. In this manner, Fielding's novel, as well as many of its 'chick-lit' successors, relies on the first-person female narrative (a mainstay of second wave feminism), as well as the use of comedy and irony (a third wave feminist trademark), to create a new kind and community of feminist authors.

'I am a child of *Cosmopolitan* culture'

Bridget Jones's Diary opens with the words 'I will not'. This declarative pro-hibition, set in boldface capital letters, introduces the title character's list of New Year's resolutions, good intentions that run the usual gamut from vowing not to 'drink more than fourteen alcohol units per week' to refusing to 'bitch about anyone behind their backs' (Fielding 1996: 2).[2] Appropri-ately, this opening immediately establishes Bridget's desire to perfect what she sees as her inherently flawed self. As such annual goals are notoriously idealistic and thus doomed from the start, *Bridget Jones's Diary* opens by highlighting not only the idea of self-improvement but also the ever-present spectre of failure that accompanies such an intent. This spectre, Alison Case argues, is further indicated in the novel's form: Bridget, she notes, calls to mind a long line of fictional female diarists who are unable to control their lives or the trajectory of their stories. Case argues that female diary narration has historically positioned the diarist as a mere witness to events as they unfold and, as such, has tended to 'deprive the narrator of the interpretive advantage of hindsight with which to shape a narrative' (Case 2001: 177). Bridget's jurisdiction over her life, she argues, as well as her ability to change herself into something new-and-improved, is necessarily undermined not only by unrealistic expectations, but also by form.

By categorizing Bridget as just another female diarist, however, Case fails to account for the importance of the historical moment in which Helen Fielding's novel is set. This moment is exaggerated by Fielding's decision to superimpose the plot of Jane Austen's *Pride and Prejudice* onto Bridget's late 1990s surroundings. While Fielding's modernization of Austen's novel does highlight similarities between the two worlds – such as women's reliance on private spaces of discourse, their ongoing attempts at self-refinement, and a perpetual interest in snagging a man – translating her predecessor's work into a contemporary setting highlights an important difference as well.

Whereas Austen's heroines bemoan their limited choices, Fielding's lament having too many. Austen's characters are given one cultural directive, to marry, while Fielding's struggle with conflicting social messages that compel them simultaneously to find a man, be independent, build a career, start a family, have sex indiscriminately and be chaste. In this light, Bridget's struggle to control her life and her narrative results not from a literary convention that emphasizes women's economic and sexual restriction, but from a cultural imperative to strive for multiple and contradictory female ideals.

The novel locates much of the cultural confusion over women's self-definition on the pages of glossy women's magazines. Janice Winship refers to the ideology contained on the pages of *Cosmopolitan* and *Marie Claire* as a 'women's world', one that is replete with messages that simultaneously pay lip-service to female empowerment while promoting women's concern with an image control that is primarily based on the purchase of consumer goods (Winship 1987). Jonathan Bignell argues that women's magazines present a set of representations, concerns and desires that construct a female identity for those who wish to 'buy into it'. Bignell identifies the significance of this wording, noting that 'the turn of phrase "buy into" is appropriate here because of the links established by feminist critical discourse between the textual production in magazines and the consumption practices of their readership' (Bignell 2004: 164). Bridget certainly is not immune to this 'women's world' or its messages. However, she is not uncritical of it. She seems conscious of the havoc that such women's magazines have wreaked upon her life. Trying to come to terms with her body image and life choices, for example, she notes regretfully that 'I am a child of *Cosmopolitan* culture [and] have been traumatized by supermodels and too many quizzes and know that neither my personality nor my body is up to it if left to its own devices' (1996: 59).

Unfortunately, what Bridget does at first appear to take from the 'women's world' of glossy magazines is a notion that the self is not fixed and unchangeable. Bridget's adoption of the 'women's world' message that the self-as-product is something to shop for, try on and adopt at will, perfectly prepares her for the genre of self-help books that emerged in force in the 1990s, primarily targeting women. Elayne Rapping notes that while the self-help genre was radical in its ability to open up dialogue on previously unmentionable or embarrassing topics, the publications also tended to depoliticize women's plights, forcing women to treat the symptoms of social problems rather than the problems themselves. Rapping also takes issue with the dependence on religion within self-help, indicting the trend of advising women not to take action against wrongdoers but, instead, to call upon a Higher Power or a Greater Good (Rapping 1996). Trish Todd, editorial director of Simon & Schuster commented on this intermingling of religion and self-help when, in the mid-1990s, she was asked about the mammoth increase in production of self-help titles. She notes, 'there seems to be a hunger for change, for a new age, and the closer we get to the millennium the more spiritual books resemble self-help books and self-help books are like spiritual books' (Davis 1996: 23).

In *Bridget Jones's Diary* the line between self-help books and spiritual guidance is nothing if not blurred. Arguably, the self-help books at Bridget's disposal do not hold for her a dominant ideology so much as a dominant theology. Bridget describes self-help books as 'a new form of religion' that helps people to 'start trying to find another set of rules' when organized religion fails them. She effaces the distinction between traditional religious formats and what she sees as their new incarnations in self-improvement, hence her comment that she has learned the 'importance of positive thought' from '*Emotional Intelligence, Emotional Confidence, The Road Less Traveled, How to Rid Your Thighs of Cellulite in 30 Days*, [and the] Gospel according to St Luke, Ch. 13' (1999: 265). Moreover, deciding that she must thin out her collection of titles she notes, 'Cannot bear to throw out *The Road Less Traveled* and *You Can Heal Your Life*', and asks herself 'Where else is one to turn for spiritual guidance to deal with problems of the modern age if not self-help books?' (1999: 264). Bridget's conflation of religion, self-help and confessional self-scrutiny is of note here and brings to mind Foucault's notion of 'technologies of the self' (Foucault 1988) – strategies of knowing and caring for the self which have developed in various historical and spiritual contexts. In a Christian context these emerge as 'a set of conditions and rules of behavior for a certain transformation of the self'. Christianity, according to Foucault, positions itself as a salvation religion, one which claims 'to lead individuals from one reality to another' – as such it has much in common with its secularized scions in the genre of self-help (Foucault 1988: 40).

Foucault argues, however, that 'Christianity is not only a salvation religion, it's a confessional religion'. Within Christianity, Foucault notes, 'each person has the duty to know who he is, that is, to try to know what is happening inside him, to acknowledge faults, to recognize temptations, to locate desires'. 'Everyone is obliged to disclose these things', he argues, everyone must 'bear public or private witness against oneself' (1988: 40). In Christianity, such confessions have historically occurred through varied means: Catholicism has required confession to a priest; in Protestantism, the individual replaced the confessor as the monitor of his or her own self. In Bridget's case, the personal diary serves as her method of self-examination: the itemized lists that begin each day's entry in her diary confess, in detail, her daily intake of calories, cigarettes and alcohol, as well as her indulgence in other practices ranging from making obsessive phone calls to thinking negative thoughts. Bridget's diary is a space in which she bears witness against herself, investigating her faults, temptations and desires. It ultimately serves as an in-house confessional: a private space of self-scrutiny, her diary is where she 'puts herself down', simultaneously recording and critiquing the self.[3]

While the title character's verbalization of the self is imperative to the confessional enterprise that she undertakes on her diary's pages, Bridget's confession is more radical than expected. Crucially, Bridget redeems herself, forgoing penance and simply justifying her own sins. Foucault argues that an individual's ability to use confessional techniques of verbalization 'without renouncing oneself constitutes a decisive break'. At moments, Bridget's diary indicates such a break, adopting a tone of deliberate self-acceptance that has largely been overlooked by the novel's critics (Foucault 1988: 49). While Bridget does censure herself at many points, she is far more likely to absolve herself, to accept herself as flawed and unchanging, often using the most outlandish criteria. A surfeit of cigarettes, for example, smoked on 1 February is written off since she 'will soon give up for Lent so might as well smoke self into disgusted smoking frenzy' (1996: 37); an increase in weight on 3 May is attributed to a phantom baby 'growing at monstrous unnatural rate' that she has not, in fact, actually conceived (117). Moreover, there is no consistency to Bridget's judgement, causing the reader to question just how serious she is about the process of reform: twenty-three cigarettes on 3 January is 'v.g.' (17) and on 18 March is 'v.v. bad' (81), just as 3,100 calories on 8 January qualifies as 'poor' (27) but nearly triple that amount on 29 April is deemed 'excellent' (111). Loath to impose categorical and consistent judgement on herself, allowing each day's experiences to shape the way that she evaluates her behaviour therein, one starts to believe that Bridget's is a confession of an unreformable self, a self ostensibly striving to improve but incapable, and possibly unwilling, to do so. The confessional diary, then, offers Bridget the tantalizing *possibility* of personal change while also affording the space in which to record the failure, non-maintenance, or simple rejection of it.

Bridget's subversive refusal to hold herself to consistent standards of judgement eventually leads to her ultimate disavowal of both her self-improvement plan and the self-improvement culture that she almost literally held to be sacred. In a chapter of *The Edge of Reason* entitled 'Mars and Venus in the Dustbin', Bridget peruses her forty-seven self-help volumes only to be staggered by their conflicting advice: alongside *The Rules* is *Ignoring the Rules*, next to *Happy to be Single* is *How not to be Single*, and flanking *How to Seek and Find the Love You Want* are both *How to Find the Love You Want Without Seeking It* and *How to Find You Want the Love You Didn't Seek*. Although she admits that without the books she will 'feel empty and spiritually at sea', she stands determined 'not to weaken', recognizing that she has 'been swayed this way and that by everyone else's idea'. The books, she haltingly resolves, are going 'In. The. Bin. I am going. To stand on. Own. Two. Feet' (1999: 265). By denying her feelings of inadequacy for failing to measure up to conflicting standards, by demoting the self-help genre from its position of higher authority in her life, Bridget ultimately affirms the unaltered self, paradoxically choosing to enact control in her life by relinquishing it altogether. Her diary, then, serves not merely as a tool with which to work through her efforts at self-improvement, but, in the end, as a rebellious record of her ultimate refusal to change.

Kelly Marsh, in an article entitled 'Contextualizing Bridget Jones', makes a similar claim in reference not to self-improvement but to consumerism, and asks rhetorically 'Would Bridget Jones be a more admirable woman, a more likeable character, a better role model if she were a more efficient consumer?' Marsh proposes that by ignoring Bridget's refusal to consume effectively, 'American critics, including American feminists, have not recognized the potential subversiveness of her position' (Marsh 2004: 56). I would add that Bridget is ultimately also a poor consumer of the self-as-product. While Bridget shops for, tries on and adopts various new-and-improved selves throughout the novel she recognizes finally that no project of improvement adequately represents her self and its needs: her ultimate intervention, it seems, is her inability to choose just one self, to 'buy into it', and to change.

'A confessional gender'

In *The Edge of Reason*, the sequel to *Bridget Jones's Diary*, the title character is given the opportunity to interview film star Colin Firth. Preparing enthusiastically for her meeting, Bridget jots down a few 'easy questions' along with some 'meaty' ones that, she admits, were hastily recorded after a few glasses of Chardonnay. Reading one such wine-muddled question during the interview, Bridget asks Firth, 'Do you think the book of *Fever Pitch* has spored a confessional gender?' Her puzzled subject responds, saying, 'Well. Certainly Nick Hornby's style has been very much imitated and I think it's a very appealing, er, gender whether or not he actually, um … *spored* it' (1999: 170). Although the substitution of the word 'spored' for 'spawned' is rather innocuous, the use of 'gender' in the place of 'genre' gets to the crux of the debate surrounding Fielding's novel. A 'confessional gender' is, to many, the same thing as a 'confessional genre': women are seen as effusively confessional creatures in a way that men are not.[4] Moreover, the mention of Hornby – and especially the mention of Hornby's *Fever Pitch* – offers a wink of recognition to this crucial double standard. *Fever Pitch* is itself a relentless personal diary, but it is a diary of a football fan. Nevertheless, when Hornby's book emerged, critics were not swept into a frenzy over the dismal state of modern man: when *Fever Pitch* hit the shelves, there was no high-profile mud-flinging about whether or not an obsession with the stereotypically male subject of sporting events was going to push the male agenda back twenty years. More commonly, praise emerged in response to this rise in male narrative introspection, classified by one critic as 'fascinating' because while 'women writers have regularly committed their growing pains to paper … emotionally honest accounts of straight male rights of passage' have been rare (Whelehan 2000: 132). Such critics were thus able to see beyond the book's obsessive football framework; they were, for example, able to recognize that football fandom may say things about our culture and the way it both shapes and reflects our selves.

Bridget Jones's Diary and its progeny were never so lucky, the controversy beginning with the very terms used in the debate. The 'chick lit' moniker that classified the first-person, female-authored genre was emptied of its original subversive content and offered, instead, as a partner to its film counterpart, the 'chick flick'.[5] Moreover, the highly-charged term 'post-feminist' was imprudently used to classify the genre, inaccurately implying that the novels sprung up in a world where the goals of feminism had been forgotten or surpassed. The controversy was not limited to terminology, however. Michiko Kakutani, in an article condescendingly entitled 'It's Like Really Weird', adopts the persona of Ally McBeal in order to write to Bridget and tell her how much they have in common, namely their 'imbecility' (Kakutani 1998: 8). Lola Young points out that publishers are simply 'paying photogenic young women to write about who they have dinner with' (Neustatter 2002: 8), a sexist charge that is reflected in Celia Brayfield's comment that young women are getting book contracts because publishers are looking for 'a twentysomething babe ... who will look hot posing naked in a glossy magazine' (Ezard 2001: 7). Before long, the brightest of female luminaries had issued their scorn: Beryl Bainbridge called *Bridget Jones's Diary* 'a froth sort of thing' (Sexton 2001: 16); Doris Lessing lamented 'these helpless girls, drunken, worrying about their weight and so on' (Ezard 2001: 7), and Fay Weldon, attempting to declare a premature death to the trend, remarked that the books are 'forgettable' and 'the genre is done out' (Wade 2002: 1).

Criticism of *Bridget Jones's Diary* and its progeny was, perhaps, to be expected, the book coming as it did at the end of a prominent and widely-documented backlash era that had concerned readers on their guard. As feminism tried to regain its footing the last thing it needed was the widespread celebration of a woman's diary of weight loss and perpetual self-modification.[6] However, such critiques too easily duplicated the larger debate about women's confessional writing as a whole. Claiming that Bridget is one of many 'helpless girls, drunken, worrying about their weight and so on', merely repeats decades-old claims that women writing about their private lives are narcissistic, solipsistic, vain. Moreover, the notion that publishers were commissioning attractive young women to write about 'who they have dinner with', that young women were getting book contracts only because they later 'will look hot posing naked in a glossy magazine', grotesquely exaggerates the notion that women's self-authority is necessarily compromised through confession, implying that the publisher–writer relationship mimics that of the analyst and the analysand, the confessor and the confessant. Instead of replaying what can certainly be read as an anti-confessional debate, attention might be focused on the ways in which confession may ultimately be associated with, rather than against, autonomy in feminist discourse.

As Alicia Ostriker argues, the confessional writer 'who attempts to explore female experience is dismissed as self-absorbed, private, escapist, nonuniversal' even though what is at the core of such writing 'is the quest for autonomous self-definition' (Ostriker 1989: 58). Interestingly enough, a large portion of Bridget's quest for self-definition in the novel surfaces through her struggle to understand her place within feminism as a whole. Indeed, if, as the above detractors suggest, *Bridget Jones's Diary* has little to no relation to the greater feminist project, it is not because the title character is unaware that feminism exists. The novel is littered with moments in which Bridget and her friends, Jude and Shazzer, strive toward feminist ideals and situate many of their behaviours within its purview. Shazzer in particular has lofty hopes for feminism's future, particularly in the way it will reform men. She explains that soon:

> There won't be any men leaving their families and post-menopausal wives ... because the young mistresses and women will just turn round and tell them to sod off and men won't get any sex or any women unless they learn how to behave properly instead of cluttering up the sea-bed of women with their SHITTY, SMUG, SELF-INDULGENT BEHAVIOUR!
>
> (1996: 126–7)

Bridget herself falls upon 'feminism' when she is trying to see female perspectives, as when, after hearing her mother's plan to leave her father for a younger man, she notes that she 'was thinking it all over and trying, as a feminist, to see Mum's point of view' (54).[7] She also classifies many of her gatherings with her friends as 'feminist rants' and is particularly thrilled when the main object of her affection admits that he's been told she is 'a radical feminist and [has] an incredibly glamorous life' (236).

While Bridget finds herself compelled by the idea of being a feminist, she has a very hard time living up to what she imagines to be feminism's ideals. Much of her frustration stems from the sense of isolation she feels after standing up for herself in the face of cruel treatment by men. Responding to a date who has just told her that their upcoming sexual encounter will not signify his status as her boyfriend, she tells him, 'That is just such crap ... How dare you be so fraudulently flirtatious, cowardly and dysfunctional? I am not interested in emotional fuckwittage. Goodbye'. Proud of herself for rejecting his crude behaviour, Bridget notes, 'It was great' and triumphantly adds, 'You should have seen his face'. However, in the very next sentence, a sentence beginning with a heavy 'But', she states, 'now I am home I am sunk into gloom. I may have been right, but my reward, I know, will be to end up all alone, half-eaten by an Alsatian' (1996: 33). Her efforts over the following days to remain 'disdainfully buoyant', to keep repeating the words 'self-respect' and 'Huh' aloud, take place in relative privacy as she wonders at the point (37). Not until she stops trying to be 'Mrs. Iron Knickers', ironically revealing through her word choice a personal confusion over whether to strive for marital union or personal asceticism, does she finally admit her frustration as well as her desire 'to burst into self-pitying tears' (37). Bridget's main concern with such polemical posturing is that she is not sure that she has got it right: she is ambivalent about what the larger project of feminism ultimately asks of her. During one gathering, for example, Bridget is startled when all of the sudden Shazzer accuses her of abandoning the feminist cause. Bridget explains that: 'It was all turning into a hideously unfeminist man-based row when we realized it was ridiculous and said we'd see each other tomorrow' (1999: 20).

While this particular example shows Bridget choosing friendship over arguing about principles, the longer and less sanitary fight that occurred in one of Fielding's newspaper columns in the *Daily Telegraph* is not as promising. In that argument, Shazzer erupts, saying, 'The trouble with you Bridge, ... you're not really a feminist'. Bridget privately remarks that she 'Could not avoid feeling hurt. Am feminist definitely. Believe in equality, give money to third-world women's charity, have own job, independent life and home ... So what was Shazzie's point?' Going on to explain exactly that, 'Shazzie' tells Bridget that she is 'obsessed by men' and is 'totally indoctrinated by the media and advertising culture into trying to improve [her]self in every area, fitting into some paternalistic, sales-led ideal'. Trying to lessen the blow, Jude pipes in, offering, 'What you mean, Shaz, ... is that your feminist ideals do not encompass the need to be loved. And Bridget is prey to the influence of whatever society and media deem to be lovable'. Bridget, practically in tears, looks at Jude 'all slim in lacy dress with bosoms heaved up by pink lejaby bra' and is utterly confused. She notes that she later forgave the women 'for making self feminism study in manner of laboratory mouse', but still 'could not help, as walked home, feeling failure, not only for failing to live up to feminist ideals, but having wrong feminist ideals in the first place' (Fielding 1998a: 4).

While they throw the word around, it is not clear whether these women – and by extension, perhaps, other women? – have a clear or shared sense of what 'feminism' means. Does, for example, wanting a man make one anti-feminist in a way that claiming not to need a man while wearing a push-up bra does not? Instead of a support system, then, feminism is often depicted throughout the novel in a category similar to self-help manuals. Just as dieting and self-improvement guides espouse multiple and often contradictory patterns for living, feminism too is a loose category with open definitions, often picked at will to suit the speaker. Moreover, feminism, like both the self-help and diet industries, has the tendency to serve as an institutional force in Bridget's life: against its tenets, Bridget judges herself and ultimately feels as though she has failed. In this sense, the 'confessional gender' takes on a new meaning. Bridget's diary is unlike the typical female confessions of the past which commonly documented women's sexual transgressions: instead of confessing transgressions of sex, Bridget confesses her sins of gender. Her diary is that of a failed feminist and the community that replaces a supposed feminist community is one that seeks a new feminism to more fully accommodate the full facets of the self.

Chick-lit and 'third wave feminism'

To be fair, the feminism that Bridget holds at a sceptical distance is an unexamined representation of feminism's second wave. Third wave feminism, of which *Bridget Jones's Diary* is arguably a part, has often been critiqued for such one-dimensional categorizations of the movement's earlier incarnation.[8] When Bridget, for example, muses that 'Germaine Greer did not have children' and asks 'But then what does that prove?' it is clear that she sees the limitations of taking one self-identified feminist's example as representative of the condition of all women (Fielding 1999: 34). Moreover, once it becomes obvious that her own mother has belatedly read *The Feminine Mystique*, Bridget observes her mother's instant disregard for her husband and children as unnatural and bizarre. Reading Bridget's denunciations of Greer and Friedan provides certain fodder for the inter-generational debate: second wave feminists might argue against Bridget's unexamined rebuff of each author's influences, quite justifiably asserting that without Greer and Friedan, Bridget – a childfree, working woman – could not exist.

But second wave feminists do not have a corner on the market of misrepresentation: feminists of the third wave have argued that they, too, feel their generation's goals and ideals are generally misunderstood. While many third wave feminists can find a place within their ideology for wedding dresses, leg waxing and stilettos, their predecessors are often quick to judge these signifiers not as the younger generation's ability to embrace multiple viewpoints and constant contradiction, but instead as evidence that the new generation has dropped the ball. Moreover, some third wave feminists are viewed by their forerunners as having, possibly, a bit too much fun: the irony and sarcasm that weighs heavily within the third wave's project is often misread as a lack of seriousness. Jennifer Baumgardner and Amy Richards sum up the difference between the general tone of the two generations in the context of the second wave publication *Ms*. The magazine, they note, 'is unable to let its hair down because it's so afraid of being fluffy (in its editorial, not its hair)'. 'There are', they continue, 'too many "You go, girls", with forced jubilation, and *Ms*. has yet to be ironic – which means the old girl has something to learn from *Bridget Jones*' (Baumgardner and Richards 2000: 117).

Within the world of the novel, Bridget's character reflects the bold strokes of third wave feminism, mainly through its refusal to be paralysed by contradictions and its willingness instead to embrace them. Bridget and her friends, for example, openly deplore unrealistic beauty standards for women at the same time that they congratulate themselves for living up to them; they realize that they do not need men while simultaneously pursuing them; and they are willing to admit that they do not need to 'have it all' even though they cannot quite figure out which part of the equation they could most likely do without. Outside of the novel's world, a community of readers emerged that largely resembled Bridget's own milieu: politically aware if not politically active, these readers were likely to qualify their relationship with feminism by stating 'I'm not a feminist but ...' or 'I *am* a feminist, but ...'. Jenny Colgan, a successful author whose work emerged in the wake of *Bridget Jones's Diary*, points out that readers coalesced around the novel and its female-authored, female-centred successors since the novels finally spoke to a group previously unrepresented in contemporary fiction. In contrast, she notes, to the female characters found in the 'thick, shiny, brick novels covered in foil' that were a mark of the 1980s, Bridget Jones and her ilk were more realistic, familiar and, quite frankly, younger. Colgan argues that detractors such as Bainbridge, Weldon and Lessing, in their sixties, seventies and eighties respectively, could not understand the lives of many young women today who 'have grown up with education as a right; with financial independence; with living on our own, with having far too many choices about getting married [and] having children', but are still saturated in the 'pressures of magazines, TV, thinness, media celebrity and love' (Colgan 2001: 6).

Colgan's is a common third wave criticism: the elder women of the movement's second wave, many argue, do not take into account the altered terrain of young women's lives. Third wave writing has developed, in large part, in reaction to this classification, offering personal accounts of personal experiences as a way to explain, first-hand, women's new realities: third wave anthologies such as *To Be Real* and *The Fire This Time* highlight the importance of the autobiographical mode in the movement with their series of personal essays written in the first-person voice. Nevertheless, critics of the third wave's concentration on the 'I' have argued that excessive personalizing is dangerous to the feminist collective, that, as Deborah Siegel sums up, 'the proliferation of the personal narrative in feminist theory displaces women with a few writerly I's' (Siegel 1997: 68). While *Bridget Jones's Diary* never claims to occupy the same category as feminist theory, its reception was marked by a similar distaste for the circulation of the personal. Imelda Whelehan, for example, notes that the fine line created between authors such as Helen Fielding and their characters on one hand 'gives the characters the credibility that makes them so readily identifiable to their readers', but on the other hand 'encourages detractors to see them as of no literary worth at all – as if they are simply confessional outpourings compressed on to the page' (Whelehan 2002: 69).

But what is it about the confessional outpouring which renders it 'simple'? Terrence Doody argues that the confession is the 'deliberate, self-conscious attempt of an individual to explain his nature to the audience who represents the kind of community he needs to exist in and to confirm him' (Doody 1980: 4). A confessor must create his own audience, Doody notes, because 'he usually feels that no available institution, no system or myth, no class structure, profession, locale, or family quite accommodates his full sense of his individuality' (1980: 22). Third wave feminists have engaged in such a practice, using the personal voice to found a version of feminism better suited to their present needs; likewise, writers of contemporary women's fiction have used the first-person narrative to tell stories about their modern lives. More than this, however, such a model of community-creation through confession has as its historical precedent in feminism in the highly successful, subversive, and not at all 'simple' consciousness-raising (CR) groups of the 1970s. Siegel concisely explains that 'the primary function of the CR group was to provide a space in which the isolated "I" could, by means of identification, collapse into collective, rescuing "we"' (Siegel 1997: 68); the confession of one, in other words, could result in the recognition of many. Siegel notes that 'if the Third Wave can return to the personal and the return to the personal enacts a return to CR, the result is CR with a difference' (1997: 68) This 'CR with a difference', third wave feminists would argue, already thrives within the movement: the third wave text *Manifesta* describes the female 'dinner party' as a CR group (Baumgardner and Richards 2000: 14); Gloria Steinem refers to the third wave anthology *Listen Up* as 'a consciousness-raising group between covers' (Siegel 1997: 68); and online websites and zine cultures offer a new form of community where third wave feminists connect, share their experiences, and unite.

Bridget Jones's Diary, in spawning the genre of chick-lit, launched a similar enterprise. The audience that Bridget's confession sought was an audience of single thirty-something women, an audience successful at work if not at love, an audience sympathetic to the same pressures of attempting to achieve idealistic standards but consistently falling short. Opponents of chick-lit argue that whether or not the novels are written by women and about women, whether or not they aim to confess and to unite, they still problematically retain the trappings of a male-ordered society. The pursuit of men, beauty and a non-smudging lipstick are not, they would argue, commonly the stuff of resistance. Moreover, it can certainly be said that even though chick-lit novels are written almost entirely in the first-person, they are not confessional memoirs that call for the social revolutions of Sylvia Plath's *The Bell Jar*, the sexual revolutions of Erica Jong's *Fear of Flying*, or the political revolutions of Doris Lessing's *The Golden Notebook*. When *Bridget Jones's Diary* does engage with the spectre of its revolutionary forebears, its tongue is always partially in its cheek. Bridget, for example, drafts several political treatises to send to Tony Blair, urging him to inform the government that they must stop touting family values unless they plan to start to 'teach all boy children that sharing the housework does not mean twiddling one fork under the tap' (Fielding 1999: 197–8).

Even while it would be inaccurate to argue that chick-lit novels have a collective political mission, the books most assuredly reveal a shared frustration and disillusionment with many aspects of women's lives. What is

unique about the genre of chick-lit is the method by which this disillusionment is shared. As Sarah Evans notes, chick-lit novels tend to explore such
discontents 'through a sharply satirical view of the world [which] differentiates chick lit from romantic fiction, where heroines are equally vulnerable
but rarely funny' (Evans 2003: 9). The *Guardian*'s analysis of the readership
for chick-lit novels reveals that 'after the earnestness of both Mother Earth
feminism in the 70s, and 80s careerism, what women most want is a good
laugh – at their own expense as much as others'. 'What the readers love', the
author notes, 'is to find their own terminal dissatisfaction with their men (or
lack of), their bums and jobs, transformed from chronic neurosis into
comedy' ('Women Want' 2001: 23). Helen Fielding, in a rare moment spent
explaining her text, takes on Bridget's telegraphic language in order to fully
indulge this claim. She notes:

> Point is not that women are retrograde ditzes, but feel that they have to
> be so perfect in every area that become incredibly hard on selves: trying
> to live life of non-independent and independent woman at same time,
> haunted by media images of anorexic teenage models running from gym
> to board meeting to nuclear family and cooking elaborate dinner parties
> for twelve. Vision of someone else – Bridget – trying so hard and spec-
> tacularly failing, ending up when guests arrive in underwear with wet
> hair and one foot in pan of mashed potato is comic release from pres-
> sures of overreaching role models. If women really are equal, surely
> allowed to laugh at selves, mark of confidence etc, etc.
>
> (Fielding 1998b: 5)

Fielding's assessment, proposing as it does that female readers unite around
and celebrate Bridget's confession of a failed self, reveals that the community
based around the novel emerged when readers recognized Bridget's story as
one they themselves might have told. Such a response not only calls upon
the CR ideal of self-revelation building community, but it circumvents the
typical confessional paradigm normally characterized by an imbalance
between the power of the confessor and the impotence of the confessant. The
tenor of the response, one built on the humour, parody and ultimate irony in
the novels, works to replace a system of judgement with one of shared
response.

   Although the irony and the parody and the undeniable humour remain,
chick-lit has grown into a community of writers and readers who share the
goal of telling more stories about women. Answering *Bridget Jones's Diary*'s
depiction of British life was author Melissa Banks, whose young female lead
was depicted working through similar issues within an American landscape. Other authors have exaggerated elements of chick-lit to different
ends: Anna Maxted took chick-lit characters' obsession with their weight to
a more serious level, depicting a main character working through the crisis
of an eating disorder; Sophie Kinsella transformed a chick-lit obsession

with shopping into a four-volume series of novels about credit-card debt, and Wendy Holden pushed the context of comedy-of-manners to its hilarious extreme.

Critics who applied the term 'post-feminist' to *Bridget Jones's Diary* – by adopting a term which popularly connotes a time after feminism, a time no longer in need of feminism – have failed to see the ways in which feminism's longer history played out on the pages of the novel. This complex history can be seen partly by way of Fielding's subversion of gender and genre expectations, partly by her engagement with long-standing feminist concerns, and partly by her invocation of a female community of readers which formed around a woman's confessional voice. Fielding's dedication of her second novel 'to the other Bridgets' acknowledges this community as well as the new writers and characters spawned, or 'spored', by this 'confessional gender'.

Notes

1 Controversy over the word 'post-feminism' largely relates to the interpreted meaning of the concept of 'post'. Ann Brooks sees 'post' as implying an ongoing transformation or change, such that post-feminism 'challenges hegemonic assumptions held by second wave feminist epistemologies that patriarchal and imperialist oppression was a universally experienced oppression' (Brooks 1997: 2). Nevertheless, popular media outlets normally invoke 'post' in a temporal sense, implying that second wave feminism – usually seen as the movement's 1970s incarnation – is no longer needed. Because of this negative connotation, many young feminists have opted for the term 'third wave' which more clearly implies both a connection to feminism and an ongoing process of change.

2 Unless otherwise indicated, all parenthetical references refer to Helen Fielding's *Bridget Jones's Diary* (1996).

3 The double meaning of 'putting oneself down' is the subject of James McGavran's work; however, the phrase is also referenced in Marsh (2004). See also Alison Case's 'Authenticity, Convention, and *Bridget Jones's Diary*' (2001), which argues that Bridget's lack of narrative control is symbolic of her lack of control over her life.

4 The notion that women are more likely than men to be seen as confessional creatures is a common one, a notion frequently argued against in recent studies of confession. Susan David Bernstein's *Confessional Subjects: Revelations of Gender and Power in Victorian Literature and Culture* (1997) is one such study that takes up this point in detail.

5 Cris Mazza coined the term 'chick-lit' in 1995 for her subversive and sexually-charged anthology *Chick Lit: Postfeminist Fiction*, a collection of rebellious female writings that aimed to disrupt the status quo. Mazza has acknowledged that the term, applied as a derivative of the chick flick, has been drained of its dissident meaning.

6 Susan Faludi's *Backlash: The Undeclared War Against American Women* (1991) gives the most detailed account of the cultural environment surrounding the feminist movement in the early 1990s.

7 Fielding's point here is to depict Bridget's mother as a throwback and a conservative. This is emphasized by the fact that she doesn't even discover the feminist texts of her own generation until they are thirty years old. The point is

not necessarily to use Bridget's mother as a generational marker between the second and third waves of feminism.

8 The term 'third wave' originated in the mid-1980s when a group of academics and activists joined to write *The Third Wave: Feminist Perspectives*, a volume that was never published, but which had planned to emphasize multicultural alliances as much if not more than age. The emphasis turned toward age in the early 1990s with the founding of an activist network called 'The Third Wave' which emphasized the term as one which applied to young feminists (Orr 1997: 30).

Bibliography

Barreca, R. (1997) 'Women's Humor', Licensed off-air recording from a broadcast by C-SPAN, originally recorded 26 June 1997 at Chautauqua Institution, Chautauqua, New York.

Baumgardner, J. and Richards, A. (2000) *Manifesta: Young Women, Feminism, and the Future*, New York: Farrar, Straus and Giroux.

Bernstein, S.D. (1997) *Confessional Subjects: Revelations of Gender and Power in Victorian Literature and Culture*, Chapel Hill: University of North Carolina Press.

Bignell, J. (2004) 'Sex, Confession and Witness', *Reading Sex and the City*, London: I.B. Tauris.

Brooks, A. (1997) *Postfeminisms: Feminism, Cultural Theory, and Cultural Forms*, London: Routledge.

Case, A. (2001) 'Authenticity, Convention, and *Bridget Jones's Diary*', *Narrative* 5: 176–81.

Colgan, J. (2001) 'We Know the Difference Between Foie Gras and Hula Hoops, But Sometimes We Just Want Hula Hoops', *Guardian*, 24 August: 6.

Davis, W. (1996) 'The Spiritual Growth of Self-help', *The Boston Globe*, 9 July: 23.

Doody, T. (1980) *Confession and Community in the Novel*, Baton Rouge: Louisiana State University Press.

Evans, S. (2003) 'Succumb to Joy of Chic Lit', *Birmingham Post*, 12 April: 9.

Ezard, J. (2001) 'Bainbridge Tilts at "Chick lit" Cult: Novelist Says Bridget Jones Genre is Just a Lot of Froth', *Guardian*, 24 August: 7.

Faludi, S. (1991) *Backlash: The Undeclared War Against American Women*, New York: Crown.

Fielding, H. (1996) *Bridget Jones's Diary*, London: Picador.

—— (1998a) 'Bridget Jones's Diary', *Daily Telegraph*, 11 July: 4.

—— (1998b) 'Bridget Jones's Diary', *Daily Telegraph*, 24 October: 5.

—— (1999) *Bridget Jones: The Edge of Reason*, London: Picador.

Foucault, M. (1988) 'Technologies of the Self', in L.H. Martin, H. Gutman and P. Hutton (eds) *Technologies of the Self: A Seminar with Michel Foucault*, Amherst: University of Massachusetts Press.

Fudge, R. (2004) 'See Dick Write: The Arrested Development of Lad Lit', *Bitch: Feminist Response to Pop Culture* 25: 73.

Hornby, N. (1995) *Fever Pitch*, London: Victor Gollancz.

Kakutani, M. (1998) 'It's Like Really Weird: Another Bad-Luck Babe', *New York Times*, 26 May: 8.

McGavern, J. (1988) 'Dorothy Wordsworth's Journals: Putting Herself Down', in S. Benstock (ed.) *The Private Self: Theory and Practice of Women's Autobiographical Writings*, Chapel Hill: University of North Carolina Press.

Marsh, K. (2004) 'Contextualizing Bridget Jones', *College Literature* 31: 52–72.

Mazza, C. (1996) *Chick-Lit: Post-feminist Fiction*, Tallahassee: Fiction Collective Two.

Neustatter, A. (2002) 'How Chick-lit Grew Up', *Guardian*, 26 March: 8.

Orr, C. (1997) 'Charting the Currents of the Third Wave', *Hypatia* 12.

Ostriker, A. (1989) *Stealing the Language*, Urbana: University of Illinois Press.

Rapping, E. (1996) *The Culture of Recovery: Making Sense of the Self-Help Movement in Women's Lives*, New York: Beacon.

Sexton, D. (2001) 'Why Beryl Wrote Off "Chick Lit" and Why She's Right,' *London Evening Standard*, 23 August: 16.

Siegel, D. (1997) 'The Legacy of the Personal: Generating Theory in Feminism's Third Wave', *Hypatia* 12: 46–75.

Wade, M. (2002) 'Weldon Dismisses "Forgettable" Chick Lit', *The Scotsman*, 12 August: 1.

Whelehan, I. (2000) *Overloaded: Popular Culture and the Future of Feminism*, London: Women's Press.

—— (2002) *Bridget Jones's Diary: A Reader's Guide*, New York: Continuum.

Winship, J. (1987) *Inside Women's Magazines*, London: Pandora.

'Women Want A Laugh: Chick Lit was Fun While it Lasted' (2001) *Guardian*, 24 August: 23.

6 'The memoir as self-destruction'

A Heartbreaking Work of Staggering Genius

Bran Nicol

Recent years have seen the flourishing of the confessional prose narrative in which the author (who is not usually famous at the time of writing) writes frankly about a distasteful or traumatic period in the past. Prominent examples include Elizabeth Wurtzel's *Prozac Nation* (1994) in which she tells of how she coped with extreme depression, and Dave Pelzer's *A Child Called 'It'* (1995) which documents the author's experience of being severely abused as a child by his alcoholic mother. These works are, in equal measure, celebrated for their extraordinary candour and criticized for their perceived exhibitionist egotism. As such they seem at once to conform to the tradition of confessional modern literature characterized by the seminal works St Augustine's *Confessions* (*c.* AD 398–400) and Rousseau's *Confessions* (1781–1789) but also represent something peculiarly of our own age insofar as they reflect an impulse within contemporary media-saturated culture – one exhibited most readily perhaps in 'reality television' – for habits, fantasies and self-impressions which normally remain private to be placed on full display.

This kind of 'obscenity', as the philosopher Jean Baudrillard might call it, is the natural condition of a culture which has undergone what he deems a complete *telemorphosis*, or transformation by the specular logic of television (Baudrillard 2002: 481). Television is symptomatic of what Baudrillard sees, expanding on some of the arguments of Michel Foucault, as the tyranny of the logic of *production* over our culture. 'The original sense of "production"', he says, 'is not in fact that of material manufacture; rather, it means to render visible, to cause to appear and be made to appear: *pro-ducere*'. Our culture is one which tries to 'let everything be produced, be read, become real, visible, and marked with the sign of effectiveness; ... let everything be said, gathered, indexed and registered' (Baudrillard 1977: 21–2). We might expect this logic of production to have a profound impact on the act of confession within contemporary culture. For as Baudrillard says elsewhere, telemorphosis represents the apotheosis of the Foucauldian notion that 'self-expression [is] the ultimate form of confession. Keeping no secret. Speaking, talking, endlessly communicating. This is a form of violence which targets the singular being and his secrecy' (Baudrillard 2001). The demand is made to everyone who inhabits contemporary world to 'confess' in this way, by making one's self visible. Televisual culture is so all-enveloping, in fact, that it indicates that we have gone beyond Foucault's understanding of production: 'We are well beyond panopticism, beyond visibility as a source of power and control. It is no longer a matter of making things visible to the external eye. It is rather a question of making things transparent to themselves' (Baudrillard 2001). This is why we might regard books like Wurtzel's and Pelzer's as the product of the same impulse as the reality television show or the Internet 'cam' site: the desire to express oneself not so much for the benefit of anyone who might be watching but as a reflex action governed by the telemorphosis of our species, an urge for contemporary subjects to 'pass their time by perpetually telling themselves their story' (Baudrillard 2002: 482).

Dave Eggers's *A Heartbreaking Work of Staggering Genius* (2000) might be regarded as a particularly accomplished example of this recent 'obscene' tradition within confessional writing. It tells the story of how Eggers lost both his parents to cancer within five weeks of each other and was forced, at the age of seventeen, to bring up his nine-year-old brother, Toph. As a result of its critical and commercial success, Eggers was catapulted out of obscurity into a state of high cultural 'visibility' (or celebrity), swiftly becoming the epitome of literary 'cool' in contemporary American writing. The effect of his self-presentation in the memoir meant that he became visible in other media: in television, print newspapers and on the Internet, where there is a vast litany of sniping attacks on him and his work. True to the Baudrillardian logic of production he was led to respond to the increased visibility by replaying his original act of confession by adding a forty-eight page appendix, *Mistakes We Knew We Were Making*, to the paperback version of his memoir in which he is even more candid about his inner self, detailing the impact of the memoir on his life after his publication. There, for example, he describes the 'involuntary chanting' in which he would indulge as he walked around Brooklyn while finishing the book: '*Oh Jesus give me give me Oh Jesus give me give me Help help no no Jesus no no no no no Help Jesus no* no' (Eggers 2001: 19) and outlines his fears that the completed book 'would alienate me from my friends and relatives' and even 'enrage many readers for one reason or another, and would compel them to come and kill me' (16–17).

Yet, as I want to suggest in what follows, though his memoir – and indeed his public profile – might be regarded as rather exhibitionist and narcissistic, Eggers's case is actually quite different to that of, say, Elizabeth Wurtzel, and in fact might even be regarded as a kind of antidote to the 'telemorphosis' of confession which Baudrillard outlines. First of all we must acknowledge that despite his absorption by contemporary television-led celebrity culture Eggers also plays a uniquely powerful role on the American *literary* scene. His celebrity rests not just on the acclaim for his memoir, nor the more limited success of his follow-up novel *You Shall Know Our Velocity* (2002), but on the high profile he enjoys as founder of two literary journals,

McSweeney's Quarterly Concern (edited by himself) and *The Believer*, as well as the publishing company begun with the proceeds of the sales of his memoir, *McSweeney's Books*. Both his journals are characterized by the high quality of their design and production, and the fact that they have achieved their success not via the conventional channels of mass marketing but through more subtle 'word-of-mouth' sales strategies. Part of their value is the way they figure as a kind of *brand* that links the work of a number of contemporary writers in the US and the UK, many of whom contribute to the journal: Rick Moody, George Saunders, Jonathan Safran Foer, William Vollmann and British writers Zadie Smith and Nick Hornby. The *McSweeney's* aesthetic also bears strong similarities to recent acclaimed independent films produced by friends of Eggers such as the director Spike Jonze and screenwriter Charlie Kaufman, such as *Being John Malkovich* (2001) and *Adaptation* (2003). The British novelist Gordon Burn recently noted that *McSweeney's* marks the resurgence of the 'coterie' of writers as a force for dictating literary trends, along the lines of the group who gathered around Ian Hamilton and his publications the *Review* and the *New Review* in the 1960s and 1970s, and included James Fenton, Craig Raine and Martin Amis (Burn 2004).

There is undoubtedly a sense that this informal collective, spearheaded by Eggers, heralds a new departure in American writing (perhaps even American culture in a wider sense, if we consider the parallel developments in film). Here is a new generation of authors with different ideals and preoccupations from earlier established US writers like Don DeLillo, Thomas Pynchon and John Updike, and who are unlike even 'blank fiction' contemporaries (who represent a different kind of cool) such as Bret Easton Ellis, Douglas Coupland and Jay McInerney. What seems to be especially distinctive about the *McSweeney's* generation is their endlessly parodic style and fondness for metafictional experiment. Each *McSweeney's* issue includes a similar range of supplementary texts, such as acknowledgements, graphs, 'rules and suggestions', graphic and typological gimmickry, and is written in a distinctive 'house' prose style which is ironic in tone and mixes the high-minded and the colloquial.

This leads us to the most important distinction between Eggers as a memoirist and Pelzer and Wurtzel, and that is the fact that the metafictional *McSweeney's* 'house style' was first adopted in *A Heartbreaking Work of Staggering Genius*, meaning that, formally, the book amounts to a considerable departure from the conventions of the confessional prose memoir. Before we get to the main story – the confession 'proper' – we have to negotiate a series of supplementary texts: a preliminary section entitled 'Rules and Suggestions for Enjoyment of This Book', a preface which discusses the story's treatment of questions like 'Dialogue' and 'Characters, and their Characteristics', an outline of contents with parodic eighteenth century chapter summaries, and an acknowledgements section. Reminiscent of Fielding's famous comment in *Tom Jones* that he has 'run into a preface, while I professed to write a dedication' (Fielding 1985: 6) this section breaks into an apparently impromptu but lengthy guide to how to interpret the book, containing a list of 'major themes' (such as 'THE UNSPOKEN MAGIC OF PARENTAL DISAPPEARANCE') and then twelve less extensively discussed 'threads'. The appendix *Mistakes We Knew We Were Making* continues in the same self-reflexive vein. It is printed upside-down and separated from the original material by a paper cover, a device that underlines its status as separate, self-contained text adjoined to the main one. Like the prefatory material it also includes a series of ironic 'Notes, Corrections, Clarifications, Apologies, Addenda', discussions of aspects of the original book (and those parts omitted from it), anecdotes about the reception of the book, and more sketches and letters. Effectively all this means that in the paperback version the ironic framing of Eggers's memoir is complete, as it both begins and ends with a self-reflexive body of texts.

At this point, though, we need to consider whether the layers of irony in *A Heartbreaking Work of Staggering Genius* – and indeed in the entire *McSweeney's* enterprise – do really constitute anything new in contemporary literature. Certainly to anyone familiar with the American metafictionists of the 1960s and 1970s (Gass, Barth, Coover and Barthelme) and the critical discourse on postmodernism which surrounded it, it is difficult to read the supplementary material in *A Heartbreaking Work of Staggering Genius* and not feel, despite the obvious originality of the voice and the story, a sense of déjà vu. Moreover, it might be argued that its predisposition towards irony not only makes the work feel like a throwback to a previous literary age but actually severely limits its potential to figure as a departure for modern confessional writing.

This is the conclusion we might be steered towards if we turn to another writer who shares Baudrillard's view (if not his terminology nor conceptual framework) about the telemorphosis of late twentieth century culture. The novelist David Foster Wallace's essay 'E Unibus Pluram: Television and U.S. Fiction' (first published in 1993 and substantially revised in 1997), argues that the conditions for writing fiction have been transformed by the increase in power of television in American culture. Because television-led media culture is now dominated by the ironic mode which was previously the preserve of serious literary fiction, irony in writing is no longer effective as a form of social or cultural critique. Wallace contends that where irony had a crucial function in the work of pioneering 'metafictionists' of the 1960s and 1970s such as Gaddis, Barth, Pynchon and Coover, in that it enabled them to mount an effective critique of the cultural and political system which constrained them, the 1990s marked a point when television itself had become supremely ironic in so far as advertisements, chat shows, dramas, and news programmes began to exhibit precisely the same kind of self-reflexivity which characterized early postmodern writing.[1] Where for the postmodern writers there was the idealistic sense that 'a revelation of imprisonment led to freedom' (Wallace 1997: 67), writers in the late twentieth century demonstrate only that they are now imprisoned themselves by the ironic mode precisely because it has become all-pervasive in wider culture and 'TV has co-opted the distinctive forms of the same cynical, irreverent, ironic, absurdist post-WWII literature that the new Imagists use as touch-stones' (Wallace 1997: 59). Television has adopted precisely the same devices of postmodernism: self-reference, intertextual allusion, rebellious experimentalism.

Ultimately Wallace regards this as evidence of a more structural flaw in the use of irony as a cultural form, one which has become exposed by this shift to an increasingly televisual culture. Irony is unproductive. It 'serves an almost exclusively negative function. It's critical and destructive, a ground-clearing [but] singularly unuseful when it comes to constructing anything to replace the hypocrises it debunks' (Wallace 1997: 67). Wallace quotes Lewis Hyde in an essay on John Berryman, to support his claim that irony 'is not a rhetorical mode that wears well': 'Irony [Hyde says] has only emer-gency use. Carried over time, it is the voice of the trapped who have come to enjoy their cage' (Wallace 1997: 67).[2]

Given the extreme degree to which *A Heartbreaking Work of Staggering Genius* employs irony we might justifiably see it as a prime case of an author becoming trapped in a cage of his own making. To exemplify his under-standing of the non-productive, incarcerating use of irony Wallace considers Mark Leyner's novel *My Cousin, My Gastroenterologist* (1990), a text which conforms to an apparent checklist of metafictional devices such as pastiche, parody and self-reference, continually sending up advertising and TV, and containing a last chapter which 'is a parody of its own "About the Author" page' (Wallace 1997: 77). Its approach to televisual culture is thus, Wallace argues, itself an ironic one: it seeks 'to "resolve" the problem of being trapped in the televisual aura ... by celebrating it', by being *'reverently ironic'* (76, Wallace's emphasis). Yet the outcome is merely that Leyner's novel is 'doomed to shallowness by its desire to ridicule a TV-culture whose mockery of itself and all value already absorbs all ridicule' (Wallace 1997: 81).

This conclusion might be applied to those points in *A Heartbreaking Work of Staggering Genius* when it turns its ironic weaponry directly onto televisual culture. At one point its main story tells of the young Eggers's application to appear on MTV's programme *The Real World*, and includes a lengthy transcription of an interview apparently given with one of the producers. *The Real World* was one of the forerunners of the wave of reality TV shows most obviously represented now around the world by *Big Brother*, which is predi-cated on the idea of presenting real individuals as they 'really' are. Sure enough his experience of applying to the show leads Eggers to acknowledge how the televisual apparatus disfigures one's 'real' personality and constructs a new one in its stead: 'Watching the show is like listening to one's own voice on tape: it's real of course, but however mellifluous and articulate you hear your own words, once they're sent through this machine and are given back to you, they're high-pitched, nasal, horrifying' (2000: 167). As if to emphasize the way that the medium disfigures the real – and the parallel between self-expression in reality TV and the confessional memoir – it becomes clear that the interview itself has become fabricated. The 'interviewer' follows an anecdote by saying *'This isn't really a transcript of the interview, is it? ... This is a device, this interview style. Manufactured and fake. ... It's a good device, though. Kind of a catchall for a bunch of anecdotes that would be too awkward to force together otherwise'* (2000: 196–7). Eggers agrees, explaining that 'squeezing all these things into the Q&A makes complete the transition from the book's first half, which is slightly less self-conscious, to the second half, which is increasingly self-devouring' (2000: 200).

What this episode reveals is that the self is something that is constructed through its representations rather than a prior entity which exists in a coherent, complete sense which can then be represented accurately. The metafictional framebreaking implies that the memoir itself, the form of fiction which is conventionally taken to be the literary mirror-image of an individual's true self, is a construction, just like the self. According to Wallace's logic this would be a pointless replication of what television already shows to be true. Everybody knows that reality television does not present people 'as they really are', but transfigures them into different beings. This, after all, is precisely why people choose to go on reality television shows like *The Real World* and *Big Brother*. This is why many who have gone through the experience complain that the programme was edited in such a way as to make them into someone different to their 'real' self.

Is this all that Eggers's memoir is, a text imprisoned in the televisual logic of the represented self, another example of the kind of 'image-fiction' which Wallace considers in 'E Unibus Pluram'? Actually, no. For here we have to consider two points about the book. First, *A Heartbreaking Work of Staggering Genius* is not, or at least not unambiguously, a work of fiction, but a work that purports to be fact. While it effectively does nothing we have not seen in previous waves of American postmodernism (Gass, Barth, Coover, Nabokov etc.), the fact is that *A Heartbreaking Work of Staggering Genius* belongs to what is still classified as a non-fictional genre: the confessional memoir. There can be no doubt, as I will argue below, that the book is generically unstable precisely because of its formal innovation. This makes it too problematic to speak about straightforward categories of 'fiction' and 'fact'. Nevertheless, the fact that it presents itself as a fundamentally true story about a real person shifts the terms of reference. It means, in particular, that the temporal logic of the relationship between contemporary fiction and televisual culture which is central to Wallace's essay must be reversed. Wallace's argument is essentially that, by the 1990s, televisual culture had caught up with postmodern fiction, thus rendering it impotent as a form of critique. With the confessional memoir the opposite is true: this form of writing needs to catch up with television and demonstrate that in the pages of a confessional memoir all is not as it seems. To put it differently, the kind of rebellious formal experimentalism that we find in *A Heartbreaking Work of Staggering Genius* is a considerable innovation in what is a rather formally conservative form of prose writing.[3]

Second, we have to acknowledge that the layers of irony in *A Heartbreaking Work of Staggering Genius* do not function as a response to televisual culture, as Leyner's do, but as an inbuilt deconstruction of his memoir itself, and by extension the confessional narrative genre as a whole. To understand this we need to acknowledge that formally *A Heartbreaking Work of Staggering Genius* needs to be described more precisely than simply 'metafictional'. In fact it figures as an excellent example of the effects of what Gérard Genette has called 'paratextuality', or the 'accompanying productions ... a heterogeneous group of practices and discourses' which surround a text (1997: 1, 2). Genette argues that there are two main varieties of paratext: epitexts, those texts 'outside' the work itself, such as author interviews, private letters and journals; and peritexts, those which occupy the same space as the main text (which appear in the same volume), such as title, dedication, preface and postscript (Genette 1997: 5). These paratexts contribute, in some cases powerfully, to the range of meanings we can draw from a main text. Sarah Brouillette has recently argued (2003) that Dave Eggers, as the man behind *McSweeney's* and the *Believer*, enjoys considerable cultural influence as an *editor* as much as an author in contemporary American literature and this makes him a fascinating case study of the significance of the *epitext* in controlling the readings of texts (such as his novel *You Shall Know Our Velocity*, which she analyses). But if we concentrate on the peritextual dimensions of *A Heartbreaking Work of Staggering Genius* we can see that rather than authorizing particular readings of the text its paratextual dimension functions as a way of shortcircuiting or warding off readings in advance. More precisely, its structure ensures we cannot be certain whether this a fundamentally genuine confession which simply uses its layers of irony as a kind of 'firebreak', a form of Foucauldian 'screen discourse' (where the act of speaking so much about something serves to conceal the 'real' of what one is speaking about) (Foucault 1990: 53) designed to protect its author, or readers, from surrendering to sheer pathos of its story, *or* one in which the ironic elements invite us to cast serious doubt on the authenticity of Eggers's response to the trauma – even of the traumatic events themselves. Both readings are valid; neither is completely persuasive. In the remainder of this chapter I want to consider in more depth how these paratexts serve to cast substantial doubt on the conventional understanding of the confessional prose memoir.

The ambiguity about how we should read *A Heartbreaking Work of Staggering Genius* is created by the fact that the complete book is neither unremittingly metafictional nor entirely 'straight'. What we have instead, as the title neatly suggests, are two very different kinds of writing which sit together rather uneasily: the 'Heartbreaking' main story, on the one hand, and the elements of 'Staggering Genius' (the supplementary texts), on the other. It is important not to overstate the distinction, for both parts are unified by Eggers's ironic tone, and the Heartbreaking story contains ironic metafictional elements, such as the fabricated MTV interview. Nevertheless the fact is that there are two different kinds of text within the whole work, both clearly separated from each other, with the prefatory texts and the appendix functioning, to use an analogy by Barthes which Genette adopts, as 'vestibules' (Genette 1997: 2), kinds of 'waiting room' in which we dwell before proceeding to the main text. The co-existence of both zones poses a challenge. Are we to read what we are presented with as essentially a *heartbreaking* narrative or an *ingenious* one? Of course the official answer, as the title suggests (fulfilling its didactic function as paratext), is both. But how can it be both?

This is where we must return to the question of the book's genre, and, more specifically, to the absence of radical formal experimentation in the genre before Eggers. The 'confessional' and the 'metafictional' figure almost as opposites in literary criticism. Confessional writing, as opposed to the simply 'autobiographical', is taken to mean work marked by an extraordinary candour about the private anguish which afflicted the author at the time of writing. Its power comes from the sense that what we read is a genuine revelation about the distress faced by the writer, and, what is more, the representation of this figure can be accepted as a faithful portrait. As the notorious case of Binjamin Wilkomirski's *Fragments* (1996) shows, confessional non-fiction loses its legitimacy if doubt is cast on the accuracy of the events it recounts or the status of the writer.[4] As Eggers says about his own memoir's veracity, 'no one, except an electorate, likes a liar. We all like full disclosure' (2000: xxviii).

Metafiction, by contrast, is a practice which is sceptical about the very nature of 'authenticity' and 'the genuine', as it questions the possibility of art representing faithfully anything in the external world without disfiguring it or remaking it in its own image. Metafiction explores what Patricia Waugh refers to as the 'creation/description paradox' (1984: 88), by which the attempt to describe something in words inevitably leads to its being effectively 'created' anew as a separate entity. The effect of metafiction – and this is why postmodern fiction has so obsessively tended to parody the nineteenth century novel – is to expose the ideologies upon which realism as a literary doctrine is founded. The realist, it suggests – and, we might add, by extension the author of the confessional memoir – has selected, interpreted and manipulated his or her material just as much as any experimental modernist or postmodernist writer. As Wallace wittily puts it, metafiction 'was really nothing more than a single-order expansion of its own great theoretical nemesis, Realism: if Realism called it like it saw it, Metafiction simply called it as it saw itself seeing it' (1997: 34).

It follows, then, that by combining the confessional with the metafictional the confessional is fatally compromised. Metafiction exposes the definition of the confessional memoir as ideologically loaded, one that depends on the pretence that terms like 'genuine' and 'faithful' are non-problematic, as well as an overly simplistic understanding of the mechanics of representation. Eggers, it seems, self-conscious to the last, is aware of this. Surely we should take as tongue-in-cheek his efforts to ensure that the paratextual dimension of the book remains as Genette advises it should be, 'subordinate to "its" text' (1991: 269). Eggers continually urges his readers to observe a strict hierarchy in which the main narrative is considered as more important than the opening collection of texts. In 'Rules and Suggestions for Enjoyment of This Book', for example, he advises us that 'There is no overwhelming need to read the preface ... no overarching need to read the Acknowledgements ... You can also skip the table of contents'. These elements are 'not necessary to the plot in any major way' (2000: v). The fact that there is no pagination to the acknowledgments, the most extensive and illuminating – not to mention subversive – of the paratexts underlines this point (even though this practice conforms to publishers' conventions regarding acknowledgements). What it seems we are presented with here is an inconsequential thirty-seven page space filled with prose which floats, disembodied, signifying apparently nothing before the book proper begins. But given its length and pertinence to what follows, it is doubtful if the reader is able to heed his advice unquestioningly.

Another way of putting this is to say that Eggers's peritexts are consciously *supplementary* in the sense that Derrida famously used the term in his reading of Rousseau in *Of Grammatology* (1976). The term 'supplement' designates something added optionally to that which is already complete, but which implies as a result, paradoxically, that the prioritized entity is actually incomplete. The very existence of the prefatory material means that, despite Eggers's disingenuous claims to the contrary, the ingenious supplementary texts are what produce, make possible, the heartbreaking dimension. They position the work as a whole, let us know how it should be read, or rather instil an uncertainty as to how far we should trust its attempts to direct us towards a reading. The 'Staggering Genius' part automatically assumes a certain priority by being what we come upon first as we open the book. But it is also given a more literal priority when Eggers explains in *Mistakes We Knew We Were Making* that

> the Acknowledgements were written before the rest of the book, as both an organizational device and a stalling mechanism. I was not looking forward to writing the first chapter of the book, and wasn't sure if I could write those thereafter, so I had a nice time fiddling with the front matter, which came easily, and helped me to shape the book in my head before starting into it.
>
> (2001: 16)

Their priority means that the Genius sections in *A Heartbreaking Work of Staggering Genius* demonstrate how any effects in literature are textual rather than 'real'. In other words, the heartbreaking elements of the story are chiefly the result of writing, as a result of the way Eggers has presented his story, and himself, rather than because of any inherent pathos in his story. It reminds us that everything in his story, like all stories – like all confessions – is narrativized, nothing is 'natural', 'as it was'. This, of course, is the implication in all works of metafiction: they remind us that writing is artifice and must not be taken as a true representation of reality, because of the very nature of representation.

In this way *A Heartbreaking Work of Staggering Genius* exposes the definition of the confessional genre as writing which is distinguished by its authenticity as contradictory at best, perhaps even entirely untenable. For, of course, the reason the reader feels that s/he is presented with a genuine story is precisely because of the rhetoric employed by that story, and rhetoric involves artifice, the imposition of an aesthetic order. *A Heartbreaking Work of Staggering Genius* suggests that there can be no more certainty about confession than there is about fiction. In fact, the resultant collapse of generic boundaries is suggested subtly but directly by the formal definitions contained in the memoir. The jacket of the book acknowledges that it is 'based on a true story' – a statement which, when considered in the light of its contents, is appropriately uncertain. A *true story* is just as much of an incongruity as the metafictional confession, for a story cannot duplicate something that happened in reality, it can only be 'based' upon it. Eggers amplifies this kind of ironic effect when he reverses the claim on the copyright page: '[t]his is a work of fiction, only in that in many cases, the author could not remember the exact words said by certain people, and exact descriptions of certain things, so had to fill in gaps as best he could. Otherwise, all characters and incidents and dialogue are real'. The result of this ambiguity is that we are forced to regard as disingenuous *all* of Eggers's claims in the supplementary material, such as his explanation that the title was chosen more or less casually in 'a round-robin sort of title tourney, held outside Phoenix, Arizona' (2000: xxii) and his (ironic) protest that 'there is almost no irony, whatsoever, within [the] covers [of the whole book]' (2001: 33). Most subversively, by implication it means we need to regard any aspect of the 'story' as potentially fabricated too.

Any confessional text, by definition, explores self-consciousness, but Eggers takes this self-consciousness to new bounds by making his text profoundly self-conscious too. As well as his own intimate confession, it is as if the text itself is confessing, telling us what *it* is, baring its own devices. It is thus a work of *metaconfession*, a confession about confession. Viktor Shklovsky famously said that Sterne's *Tristram Shandy* is the 'most typical novel in world literature' (1989: 210) because of the extreme degree to which it foregrounds the sheer artificiality of presenting a fictional world, something which, by definition, is a property of all novels – but tends to remain hidden. By the same token we could call *A Heartbreaking Work of Staggering Genius*, for all its singular innovation in this genre, the most typical confessional work in literature, because it demonstrates how confession in writing is always a matter of textual effect, it can never accurately represent the real. In fact it suggests that the real self is actually fiction, always framed by the discursive and textual network of representation in which we must present ourselves.

The book thus stands as a counterpart to the arguments developed in recent work in the academic study of autobiography. Over the last couple of decades the theory of autobiography has undergone a shift in how it conceives of the relationship between the human subject and the representation of this subject in writing. Previously, for example, in Olney (1972) or Weintraub (1978), it was assumed that autobiography reflected the 'fact' that the human being was a coherent, unique individual who could effectively transcend his or her historical and social circumstances. The function of the written form, the autobiography itself, was to exemplify what was considered a natural human goal to journey through life and arrive at a kind of self-reflective wholeness. Now, however, as a result of the influence of thinkers in the poststructuralist tradition such as Derrida, Barthes and Foucault, whose work has taught us that the human being is subject to ideological and historical forces so that we are fragmented beings written by our socio-historical position, autobiography theory has focused on how the memoir reveals that the self is effectively a fiction which we preserve. Works such as Paul John Eakin's *Fictions in Autobiography* (1988) and Leigh Gilmore's *Autobiographics* (1994) inform us, like *A Heartbreaking Work of Staggering Genius*, that although it may pretend otherwise, autobiography is subject to precisely the same laws of selection, ordering and narrativization as fiction.

But rather than simply echoing this view of the self as construction *A Heartbreaking Work of Staggering Genius* in fact develops an interesting variation on the theme by implying that what is shown to happen to the subject in autobiographical writing may equally be thought of as a deconstruction or even a destruction. Essentially, of course, this is saying the same thing: the conception of the self as singular, autonomous individual is outdated and untenable. But it marks a notable shift of emphasis from the perspective of the theorist or critic of autobiography to that of the writer – giving us a judgement on writing autobiography from 'inside' the cage, as it were, rather than outside. In the extended acknowledgements section Eggers considers what he calls the 'memoir as self-destruction' theme which runs through the book. Producing the confessional text, he says (appropriately combining a metaphor commonly used in the confessional tradition, by John Berryman, for example, with a more irreverent late twentieth century one) 'can and should be the shedding of a skin, which is something one should do, as necessary and as invigorating as the occasional facial, or colonic' (2000: xxxiv). This is because the act of coldly, cruelly presenting oneself as one was (but no longer is) is a means of 'killing that person' as a way of saying: '[t]his was me then, and I can look at this person, from the distance I now have, and throw water balloons on his stupid fat head' (2001: 20).

A more literal dramatization of the notion of confession as self-destruction can be found in the many passages in the book where Eggers writes of his paranoid fear of always being on the point of violent death – something which, he explains in *Mistakes We Knew We Were Making*, dogged him as a consequence of his self-exposure in prose:

> For years I feared the opening of every elevator, half-convinced that from the open doors would come a bullet, for me, shot by a man in a tan trenchcoat. I have no idea why I feared this, expected it to happen. I even knew how I would react to this bullet coming from the elevator door, what word I would say. That word was: *Finally*.
>
> (2001: 16–17)

With this word we pass back through the 'vestibule' into the original text, for 'finally' is the last word in the main story and concludes a tumultuous two-page stream-of-consciousness monologue with an explicit plea to the readers of the memoir to kill him: 'Oh do it, do it, you motherfuckers, do it do it you fuckers finally, finally, finally' (2000: 437). Thus the writing of the memoir is envisaged as as a masochistic act in which he expects to be slaughtered for his 'full disclosure'. It suggests that one way of conceiving of the main narrative in *A Heartbreaking Work of Staggering Genius*, most obviously the tale of the author's response to the deaths of his parents, is that it is really the story of its author's own metaphorical act of self-destruction – a story which neatly parallels the self-*deconstruction* effected by its paratexts.

Its sheer complexity, then, the depth of its layers of irony and its resultant capacity to resist readings, means that *A Heartbreaking Work of Staggering Genius* cannot be seen as simply a literary equivalent of the form of self-expression-as-confession which Baudrillard regards as symptomatic of the telemorphic condition of twenty-first century culture. It is altogether too ambiguous, it preserves too many of its author's secrets, to be regarded as properly obscene, in the Baudrillardian sense. Nor can it be easily condemned along the lines of Wallace's alternative take on the hegemony of televisual culture as a work whose ironic approach to dealing with self-disclosure is diluted by the predominance of the ironic mode in television. By stopping well short of claiming it is a total fabrication but nevertheless allowing the suspicion to reign that it might be, *A Heartbreaking Work of Staggering Genius* injects a degree of uncertainty into the confessional memoir about the nature of the distinction between the real and fake which is more unsettling than Wilkomirski's outright bogus memoir. Its capacity to resist alternative readings (i.e. the uncertainty as to whether we should finally treat it either as a genuine account cloaked in self-protective irony or a complete deconstruction of the confessional genre) gives it a peculiar seductive power. Baudrillard's critique of the dominant logic of production in contemporary culture is bound up with his desire that this be opposed by the logic of seduction, the force that 'withdraws something from the visible order and so runs counter to production, whose project is to set everything up in clear view' (Baudrillard 1977: 21–2). In his contention about the state of ultimate visibility exemplified by reality television, Baudrillard argues that the endpoint of Foucault's self-expression-as-confession is not only a kind of violence against 'the singular being and his secrecy' but 'also a form of violence against language. In this mode of communicability [i.e. reality television], language loses its originality. Language simply becomes a medium, an operator of visibility. It has lost its symbolic and ironic qualities, those which make language more important than what it conveys' (Baudrillard 2001). The densely metafictional form of *A Heartbreaking Work of Staggering Genius* draws instead on the ironic power of language, and this causes it to function as, at the same time, both a seductive operator of invisibility and a demonstration that more conventional confessional memoirs use language as a medium simply to produce visibility. The book's irony causes us to focus on the role of language in producing – and hiding, perhaps destroying – the subject, and as such gestures towards an alternative way of confessing in contemporary culture than telemorphic self-expression.

Notes

1 See Maltby (1991) for an excellent and extensive argument along these lines. Wallace is by no means the first to consider the significance of irony in contemporary culture; a predisposition towards irony has been regarded, by those both appreciative and disapproving of postmodernism, as the most typical feature of postmodern culture. Fredric Jameson (whose famous critique Wallace in some way echoes) has noted the tendency towards the kind of 'blank irony' favoured in postmodernist works, which functions as an empty reflex gesture, lacking any kind of critical edge (Jameson 1991: 18). Others, such as Charles Jencks (1985), Linda Hutcheon (1988, 1989) and Umberto Eco (1983), have argued that the postmodern predisposition towards irony actually reflects a more valuable sense of self-awareness about the 'postmodern condition'. The value of Wallace's piece, besides its status as a polemical essay on the viability of contemporary fiction by a practitioner-critic in the tradition of Philip Roth's 'Writing American Fiction' (1961) and John Barth's 'The Literature of Exhaustion' (1968), is that he opens up a potential realignment of the co-ordinates of the debate about postmodernism and contemporary fiction by tracing the interconnections between postmodern US fiction and televisual culture.
2 Lewis Hyde, 'Alcohol and Poetry: John Berryman and the Booze Talking', first published in the *American Poetry Review* and issued as separate pamphlet (Hyde 1986).
3 I am here distinguishing between confessional narratives in prose and confessional poetry. Confessional poetry can be regarded as more of a departure from previous ways of dealing with personal expression in poetry, as it emerged in response to the formal, modernist, poetics of restraint (as voiced by the likes of T.S. Eliot and John Crowe Ransome). As a result it was celebrated as a radical 'breakthrough' by critics such as A. Alvarez.
4 To considerable acclaim Wilkomirski published *Fragments: Memories of a Wartime Childhood* (1996), which purports to be a memoir of being caught in a Nazi concentration camp at the age of three. An article by Philip Gourevitch ('The Memory Thief', *The New Yorker*, June 14 1999) later voiced doubts as to the validity of his account, alleging that Wilkomirksi did not spend any of his childhood in concentration camps, is not Jewish, and not even called Wilkomirski. See also Maechler (2001).

Bibliography

Baudrillard, J. (1977) *Forget Foucault*, trans. 1987, New York: Semiotext(e).

—— (2001) 'Dust Breeding' (*'L'Elevage de Poussière'*), trans. F. Debrix, *Libération*, 29 May. Available online at: http://www.ctheory.net/text_file.asp?pick=293 (accessed 9 December 2004).

—— (2002) 'Telemorphosis', in T. Levin, U. Frohne and P. Wiebel (eds) *CTRL {SPACE}: Rhetorics of Surveillance from Bentham to Big Brother*, Cambridge: The MIT Press.

Brouillette, S. (2003) 'Paratextuality and Economic Disavowal in Dave Eggers' *You Shall Know Our Velocity*', *Reconstruction: Studies in Contemporary Culture* 3 (2). Available online at: http://www.reconstruction.ws/032/brouillette.htm (accessed 9 December 2004).

Burn, G. (2004) 'The Believers', *Guardian*, 27 March. Available online at: http://books.guardian.co.uk/review/story/0,12084,1177959,00.html (accessed 9 December 2004).

Derrida, J. (1976) *Of Grammatology*, trans. G.C. Spivak, Baltimore: Johns Hopkins University Press.

Eakin, P.J. (1988) *Fictions in Autobiography: Studies in the Art of Self-Invention*, Princeton: Princeton University Press.

Eco, U. (1983) *Reflections on The Name of the Rose*, London: Weidenfeld and Nicolson.

Eggers, D. (2000) *A Heartbreaking Work of Staggering Genius*, London: Picador.

—— (2001) *Mistakes We Knew We Were Making*, London: Picador.

Fielding, H. (1985) [1749] *Tom Jones*, London: Penguin.

Foucault, M. (1990) *The History of Sexuality: The Will to Knowledge*, Volume 1, London: Penguin.

Genette, G. (1991) 'Introduction to the Paratext', trans. M. Maclean, *New Literary History*, 22 (2): 262–72.

—— (1997) *Paratexts: Thresholds of Interpretation*, trans. J.E. Lewin, Cambridge: Cambridge Univesrity Press.

Gilmore, L. (1994) *Autobiographics: A Feminist Theory of Women's Self-Representation*, Ithaca: Cornell University Press.

Hutcheon, L. (1988) *A Poetics of Postmodernism*, London: Routledge.

—— (1989) *The Politics of Postmodernism*, London: Routledge.

Hyde, L. (1986) *Alcohol and Poetry: John Berryman and the Booze Talking*, Dallas: Dallas Institute of Humanities & Culture.

Jameson, F. (1991) *Postmodernism, or The Cultural Logic of Late Capitalism*, London and New York: Verso.

Jencks, C. (1986) *What is Post-Modernism?*, London: Academy.

Maechler, S. (2001) *The Wilkomirski Affair: A Study in Biographical Truth*, London: Picador.

Maltby, P. (1991) *Dissident Postmodernists: Barthelme, Coover, Pynchon*, Philadelphia: University of Philadelphia Press.

Olney, J. (1972) *Metaphors of Self: The Meaning of Autobiography*, Princeton: Princeton University Press.

Shklovsky, V. (1989) 'The Parody Novel: Sterne's Tristram Shandy' [1921], *The Review of Contemporary Fiction*, 1–2: 190–212.

Wallace, D.F. (1997) 'E Unibus Pluram: Television and U.S. Fiction', in *A Supposedly Fun Thing I'll Never Do Again: Essays and Arguments*, London: Abacus.

Waugh, P. (1984) *Metafiction: The Theory and Practice of Self-Conscious Fiction*, London: Methuen.

Weintraub, K. (1978) *The Value of the Individual: Self and Circumstance in Autobiography*, Chicago and London: Chicago University Press.

Wilkomirski, B. (1996) *Fragments: Memories of a Wartime Childhood*, New York: Random House.

7 Truth, confession and the post-apartheid black consciousness in Njabulo Ndebele's *The Cry of Winnie Mandela*

Yianna Liatsos

> The African oppressed appear to have been reduced to the status of being mere bearers of witness. They do a good job of describing suffering but they cannot define its quality ... To define is to understand, while to describe is merely to observe.
>
> Njabulo Ndebele, 'Noma Award Acceptance Speech'[1]

In the acceptance speech he gave in 1985 on receiving the Noma Award for his collection *Fools and Other Stories*, Njabulo Ndebele traced the genealogy of his inspiration to the indignation expressed in Solomon T. Plaatje's 1916 volume *Native Life in South Africa* (Ndebele 1994: 159). Writing three years after the Native Land Act limited the land ownership rights of Africans to demarcated reserves, essentially inaugurating the official rule of segregation that was to reach its culmination in the form of apartheid, Plaatje noted the discord evident in the responses to the Act. While the ruling whites 'content[ed] themselves with giving contradictory definitions of their cruelty' the natives gave 'no definitions of legislative phrases nor explanations of definitions. All they [gave] expression to [was] their bitter suffering' (Ndebele 1994: 159). Ndebele's epigraph in the present essay was written almost seventy years later and expands both on the implications of Plaatje's claim and on the black literary production of his own time – whose predication, according to David Attwell, was 'that writers provide the solace of truth, of political faith, not fictive irritants ... which leave readers with fewer defenses against the collective trauma [of apartheid] they inhabit' (1993: 15).

According to Ndebele the political agenda of liberation that obliged black writers during the latter part of the apartheid era – mainly in the 1980s – to follow, by and large, the wider international trend of protest literature, signalled not so much the political rebellion as the imaginative impoverishment of black South African consciousness. Generated primarily in the twentieth century among peoples fighting for national liberation and independence, protest literature aimed to tell truth to power by testifying the experience of deprivation and repression suffered by civilians and concealed by colonial occupying forces or authoritarian regimes.[2] Ndebele's contention was that by 'testifying' everyday repression under apartheid, a writer is not necessarily being polemical: if truth-telling entails mere observation, it risks being little more than a dull response to an action initiated by those who possess sociopolitical agency. Worse still, protest literature tends to generate static images 'of passive people whose only reason for existing seemed to be to receive the sympathy of the world' (Ndebele 1994: 160). For Ndebele, the effect of this is to 'promote a negation ... a fixed and unhistorical image with the result of obscuring the existence of a fiercely energetic and complex dialectic in the progress of human history' (1994: 160).

In 'The Rediscovery of the Ordinary', an essay written a year after the Noma speech, Ndebele expands on the limitations of black South African protest literature by specifically commenting on its production of spectacular effects:

> Everything ... points to spectacle: the complete exteriority of everything ... we have spectacular ritual instantly turned into symbol ... Thinking is secondary to seeing. Subtlety is secondary to obviousness. What is finally left and what is deeply etched in our minds is the spectacular contest between the powerless and the powerful. Most of the time the contest ends in horror and tragedy for the powerless.
>
> (1994: 46)

By reducing the complexity of lived reality under apartheid to a barely varied series of episodes whose recurrence confirmed the unremitting victimization of innocent blacks at the hands of whites, protest literature, according to Ndebele, essentially espoused the Manichean doctrine employed by the apartheid system itself. The depiction of the white state oppressors as dissolute murderers and of the non-white civil society as virtuous victims, unwittingly observed the imaginative guidelines of the repressive social order without challenging its binary structure. 'Telling truth to power', in this respect, did not entail the demystification of the logical framework of this power but confirmed its seat.

From W.E.B. Du Bois and Plaatje writing at the turn of the twentieth century, to Frantz Fanon and Stephen Biko writing during the anti-colonial struggle on the African continent, the idea that blacks have compounded their long period of victimization by turning it into the essence of their identity became the catalyst for a tenet of radicalism. Within the Black Consciousness Movement, the South African anti-apartheid organization created in the late 1960s by Biko, the 'complicitous victim' neurosis was perceived as the most important obstacle preventing the liberation of black South Africans (Sanders 2002: 178). In his essay 'We Blacks' Biko defined the South African black man – and it was exclusively the black male subject that the Black Consciousness Movement was centred on – as 'a shell, a shadow of a man, completely defeated, drowning in his own misery' (Biko

1978: 29). According to Biko, the way 'to pump back life' into this 'empty shell' was to remind the black South African 'of his complicity in the crime of allowing himself to be misused and therefore letting evil reign supreme in the country of his birth' (1978: 29). Biko envisioned this realization as emerging from the kind of 'inward-looking process' that escapes the confines of apartheid's normative subjugation so as to question its meaning and authority and to conceive of a substitute.

An outspoken supporter of Black Consciousness himself, Ndebele saw the political role of black South African writing as a potent medium in the struggle for the emancipation of the black imagination. Adopting Herbert Marcuse's assertion that the interiority of subjectivity has political value both as 'a counter force against aggressive and exploitative socialization', and as the 'realization' of the 'inner resources of the human being ... passion, imagination, conscience', Ndebele claimed that literary writing committed to sociopolitical transformation needed to abandon 'the spectacular rendering of a familiar oppressive reality' and concentrate on 'the essential drama in the lives of ordinary people' (1994: 55). Although questions such as 'Will I like my daughter's boyfriends or prospective husband?' or 'What will my child become?' may appear insignificant before the 'serious' agenda of 'the people's liberation', Ndebele understood these 'ordinary' instances of self-reflecting questioning – instances of private confession – as potent catalysts reviving the unlimited inventiveness and power of social imagination at large (1994: 55). 'The mechanisms of survival and resistance that the people have devised are many and far from simple' (1994: 160), Ndebele asserted to fellow writers in his Noma speech, encouraging them to go beyond the spectacular agenda of the liberation struggle in order to conceive the full intricacy of the non-white South African social imaginary.[3] 'The task is to understand [these mechanisms], and then to actively make them the material subject of our imaginative explorations' (1994: 160).

Since the first articulation of Ndebele's ideas in the mid 1980s, the dream of 'the people's liberation' has become a reality and South Africa has transformed from the last stronghold of state-sanctioned racial segregation to an exemplary constitutional democracy. In the transition, the credo of 'telling truth to power' that once inspired South African literature became official policy when the first nonracial democratic parliament passed the 1995 National Unity and Reconciliation Act instituting the South African Truth and Reconciliation Commission (TRC). My interest in this essay is to read Ndebele's latest novel, *The Cry of Winnie Mandela*, as the author's response to the Manichean spectacle of the apartheid experience which, I would argue, in post-apartheid South Africa has found new expression in the historical memory codified by the TRC public hearings. More specifically, I will examine how Ndebele's novel explores the nuance and complexity of the 'ordinary' past and present-day black consciousness by engaging the historical memory of Winnie Madikizela-Mandela in an alternative way to that employed by the TRC 'Winnie hearing' – formally known as 'A Human

Rights Violation Hearing into the Mandela United Football Club'. The aim of this essay is to show how in 'rediscovering the ordinary' dimension of the black woman's consciousness, Ndebele's novel transforms one of the most controversial mnemonic representations of that consciousness, publicly embodied by Winnie Mandela, from 'a South African tragedy' as Alex Boraine called it (2000: 221–57), into a less dramatic and more paradoxical emancipatory opening of the South African social imagination.

The South African truth commission which was founded, much like previous and subsequent truth commissions, on the negotiated settlement between the past authoritarian regime (the Afrikaner National Party, or NP) and the resistance movement led by the African National Congress (ANC), employed a unique amalgamation of three different models of confession; the religious, judicial and psychoanalytic, in order to reveal the hidden truth of the human rights violations that had taken place during the apartheid era, and promote the unity and reconciliation of the South African people. More specifically, in its effort to carry out its assigned four-fold task of establishing 'as complete a picture as possible of the causes, nature and extent of the gross violations of human rights' committed between 1 March 1960 to May 10 1994; offering amnesty 'to persons who [would] make full disclosure of all the relevant facts relating to acts associated with a political objective'; 'making known the fate or whereabouts of victims'; and recommending appropriate reparations to apartheid's victims, the TRC was divided into three committees, two of which elicited public confessions (open to the audience as well as radiocasted and televised) from the designated 'perpetrators' and 'victims' of apartheid: the Amnesty Committee (AC) and the Human Rights Violations Committee (HRVC) respectively.[4]

According to Peter Brooks, who has suggested a structural uniformity in the character of confession in law, religion and psychoanalysis (sharing primarily the oral quality of the confessional narrative and the requirement for an interlocutor's response), the tension between the modern judicial and the Christian (primarily Catholic) models of confession is that whereas the latter model rewards absolution, the former model administers conviction (Brooks 2000: 96). In the case of the AC hearings, whose aim was to recover the concealed historical truth of the apartheid era from its designated perpetrators in exchange for the amnesty already agreed upon in the interim constitution, the legal equivalent of absolution *was* in fact gifted: amnesty was made available to anyone who had perpetrated a crime against humanity during the apartheid era as long as:

1   the crime confessed had taken place between 1960 and 1994;
2   the perpetrator disclosed the truth about his/her involvement in the crime;
3   the crime confessed had a political motivation and nature – rather than personal;
4   the crime confessed was proportional to the political motive.

Amnesty as sociopolitical absolution in turn confused the performative distinction of the legal and religious confessional rituals: on the one hand it Christianized the confession to be offered by perpetrators in the pseudo-judicial setting of the commission hearings, and on the other hand it transformed the predominantly private character of modern Christian confession and absolution into a public spectacle that systematically assumed a moralistic and shaming tone vis-à-vis the perpetrators' confessions. The commissioners, judges and lawyers participating in the AC hearings repeatedly blurred the boundaries between a cross-examination that measures the veracity of a perpetrator's confession and a shaming ritual that reduces these same perpetrators to powerless villains. Thus by demanding that perpetrators confess publicly their crimes against humanity, the AC hearings tacitly expunged a kind of compensation for the punishment such perpetrators would have suffered had they been prosecuted. In the words of the chairperson of the TRC, Archbishop Desmond Tutu, 'the perpetrators don't get off scot-free: they have to confess publicly in the full glare of television lights that they did those ghastly things. And that's pretty pretty tough' (Reid and Hoffmann 2000). Charles Villa-Vicencio, director of research at the TRC, similarly claimed that 'public censure of those responsible for gross violations ... is a form of justice that, in a certain way, is as severe as languishing in prison' (cited in Ntsebeza 2000). Putting aside the contestable merit of the latter's analogy, Tutu and Villa-Vicencio's claims unmistakably confirm that the public degradation of the perpetrators was in fact rationalized as a means of balancing the otherwise badly unbalanced historical scales: if the victims who suffered the crimes confessed by the perpetrators were not allowed retribution by means of seeing those perpetrators receive state-sponsored punishment for their crimes, they would nevertheless recover some solace in witnessing the perpetrators be humiliated (an experience all too familiar to non-white South Africans living under the apartheid rule). As human rights lawyer George Bizos has suggested, the largely non-white audience that witnessed the mighty of the past being cross-examined and challenged by the lawyers and commissioners of the AC hearings, achieved an emotional catharsis that would not have been available to them otherwise, considering the pact of amnesty that came with the negotiated settlement (Reid and Hoffmann 2000). By using confessions to perform public shaming rituals, then, the AC hearings coupled the absolution granted to the perpetrators with the purgation of historical affect for the audience. In more ways than one, the dilemmas of transitional justice were mastered, at least in part, through spectacular effects.

Conversely, the HRVC hearings enveloped the narratives to be given by the designated 'victims' of apartheid within a therapeutic discourse that solicited a psychoanalytic confession. Before proceeding with my analysis I want to make a brief clarification of how I employ the concept of confession in the context of the HRVC. Customarily anchored in conscious choice and free will, confession, according to Brooks and Michel Foucault before him, functions as a critical self-reflective ritual that 'delves into the subject's past and into the subject's deepest and most hidden thoughts and wishes, in order to account for the individual self' (Brooks 2000: 102). Testimony, on the other hand, typically conveys descriptions of events either witnessed or personally experienced and in either case understood to have originated outside the narrator's personal volition. In other words, we traditionally confess something we did whereas we testify something we witnessed or experienced from without. Accordingly, the narratives given by victims and witnesses are understood as testimonies since the storytellers are not expected either to disclose personal secrets or embark on an investigative journey of personal incentives, but to describe events under dispute to the best of their recollection.

Nevertheless, the choice of the HRVC to prioritize the therapeutic potential of the narratives told by apartheid's victims (offering them the opportunity to tell their stories in an uninterrupted fashion and 'in their own words') over the quality and accuracy of information of those narratives (little, if any cross-examination was employed), entailed treating the emergent narratives more as psychoanalytic confessions than as testimonies (Slye 1999). Quoting Freud's claim that whereas 'in confession the sinner tells what he knows, in analysis the neurotic has to tell more', Brooks explains that in its psychotherapeutic orientation confessional discourse has a distinct double character that subverts the logic of the religious and judicial confessional acts: 'the referential matter of the [psychoanalytic] confession ... is not necessarily the meaning or the truth of the confession, that which is intended by the speech act' (2000: 116–17). Released from the burden of referential accuracy (the first, conscious scope of psychoanalytic confession and the exclusive dimension of both judicial and religious confessions), confessional truth in the psychoanalytic context becomes associated with intention or desire – the second, unconscious scope of psychoanalytic confession.

The therapeutic value of this doubleness becomes particularly evident when the psychoanalytic confessional act is employed to address the memory of a traumatic event. If trauma, according to Freud, is shielded and repressed by and from consciousness at the moment it forms, and is subsequently experienced in the form of a neurotic pattern whose repetition signals the presence of a still unrevealed but existent traumatic kernel, then confession allows the analyst to investigate more extensively the hidden crevasses of the analysand's conscious memory and thus ascertain its gaps and fissures. In turn, the aim becomes to bridge the gap created by traumatic dissociation between the unconscious and conscious layers of the confessing consciousness in such a way as to allow the patient not so much to become cognizant of the actual trauma, whose origin remains permanently beyond the scope of conscious knowledge, but to recover 'that truth of mind and emotion that offers a coherent and therapeutic life's narrative to the analysand [and] which is not wholly dependent on referential truth or correspondence to a set of facts' (Brooks 2000: 118). Donald Spence has called this truth which overcomes traumatic dissociation 'narrative truth', claiming that though a traumatized psyche can never recover the actual historical moment that produced its traumatic experience, it can nevertheless be 'healed' via the construction of a viable narrative that gives the patient coherent and meaningful continuity from the past to the present (1982: 280). Unlike religious and judicial confession which aims to reveal the already existent but hidden truth of a past action, psychoanalytic confession is thus performed in order to construct (remember) a truth whose original and ever-elusive traumatic force has fractured memory.

To summarize then, by constructing their storytellers as the distraught victims of apartheid suffering traumas whose origins can never be fully and factually known, the HRVC hearings were geared less toward recovering the historical truth of the apartheid memory among the victims and more toward assisting these victims in establishing some type of narrative truth that would help them achieve the proverbial 'closure'. Yet insofar as the closure to emerge from the HRVC hearings needed to cohere with the larger agenda of the TRC to promote what Judge Ismael Mahomed, in his defence of the TRC at the Constitutional Court, called the 'reconciliation and rapid transition [of South Africa] to a new future' (Bizos 1998: 234), it was sought after as an efficient resolution rather than as an attentive examination of the confessional narratives it helped stage. In other words, apartheid's designated victims had little chance to engage in the kind of confessional, self-reflective examination of their own past motives and experiences that Ndebele had envisioned as capable of sharpening the individual and social black consciousness. Rather, the confessions of the designated victims were reduced to a kind of testimonial spectacle whose quality resembled that of the testimonial/protest literature Ndebele criticized in the 1980s, constructing innocent victims pleading to be rescued from the abuses of villainous masters. Furthermore, as Mahmood Mamdani has suggested, by choosing to define the victims of apartheid as those individuals who suffered from unlawful treatment at the hands of the apartheid regime, the TRC failed to distinguish between law (what is legal) and right (what is legitimate) and attended to the stories of only those victims who suffered a gross violation *within* the context of the apartheid laws (Mamdani 2000: 180–1). Only those victims who suffered the kind of exceptionally violent treatment – torture, rape, the murder of a loved one – that was unlawful during the apartheid era had a chance to tell their stories in the HRVC hearings, leaving the greater non-white South African population that suffered the more ordinary and systematic subjugation of the apartheid system – dislocation, abject poverty, ceaseless humiliation – largely absent from the historical memory to be constituted and publicly recognized through the hearings. Accordingly, if the AC hearings performed the kind of shaming ritual that publicly exposed and debunked the corrupt past authority of apartheid's perpetrators, the HRVC hearings staged a drama whose spectacularly harrowing details overwhelmed the opportunity provided by the

hearings to generate the kind of self-reflection that would allow the designated 'victims', in interchange with their audience and perhaps even the perpetrators, to produce viable 'narrative truths' that would assist them with
overcoming their traumatic past without reducing it into a time predeter-
mined to be understood as 'horror and tragedy for the powerless' (Ndebele
1994: 46).[5]

On whatever level the TRC public hearings achieved the task of promoting national unity and reconciliation, they did so by employing the type of
confessional discourse that fell short of illuminating the complexity of living
through apartheid. Perhaps more than most of the other TRC hearings, the
Winnie Mandela special hearing exposed how the dramatic dualism of
'victims' and 'perpetrators' and the emphasis on closure/reconciliation were
too limiting for contextualizing the historical memory of apartheid and for
coming to terms with its nuances and conundrums.

Widely known as one of the driving forces behind the anti-apartheid
struggle during the twenty-seven years her husband, Nelson Mandela, was
in prison, Winnie Madikizela-Mandela has amassed epithets that make
evident her iconic stature and commanding aura. The best known of them,
'the Mother of the Nation', paints her as a veritable Marianne embodying
South Africa and leading her children to their freedom. The scandals that
arose in the late 1980s involving Winnie Mandela as the head of a vigilante
group – 'the Mandela United Football Club' – that spread terror across the
township of Soweto, temporarily subsided during the country's sociopolitical transition period of 1990–1994, only to resurface in several of the
HRVC hearings held in Soweto in 1996. Accusations raised against the club
included abductions, assaults, torture, mutilation, murders and attempted
murders of children, women and men. When the TRC subpoenaed Mandela
for a private hearing behind closed doors, she demanded the hearing be held
'as an open and public hearing, presumably so that she might be able to
respond to all the suspicions, allegations, and innuendos leveled against her'
(Tutu 1999: 167). Having decided not to apply for amnesty for any of the
crimes she was accused of, however, Mandela was not obliged to – and did
not – offer a confession.

Analyses of the TRC that discuss the nine-day special investigation
hearing held in 1997 depict it as a messy affair. The widespread reverence
among black South Africans for Winnie Mandela, whose mythic stature per-
sisted even after the struggle against apartheid was over, produced much
controversy over holding the hearing in the first place. Even her black
victims were so intimidated by her legacy that, according to Antjie Krog,
while testifying against her they found it difficult to look in her direction
(Krog 1999: 322). Moreover, Mandela's arrogant disposition towards the
commission and the victims magnified the imbalance of power her aura produced, and 'her contemptuous attitude towards certain witnesses and her
reprimands to those who asked her questions that she did not like' only
served to undermine the proceedings further (TRC *Report* 2: 581). It was the

combination of these factors that made controversial Tutu's plea to Mandela for an apology. In concluding the hearings with a long and intimate speech in which he publicly declared their past closeness ('We have had a very close relationship with the Mandelas'), his love ('I speak to you as someone who loves you very deeply') and his respect for her projected onto the entire South African nation, Tutu appealed to Mandela to apologize and ask for forgiveness: 'I beg you, I beg you, I beg you please ... you are a great person and you don't know how your greatness would be enhanced if you were to say, "Sorry, things went wrong, forgive me". I beg you' (Tutu 1999: 172–4). When Mandela offered the procured apology – 'It is true ... things went horribly wrong and we were aware of the fact and there were factors that led to that, for that I am deeply sorry' (Tutu 1999: 174) – it was predominantly understood as a half-hearted paying of lip-service to the politics of reconciliation, though several commentators of the TRC hearings saw it in a positive light nevertheless. In fact it seems that for every account that has interpreted the exchange between Tutu and Mandela as 'a poignant and emotional moment' (Tutu 1999: 175) and the creation 'of some kind of beginning' (Krog 1999: 340), another saw it as an instant that 'left the Commission wide open to the charge of bias' (Boraine 2000: 252–3) or as an altogether 'false note' (Meredith 1999: 270).

Ndebele's latest novel stirs up the contentious memory of the Winnie Mandela legacy and hearings without settling on either side of the debate. In assuming the form of a historiographic metafiction, the novel challenges the stable boundaries separating fact from fiction to explore the potential of their cross-fertilization. It comments on the historical memory of apartheid and the place of Winnie Mandela in it while remaining conscious of its own fictionality. Coupled with the oral quality of the narrative, the metafictional dimension of *The Cry of Winnie Mandela* also blurs the boundary, painstakingly set out by Walter Benjamin, between a novel and a storytelling performance and, consequently, between the reading and listening experience (Benjamin 1968: 83–109). This melange of seemingly dissonant narrative properties simultaneously debunks the exclusive logic of distinct narrative structures (historiographic, novelistic, storytelling) while guarding the most potentially transformative elements of their discourses (historical awareness, detached and self-conscious reflexivity, relating to others by sharing experiences).

We are confronted with the unsettling effects of this melange on the very first page of the novel, when its narrator/storyteller directly invites the readers/listeners into a heedful exploration of an imaginary text: 'Let's begin with a blurb of an imaginary book about a South African woman during the long years of struggle against apartheid' (Ndebele 2003: 1). As the narrator/storyteller proceeds to explain, the imaginary book recounts 'a great South African story not yet told', that 'of four unknown women and ... of South Africa's most famous woman, who waited' (1). The reader of *The Cry of Winnie Mandela* is thus promptly alerted that the character of Winnie

Mandela, already foretold in the title, will be imaginatively re-inscribed in a novel that stages a storytelling performance of an imaginary book which centres on a still untold South African historical experience. In other words, the reader enters the novel knowing that the Winnie Mandela to be found there will be a series of imaginary effects inscribed across two narrative layers, one historical, the other fictional, that are contrapuntally entwined in a moebius strip without beginning or end.

The novel further complicates the character of Winnie Mandela by tacitly removing her from the precarious public pedestal where she is usually placed to remember her as one among the millions of 'Penelope's South African descendants' whose historical lives 'have unremittingly been put to the test by powerful social forces that caused their men to wander away from home for prolonged periods of time' (4–5). In fact, it is the experience of belonging to Penelope's genealogy rather than Winnie Mandela herself that is the focus of Ndebele's novel, and the greater part of the text concentrates on four women who comprise a random sample of Penelope's all too ordinary black South African descendants trying to come to terms with their own pasts. This becomes the first and most obvious instance of how Ndebele's novel departs from the conceptual framework of the TRC (centred on dramatic crimes to disclose the historical memory of apartheid) to explore a more ordinary yet no less poignant historical experience that has moulded the consciousness of black South African women. Their experiences were not only historically marginalized by the white South African authority, but also by the black anti-apartheid resistance, including the Black Consciousness Movement, which conceptualized the 'humanity' it sought entry into as male (Sanders 2002: 177).

In the first part of the two-part novel we get a brief description of the lives of each of the four women by the novel's storytelling narrator. We find out that the first woman, 'Mannete Mofolo, enters the genealogy of Penelope when her husband leaves their impoverished homestead to work in the mines. When he subsequently abandons his family, 'Mannete takes upon herself the responsibility of providing for her children without altogether relinquishing hope for her husband's return. The husband of Delisiwe Dulcie S'khosana, the second descendant of Penelope, leaves their township home for medical studies in Scotland. His studies continue for years, and she copes with his absence by having short-lived affairs, one of which unexpectedly leaves her pregnant. When on their fourteenth year apart her husband finally returns and finds Delisiwe with a four-year-old child, he divorces her, remarries and abandons the township where she had fantasized he would return to become the first black doctor for the rich white suburbs. Mamello Molete, the third descendant and only character in the first part of the novel to speak in her own voice, takes care of her husband's ageing parents while he is in the anti-apartheid resistance. When the transition period of 1990–1994 begins and political prisoners are granted their freedom, Mamello's husband files for divorce, marries a white comrade from the resistance movement and moves to the white northern suburbs of Johannesburg. After repeated attempts to get her husband back, and after five emotional breakdowns, Mamello begins to reconstitute her life without him. Penelope's fourth descendant, Marara Joyce Baloyi, is married to a philanderer whose excesses she finances. Committed to a tradition which demands that she remain faithful, Marara stays with her husband until his death, spending thousands of rand on an elaborate burial that demonstrates her love for him – a false 'cover' since 'in truth he had become a rag towards which she no longer felt any emotion' (30).

It is in the second part of the novel that Mandela first enters the narrative as an imaginary interlocutor in a game that the four women devise when they come together, in their narrator/storyteller's imagination, to form a traditional *ibandla*, or 'gathering'. More specifically, during one *ibandla* meeting Mamello, the self-proclaimed madwoman of the group suggests playing a game of carrying on imaginary conversations with Winnie Mandela (38). When the others respond with perplexity as to the choice of the interlocutor ('Why Winnie? Why not Albertina Sisulu? Why not Urbania Mothopeng? Why not Veronica Sobukwe? Why not Ntsiki Biko?')[6], Mamello explains,

> All these other remarkable women waited too, but ... their waiting was not significantly different from ours ... there was a silent, almost private dimension to their waiting ... Only Winnie was meant to be spoken about. Only she was the subject of daily conversation ... Only Winnie was history in the making.
>
> (39–40)

Describing the public persona of Winnie Mandela not as a spectacle that has set her place in the historical memory of South Africa in stone, but as a force whose ever-mutable form, promising no 'foreknown destinations' (40), rebuts all monolithic representations, Mamello hopes that an intimate conversation with Mandela will help transform the four women's understanding of the past and their relationship to their present identities as Penelope's descendants. 'I'm just looking for a way we can look at ourselves', she explains, 'a way to prevent us from becoming women who meet and cry. Or, if we do meet and cry, that we do so out of choice' (40).

The desire to create choices, perhaps inadvertently attracting Mamello to Mandela's life as an alternative version of her own, becomes one of the driving forces impelling the second part of Ndebele's novel forward, and the second instance where the novel departs from the conceptual framework of the TRC hearings to explore alternative ways of examining the historical memory of apartheid. If the HRVC hearings defined apartheid's victims as being in need of a narrative truth that would heal their traumatic past experiences, the second part of Ndebele's novel rethinks the very syllogism of victimhood as an already constructed imposition of narrative truth onto one's past. Rather than constructing victims that it can then proceed to heal, Ndebele's novel constructs victims who want to redefine their past experience and escape the confines of victimization. As Mamello says, 'I want to reclaim my right to be wounded without my pain having to turn me into an example of woman as victim' (28).

Mamello's subsequent proposal that the four women play a game to remedy the burden of understanding themselves as historical victims, brings to mind Jean-François Lyotard's assertion, expressed in *Just Gaming*, that history becomes tragic fate only when the individual refuses to respond with a ruse that revises and reinterprets what otherwise appears as an inescapable historical pronouncement (Lyotard and Thébaud 1985: 42). In contradiction to the positivist (legal/historiographic) and religious (Christian) frameworks of the TRC, which divided the cast of the apartheid historical memory into resolute 'victims' and 'perpetrators', the second part of Ndebele's novel has the four women of the *ibandla* engage in the kind of pagan gaming which motivates each of them to respond to society's normative – oracle – framework and rethink her belonging to Penelope's genealogy through intricate ruses that are produced by and in turn evoke imaginative openings.

Moreover, by vocalizing their one-way exchanges with Winnie Mandela within the intimacy of the traditional *ibandla* which provides a ceremonial familiarity and trust, the four women express their past experiences and questions to Mandela in the spirit of partaking in a traditional storytelling performance – which according to both Benjamin and Ndebele,[7] promotes the exchange of experiences without deluding their mnemonic density and opacity into formulaic or conclusive accounts. In turn, the imaginary discussions the women share with Mandela initiate a complex dialectic whereby their thoughts are both directed outward, in the form of questions and reflections seeking to make sense of Mandela's life, as well as inward, in the form of confessional reflections that aim to revise the mnemonic narratives through which each of the four women constructs her personal identity. In their inward, confessional modality, these exchanges seek neither absolution nor understanding from their audience – the other women of the *ibandla*, Mandela, and the reader/listener. In fact, the formal, imaginary character of the stories shared among the women free us from the burden of a moral response altogether. Much in the spirit of employing the *ibandla* and the game to create choices, the four protagonists of Ndebele's novel allow their audience to choose their response to the narratives unfolding before them. In the meantime, the women proceed with confessional exchanges that transform them from generic and passive victims who experience the past as a forlorned fate, to uniquely astute storytellers who know the present as a set of choices.

Thus what begins as Delisiwe S'khosana's inquiry into Winnie Mandela's notorious infidelity with different lovers during the years that Nelson Mandela was in prison, transforms into Delisiwe's confession of the emotional charge with which she engaged her own affairs or 'sins of commission' as she calls them. More a needy and fiery *magogo*, or 'old woman', than a discarded Penelope, Delisiwe describes her affairs not as a trail of submissive capitulations – she admits 'I have felt sometimes that I used the fantasies of being in love to justify the real desire for a fuck' (Ndebele 2003: 46) – but as a set of contingent choices whose repercussions she has accepted 'without having to respond to blame or any need for self-justification' (51). Similarly, as Marara Baloyi engages in her imaginary conversation with Winnie Mandela she begins a process of self-reflection that transforms the past tragic vision of her life from one of inescapable victimization into one that was chosen.

The intimate knowledge the four women develop about their own histories while engaging Winnie Mandela in an imaginary dialogue, is in turn projected onto Mandela's past as a desire to understand and accept the paradoxes of her life beyond spectacular representations – both of the glamorous and the denigrating kind. This kind of 'good faith' with which the four women question the more unsettling aspects of Mandela's life does not mean, however, that their exchanges shy away from difficult questions and observations. Mamello Molete, who becomes intimately familiar with political posturing when her husband responds to her pleas for an explanation of their divorce by employing the wooden language of liberation rhetoric (24–6), says to Mandela in a tone that resembles Ndebele's own:

> So much about you ... rises to significance only to descend into banality ... You become the most dramatic, most visible manifestation of the culture of political posture that may have had its use at a particular time, but which now bedevils our ability to recognise the real needs of a new society ... You personify extreme political perception unmediated by nuance.
>
> (62)

In avoiding drawing as monolithic a judgement on Mandela's public character as she claims Mandela herself to have done, Mamello couples this pronouncement with an ambivalent metaphor: she compares Mandela to the figure of Quesalid, the Kwakuit Indian who in his effort to expose the fraudulence of shamanism, trained to become a shaman only to fall in love with the power consequentially bestowed upon him by his people. Mamello, who believes that at some point between being imprisoned, tortured, displaced, feared and revered, Winnie Mandela became 'some kind of Quesalid', suggests that Mandela 'won' the TRC special hearing that bears her name precisely because the public spectacle the hearing evoked was one she had already learned and mastered. It was this mastery that allowed Mandela to confidently respond to Justice Stegmann's caustic remark during the hearing that she was a 'calm, composed, deliberate, unprincipled and unblushing liar', 'It's your opinion, your Lordship. A black face cannot turn red from blushing even if it wanted to. Find another language to describe me' (65). Not knowing the language that may reveal another, more private side of Mandela's public Quesalid nature, and unable to resolve the tension between her admiration for and profound doubts of Mandela's character, Mamello concludes her conversation by asking Mandela to explain how she has succeeded or failed to shut out 'the trauma of mental and ethical agonies' (65).

When 'Mannete Mofolo finally takes her turn to address Winnie Mandela, this first descendant of Penelope adds yet another dimension to the intricate dialectic evoked by the imaginary game the women play. A seasoned storyteller who has accumulated experiences through years of seeking her husband in her mind 'long after the physical search ended' (80), 'Mannete has only counsel to give. Resembling the figure of Walter Benjamin that Martin Jay draws in his essay 'Against Consolation' (Jay 1999: 221–39), 'Mannete's consciousness has been moulded by the kind of melancholy that comes from remaining attached to a lost object of love, refusing 'to seek some sort of ... symbolic equilibrium through a process of ... mourning that would successfully "work through" the grief' (Jay 1999: 225). This is a different version of the psychoanalytic model that masters traumatic experience by producing a narrative truth in its place. Instead, 'Mannete uses her stubborn attachment to become intimate with the dissociative experience that is born from trauma and which the HRVC hearings, in their psychological postulation, sought to heal. 'Mannete's dissociation in turn initiates a dynamic private dialectic that resembles the quality of critical reflection and self-questioning that J.M. Coetzee ascribed to the secular literary confessional consciousness.

In his essay 'Confession and Double Thoughts: Tolstoy, Rousseau, Dostoevsky', Coetzee claims that confessional literature exposes the contradictory character of all self-reflective investigations: aware of its conscious motives and pursuits, that is, of what it knows, consciousness proceeds toward certainty; aware of its unconscious desires, that is, of its capacities to manipulate, contradict and falsely rationalize, it doubts itself. The double character of the secular literary confessional consciousness Coetzee describes here resembles that of psychoanalytic confession. The difference between the two is that whereas the latter is geared toward the resolution of its inherent contradiction via the creation of a narrative truth, the former is committed to the idea of truth that constitutes it in the first place. As Coetzee asserts, 'because the basic movement of self-reflexiveness is a doubting and questioning movement, it is in the nature of the truth told to itself by the reflecting self not to be final' (1992: 263). A secular self-confrontation in the form of confession, then, can never reach absolution, or the secular equivalent of 'coming to terms with' or 'working through' one's past traumas.

Confessional, in that it doggedly accepts its Sisyphean self-reflective and self-doubting composition, 'Mannete's address to Winnie Mandela mirrors the open-ended dialectical exchange between inward reflection and outward attentiveness that 'Mannete has been engaging on her own. As she suggests to the other three women of the *ibandla*, 'Perhaps the only game I can play is with myself ... My game is a test of how to express my silences. Thoughts that have lived without a voice' (Ndebele 2003: 78). Thus begins her long storytelling meditation on her own and Mandela's life, in which 'Mannete counsels her audience – the women of the *ibandla*, Mandela, and the reader/listener – on how to 'separate the desire for a moral outcome from the process of getting to it' (83), and become acquainted with the patience and tolerance for ambivalence entailed in the creation of choice.

'Mannete's assertions here capture the effects that the formal aspect of Ndebele's novel has on its reader. The constant oscillation between fact and fiction prevents the reader from 'forgetting' that she is witnessing the imaginary creation of an alternative reality to which she is called to participate by reorienting her focus from the plot – which is directed toward the closing 'Finis' – to the narrative process unfolding before her. Furthermore, by collapsing the demarcation lines between the experience of studying a historiographic account, reading a novel and listening to a storytelling performance, *The Cry* becomes a hybrid text that invites us to confront the ambiguity of passing through history and living to tell about it. In particular, while the storytelling performances that are staged in Ndebele's novel convey historical experience in its full weight, precisely because they do not explain away its impact in the lives of their characters, the actual novelistic form of the text invites personal reflection and contemplation over the transcendental homelessness that, by its very nature, historical progression creates – a Benjaminean 'storm blowing from paradise' of sorts (Benjamin 1968: 257–8).

The irreconcilable formal tension of Ndebele's text is coupled with the dizzying overlay of narrative threads, whereby as the novel progresses, the characters in the imaginary narrative of one storyteller come alive to imagine stories of their own. In turn, the inventing capacity of imagination becomes the antidote to the pile of debris that historical progression leaves behind. In other words, if the angel of history can only fantasize about making whole what has been broken, the equivalent angel of fiction can proceed to imagine an alternative redemption by giving voice and agency to the lives that constitute the historical debris itself – those 'ordinary' masses of history represented in *The Cry* by the four women. By the time Winnie Mandela enters the imaginary game of the four imaginary women whose untold story is found in the imaginary book that the novel's primary narrator makes up, the orchestration of narrative layers enters a new stage of perplexity, not least because it suspends altogether the boundary between the imaginary and the historically real.

Winnie Mandela enters the *ibandla* of the four women compelled by 'the burden of a double consciousness' imposed by their exchanges (86). 'Since you began to talk to me', she explains, 'my dreams have been a cinema screen showing a movie I am watching, while at the same time being the main actor' (86). And she continues:

> Not only do I see myself in the past and in the present all at once, but I am in the past and in the present all at once ... Your voices have brought me into that state of being in which I can see something in me deeply, but find I lack the language or other means to express. Being in and out all at once may take away language, take away the capacity for reflection and the vital sense of identity. Now I know. I have lived in that in between space from which my serenities and terrors have emerged.
>
> (86–7)

Thus eloquently articulating the 'all at once' impression that Ndebele's novel evokes, Winnie Mandela also points to the elusive but critical difference between a 'double-consciousness' that reveals the source from which both 'serenities and terrors emanate' and the dissociation inherent in the Quesalid experience. While double-consciousness produces the moebius-strip effect that Coetzee attributes to the literary and secular confessing consciousness, the Quesalid-type dissociation 'takes away the capacity of reflection and the vital sense of identity' rather than enhancing them. In other words, unlike the life that Mandela lived during the apartheid years, whose doubleness signalled the presence of a traumatic if not manipulative dissociation that resisted critical reflection and responsibility, the 'double consciousness' the four women of the *ibandla* employ in their exchanges with Mandela stimulates a dialectical process of self-reflection that also affects her own consciousness and her decision to adopt the mode created in the *ibandla* and become another character in the story, 'certain in the knowledge that [she] could never be entirely [her] own creation, even less [ours]'. As she declares 'I, too, will speak to Winnie' (91–2). Mandela accordingly brings her 'private' self in conversation with her 'public' persona in order to break the spell of self-negation that had attended her role as 'weapon of resistance' (94). Her interlocutors, the women of the *ibandla* and the reader/listener, proceed to witness Mandela's confessional self-examination as a journey through time which is neither linear nor coherent, but which brings Mandela face to face with those instances of her life that are public knowledge and which were already addressed, however briefly, by her fellow *ibandla* members.

Having been challenged to confront our ambiguous function as audience when we witnessed the single narrator/storyteller of the first part of the novel transform into the four different storytelling voices that led in the second part of the novel, we are now asked to reconfigure our position vis-à-vis the text once more. That is, where we unquestionably identified with the original second-person address 'you' that the single storyteller of the first part of the novel employed to address us, we were then given a choice to identify or refuse to identify with the 'you' employed by each of the four women in the second part of the novel, as they addressed each other and Winnie Mandela. With Winnie Mandela's double-consciousness effect, we

are now given a similar choice to identify with the 'you' employed by
Mandela to address her own public personality. Ndebele's novel, which has
been giving us the option of fluctuating between the function of a storytelling audience and a novelistic reader at our own will is here giving us the
option of confronting the controversial life of Winnie Mandela by embodying it (and thereby also, implicitly, challenging us to reflect on our choice of
either identifying with Mandela or keeping our distance). Thus we accom-
pany Winnie Mandela, with variant degrees of intimacy, as she contemplates
experiences from her early 'Penelope years' when she was interrogated, tortured and banished for her activities in the anti-apartheid movement. We
continue to follow her as she reflects on the motives that inspired and sustained the Mandela United Football Club, travels to the Victor Verster
Prison to receive Nelson Mandela upon his release, contemplates how her
husband's restored freedom may entail the end of her independence, and
concludes that in the TRC special hearing she *did* become a Quesalid who
refused to 'truth [her]self out of business'. 'The point about people such as
Quesalid and myself', she explains, 'is that they are intimately in touch with
their own folly, but choose to live with it. In time they find they are unable
to live without it' (112).

When at the end of her self-reflective mnemonic journey Mandela goes
back to speak in a single voice that restores the distance between herself and
her audience, we learn that this confession we had the option of undertaking
with her does not add up to the traditionally-anticipated plea for forgiveness
and exoneration. Ever aware of her iconic status and of the scapegoating
politics it can attract, Mandela concludes this 'game' confession by declaring
that she will not become 'an instrument for validating the politics of
reconciliation' as she did in her special hearing, but will instead take solace
in the tolerance for ambiguity and nuance that the double-consciousness
affords her:

> For me, reconciliation demands my annihilation. No. You, all of you,
> have to reconcile not with me, but with the meaning of me. For my
> meaning is the endless human search of the right thing to do. I am your
> pleasure and your pain, your beauty and your ugliness. Your solution
> and your mistake ... All that has gone before and all that is yet to come
> are the burdens and joys of our responsibility. Give me the trust to
> accept it. You and I, in that country known by a cardinal point. A
> country known as a direction, but hopefully, as well, a destination. As
> the world carries us, so do we carry it too. We who are here now, to
> stay. At home.
>
> (113–14)

By refusing to resolve Mamello Molete's dilemma over admiring or doubting her character, Winnie Mandela instead demands a recognition of the
inherent doubleness of consciousness and conscious – wilful – choice. By

questioning the desire to transcend a traumatic past and inaugurate a politics of reconciliation that aims to sanitize and bring under control the imaginative drive, Ndebele's novel debunks the idea of emancipation through transcendence for the more humble idea of emancipation through acceptance, the kind of acceptance Mandela asks of her audience after claiming to embody the unresolved contradictions of the past and the future. A Quesalid who developed ruses in response to a racist, patriarchal history and to a marriage ('[Nelson Mandela] always pronounces like an oracle') that constrained her consciousness and imagination, Mandela interprets her doubleness as 'the endless human search for the right thing to do' (97). Endless, in that it remains always at least double by virtue of providing choices, this human search becomes a feminist sociopolitical ethic that complicates both the TRC's construction of apartheid's spectacular historical memory, and reconfigures the polemics of the Black Consciousness Movement in a post-apartheid context.

Where the TRC aimed to reconcile the past in a way that, in 'Mannete's language, prioritized 'the moral outcome' over 'the process of getting to it', Mandela's concluding declaration insists on prioritizing the process of examining and understanding the historical forces at work during the apartheid era over the attainment of a strained reconciliation. Where the South African truth commission desired to abolish the contradictory perspectives that undermined the creation of a single, moral conclusion of apartheid's historical memory, Mandela advocates a dual orientation toward the past, whose contradictory insights stimulate the imaginary deftness – that which, according to Ndebele, is contained in 'the ordinary' life of the South African black consciousness, and constitutes the formal effects of his latest novel.

More importantly, however, Ndebele's latest novel transforms the Black Consciousness Movement through its gendered reading that evokes a feminist understanding of double-consciousness not as an affliction to overcome, but as an insight into the limitless possibilities of the imagination to discover, rethink, re-imagine and understand the historical circumstances that gave it birth. In its feminist rendition and as a sociopolitical ethic, double-consciousness radically undermines the 'us' and 'them' identification that is involved in master/slave struggles, while also complicating the idea of complicity that the Movement had desired to transcend. Inspired by communal storytelling and confessional self-reflection, Ndebele's novel articulates and performs the kind of double consciousness that is not a source of torment but of power and imagination – the kind of feminist doubleness articulated by Gloria Anzaldúa, whose role as a thinker of *mestiza consciousness* makes her a philosophical partner to Ndebele's latest novel.

Emerging from a patriarchal society that is marginalized in its own land by a settler culture, Anzaldúa imagined the liberation of herself and her people as involving less an emancipatory power struggle than an affirmation of the doubleness of all life, what she has called the *mestiza* or *borderland consciousness*. An alternative to the male, Quesalid experience, whose complicity bespeaks less his desire to dominate than his belief that there is a single hidden truth that remains concealed by virtue of his becoming a compliant shaman, the feminist experience that Anzaldúa proffers accepts at once the 'duality in life, a synthesis of duality, and ... something more than mere duality of a synthesis of duality' (Anzaldúa 1987: 46).

In envisioning post-apartheid South Africa as a 'borderland' home, a 'dot ... in the world map that lays out journeys towards all kinds of human fulfillment' (114) Ndebele's novel employs this ethic of double-consciousness to re-imagine the present and future South Africa by radically reconstructing the identity politics that supported the apartheid logic in the first place. By writing a novel that engages the historical memory of apartheid through one of its most ambiguous figures, Winnie Mandela, Ndebele engages in a genealogical search that undermines the unitary character of the historical past – made of victims and perpetrators – as it was produced through the TRC hearings. Abandoning the witness stand, from where the black writer can only passively describe the historical trauma his/her people have suffered as a static experience of victimization that takes on the label of 'historical truth', Ndebele's novel consciously employs the kind of 'systematic dissociation of identity' that Nietzsche and Foucault imagined as the antidote to historic ossification (Foucault 1977: 161). In so doing *The Cry* creatively defines the 'distinct and multiple elements' that make black consciousness a *sujet en proces*, an imaginary force of ever-renewed discovery and invention without beginning (grand or traumatic) or end (Foucault 1977: 161–2). By transforming this dissociation of identity from an unconscious trauma into a reflective double-consciousness that is not to be transcended but embraced as an occasion for critical reflection in the form of a personal confession, Ndebele thus re-evaluates the relevance of the Black Consciousness Movement in a post-apartheid world order. It seems that if the problem of the twentieth century was the problem of the colour line, the problem of the twenty-first century, according to Ndebele, has become the problem of historical identity. In addressing this problem, Ndebele trades in the future-oriented, emancipatory politics of the Black Consciousness Movement for a more complicated political ethic that reinvents the historical past, which present-day unitary identities claim as their heritage, as an imaginative game.

When at the end of *The Cry* the single narrator that opened the novel returns to imagine the now five women of the *ibandla* meeting Penelope while taking a trip to Durban, Ndebele's novel transforms into a surrealistic constellation of meaning that reinvents Penelope's genealogy from its roots. By adopting what Benjamin had called a 'historical materialist' approach, whereby 'history ... is not homogeneous, empty time, but time filled by the presence of the now', Ndebele's novel imagines how the transformation of consciousness that ensues from the exchanges that take place in an *ibandla* of five women, simultaneously ascertains the transformation of an entire genealogy starting with Penelope herself, and discovers an entire new genealogical progression (Benjamin 1968: 261). As Penelope explains to the five women in sharing with them an 'untold story' that resonates with their own, when at the end of the Homeric epic Odysseus departed from their home once more to go and perform cleansing rituals, she decided to leave him. 'It has never been told that when he returned I was gone', she explains. 'I went on my own cleansing pilgrimage' (Ndebele 2003: 120). And she continues:

> I travel around the world to places where women have heard of me, attempting to free them from the burden of unconditional fidelity I placed on their shoulders. I've come to join you briefly on your holiday trip ... to affirm it for what it is: a signal gesture by five women who are finally at peace with themselves and the world.
>
> (120)

By thus complicating our understanding of history through an awareness of how imagination works, *The Cry of Winnie Mandela* introduces us to a political ethic that centres on choice in the most radical way possible: by affirming the ever-double, contrapuntal relation of past memory and present imagination that such an ethic necessitates, and thus the open-ended ambiguity of all belief systems.

Acknowledgements

I would like to thank Mary Keller, Derek Attridge, Larry Mintz, Ana Soto-Canino, Jo Gill and my unknown outside reader for their thoughtful and immensely helpful feedback on this essay.

Notes

1 Founded in 1979, the Noma Award is open to African writers and scholars whose work is published in Africa.
2 Ndebele's term for the black literary writing he is critiquing is 'protest literature'.
3 I am employing Cornelius Castoriadis' notion of the 'social instituting imaginary' – the creative property both of society and of individuals. In Castoriadis' words 'the individuals are made by the *instituted* society, at the same time as they make and remake it' (Castoriadis 1991: 145–6). See also Castoriadis (1987).
4 Alongside the Amnesty Committee (AC) which centred on recovering the historical truth of the apartheid past from the perpetrators, and the Human Rights Violations Committee (HRVC) which focused on recovering the same historical truth from the victim's perspective, the Act – the Promotion of National Unity and Reconciliation Act, No. 34 of 1995, http://www.doj.gov.za/trc/legal/act9534.htm – established the Reparations and Rehabilitation Committee (RRC) which addressed questions of material compensations and support for the victims.
5 This is not to suggest that the TRC did not also accommodate confessions that exceeded the dualistic framework of 'victims' versus 'perpetrators'. There are countless examples of perpetrators who refused to be shamed or to ask for

amnesty/absolution, victims who refused to be healed or forgive or even tell their story, bystanders who saw their apathy as tacit support of the apartheid rule and asked for amnesty, and so on. The capacity of the TRC to allow for these narratives to surface and to contradict its own conceptual categories, pointed to its commitment toward a catharsis of the historical past which not only desired to purge a disquieting historical memory and its affect, but it also, paradoxically, intended to clarify and understand the very contours and emotional bearings of this disquietude. Moreover, the TRC hearings did occasionally manage to provide a very material type of closure to victims' families by ordering and supervising exhumations of their loved ones' missing bodies.

6 Albertina Sisulu was the wife of Walter Sisulu, the Secretary General of the ANC. Urbania Mothopeng was the wife of Zephaniah Mothopeng, a PAC activist who is best known for having organized the Soweto uprisings of 1976. Veronica Sobukwe was the wife of Robert Sobukwe, the founder of PAC who was imprisoned for incitement during the Sharpeville Massacre of 1960. Ntsiki Biko was the wife of Stephen Biko, the founder and leader of the Black Consciousness Movement who died in detention after being tortured.

7 In his essay 'Turkish Tales and Some Thoughts on South African Fiction', Ndebele employs Benjamin's theories on storytelling effects to imagine alternative narrative approaches to black protest literature (Ndebele 1994: 17–40).

Bibliography

Anzaldúa, G. (1987) *Borderlands/La Frontera*, San Francisco: Aunt Lute Books.

Attwell, D. (1993) *J. M. Coetzee: South Africa and the Politics of Writing*, Berkeley: University of California Press.

Benjamin, W. (1968) 'The Storyteller', in H. Arendt (ed.) *Illuminations*, trans. H. Zohn, New York: Schocken Books.

—— (1969) 'Theses on the Philosophy of History', in H. Arendt (ed.) *Illuminations*, trans. H. Zohn, New York: Schocken Books.

Biko, S. (1978) *Steve Biko: A Selection of his Writings*, London: The Bowerdean Press.

Bizos, G. (1998) *No One to Blame? In Pursuit of Justice in South Africa*, Cape Town: David Philip Publishers.

Boraine, A. (2000) *A Country Unmasked: Inside South Africa's Truth and Reconciliation Commission*, New York: Oxford University Press.

Brooks, P. (2000) *Troubling Confessions: Speaking Guilt in Law and Literature*, Chicago: Chicago University Press.

Castoriadis, C. (1987) *The Imaginary Institution of Society*, trans. K. Blamey, Cambridge: The MIT Press.

—— (1991) 'Power, Politics, Autonomy', in D.A. Curtis (ed.) *Philosophy, Politics, Autonomy: Essays in Political Philosophy*, New York: Oxford University Press.

Coetzee, J.M. (1992) 'Confession and Double Thoughts: Tolstoy, Rousseau, Dostoevsky', in D. Attwell (ed.) *Doubling the Point*, Cambridge: Harvard University Press.

Felman, S. (1995) 'Education and Crisis, or the Vicissitudes of Teaching', in C. Caruth (ed.) *Trauma: Explorations in Memory*, Baltimore: The Johns Hopkins University Press.

Foucault, M. (1977) 'Nietzsche, Genealogy, History', in D.F. Bouchard (ed.) *Language, Counter-Memory, Practice: Selected Essays and Interviews by Michel Foucault*, trans. D.F. Bouchard and S. Simon, Ithaca: Cornell University Press.

Harlow, B. (1987) *Resistance Literature*, New York: Methuen.

Jay, M. (1999) 'Against Consolation: Walter Benjamin and the Refusal to Mourn', in J. Winter and E. Sivan (eds) *War and Remembrance in the Twentieth Century*, New York: Cambridge University Press.

Krog, A. (1999) *Country of my Skull: Guilt, Sorrow, and the Limits of Forgiveness in the New South Africa*, New York: Three Rivers Press.

Lyotard, J.-F. and Thébaud, J.-L. (1985) *Just Gaming*, trans. W. Godzich, Minneapolis: University of Minnesota Press.

Mamdani, M. (2000) 'The Truth According to the TRC', in I. Amadiume and A. An-Na'im (eds) *The Politics of Memory: Truth, Healing and Social Justice*, New York: Zed Books.

Meredith, M. (1999) *Coming To Terms: South Africa's Search for Truth*, New York: Public Affairs.

Ndebele, N.S. (1994) *South African Literature and Culture: Rediscovery of the Ordinary*, Manchester: Manchester University Press.

—— (2003) *The Cry of Winnie Mandela*, Claremont, South Africa: David Philip Publishers.

Ntsebeza, D.B. (2000) 'The Uses of Truth Commissions: Lessons for the World', in R.I. Rorberg and D. Thompson (eds) *Truth v. Justice*, Princeton: Princeton University Press.

Promotion of National Unity and Reconciliation Act (1995) No. 34. Available online at http://www.doj.gov.za/trc/legal/act9534.htm (accessed 28 November 2004).

Reid, F. and Hoffmann D. (2000) *A Long Night's Journey Into Day*, San Francisco: California Newsreel (Video recording).

Sanders, M. (2002) *Complicities: The Intellectual and Apartheid*, Durham: Duke University Press.

Slye, R.C. (1999) 'The Truth About the Truth Commission', *South African Review of Books*. Available online at: http://www.uniulm.de/~rturrell/sarobnewhtml/trcindex.html (accessed 23 January 2004).

Spence, D. (1982) *Narrative Truth and Historical Truth: Meaning and Interpretation in Psychoanalysis*, New York: W.W. Norton.

Truth and Reconciliation Commission [TRC] (1998) *Truth and Reconciliation Commission of South Africa Report*, Volumes 1–5, Cape Town, Juta.

Tutu, D. (1999) *No Future Without Forgiveness*, New York: Doubleday.

8 Personal performance

The resistant confessions of Bobby Baker

Deirdre Heddon

The concerns of this chapter are the relationships between confession and performance. This contribution might initially appear to sit uneasily in a collection that specifies 'writing' in its title, but performance, like writing, is always a 'text', and it is the textual instabilities of specific, live performance work that interest me here. Through examining the work of British performance artist, Bobby Baker, I propose the potential difference that the context of live performance makes to the confessional act. In live performance, the process of textual inscription and reinscription is a visibly embodied practice that is performed.

Performance texts, like written texts, are capable of complex engagements with the matter of experience, with the problematics of memory and its potential representation, with the intricate relationships between lived life and its telling. Weaving and layerings and shifting perspectives are common devices of the contemporary confessional performance, just as they are of the written confessional text. One difference pertains, however; in the performance text, there is an additional layer with which to play, an extra ingredient to be thrown into the mix: the live, and present, authoring body. The live presence of the confessing subject prompts a questioning of the subject of confession. Who is confessing? What is being confessed? Does the literal performance of confession render its truth-status 'suspect', as the act of confessing reveals the necessarily performative nature of all confessional acts? Such a revelation might, arguably, be more transparent in the live act that is witnessed by the spectator in shared time and space.

An important property of most performance art that distinguishes it from more conventional dramatic productions is that in performance art the author and performer are typically the same. As such, the 'author-performer' potentially has far more control over the subject of representation. Translating this to the realm of autobiographical, confessional performance art, the subject has greater control over the representation of her or himself. This might also distinguish it from the gamut of currently available mass-mediated confessional opportunities. The word 'representation' is also important here. Within the frame of live performance, it is difficult to confuse the *re*presented with any realm of the 'real'.

The histories of performance art and autobiographical, confessional performances are, from the outset, linked. During the early 1970s, women, particularly in the USA, turned to performance art as a means of attaining some control over representations of themselves. Placed within the context of the second wave feminist movement, most particularly consciousness-raising activities, performance art (a relatively new practice, and therefore one without a dominant male genealogy) became a means by which women could both explore and represent hidden aspects of their everyday lives. Performance art enabled women to make visible that which had been forbidden, denied, or erased within the dominant art movements. Such a turn to the everyday frequently involved the confession of personal details.

The attraction of personal material within performance art has remained constant, perhaps unsurprising given the contemporary cultural appetite to both confess and consume confession. I would argue, however, that autobiographical, confessional performances often attempt to position themselves as 'resistant' acts within this flow, with Baker's work just one example of such 'counter' activity. What is surprising, however, given this continuing (and in fact increasing) performance practice, is the dearth of critical analysis that accompanies it. Commentary, where it does exist, is often little more than unsubstantiated generalisation:

> The dangers in autobiographical art are legion: solipsisms that interest an audience of one.
>
> (Weisberg 1980: 107)

> Performance art is famously resistant to dealing with the outside world; its politics, when present at all, not only spring from autobiographical impulses but remain limited by them. Constricted themes, narrow skills, and inflated, needy egos plague this kind of theater.
>
> (Munk 1997: 135)

> The temptation of autobiography is to shrink the complex social and historical determinants of personal history into a singular and singularly unproblematized wrapper of identity. This impoverished site is vulnerable to the imputation that a politics whose only sure referent is the self is hardly a politics at all.
>
> (Larsen 1995: 31)

> It is as often an ego show as a revelation; the virus of the 'I – Did – It – My – Way/I – Gotta – Be – Me' strain afflicts the larger number of such acts, particularly in the performance art area which presents amateurish

staging techniques and mini-personalities as often as original methods and subjects.

(Howell 1979/1980: 158)

Solo performance is, of course a field rife with self-indulgence and incipient monumental egotism, and I have sat through as many shows demonstrating this as anyone – typically performed by frustrated and mediocre New York actors trying to jump-start their me-machines with sitcom-shallow autobiographical monologues.

(Kalb 2000: 14)

Against the backdrop of such 'critique', Bobby Baker's fears, admitted in her performance *Drawing on a Mother's Experience*, appear to be justified:

I got very worried because I read a review in the *Guardian*, of course, about the Edinburgh Festival. There was some heavy criticism about all these shows by aspiring artists which smacked of the confessional box, and I blushed. This is just what I was about to do.

(Baker 1988)[1]

Given the historical link between women and autobiographical, confessional performance, it might not be too cynical to suggest that such critical responses belie deeper prejudices. Irene Gammel, considering the 'danger' of confessional forms for women, writes that:

the female voice relating personal experience, like the sinner's and the patient's, belongs not to the realm of abstract and official *langue* but to *parole*, to familiar and intimate speech … the confessional mode is dismissed as 'raw', 'narcissistic', and 'unformed' … A history of confessional readings has created the perception of women obsessively confessing their secrets, reinforcing stereotypes of the female psyche as fragmented and, what is perhaps even worse, as 'needy'.

(1999: 4)

The confession is considered a 'feminised space', and in a social world in which the 'feminine' continues to signify negatively, it is accordingly routinely devalued. The confessional performance, then, carries within it multiple risks for the female performer. It also, however, carries within it potential. If, as Foucault suggests, confession is a technique through which 'truth' is both produced and maintained, then the very operation of the confessional mode affords the opportunity for counter-discursive stories, the forging of other truths, other possible lives. As avenues for confession have multiplied, is it possible that so too have the stories that are being confessed? Equally, is it not also possible to play with the mode of confession, acknowledging its role in the construction of truth? 'Truth telling' is the very condition upon which the confession rests. As Jessie Givner states, 'the very etymological traces of the word confession (confessus, meaning "incontrovertible, certain, beyond doubt") suggest that absolute truth is the basis of the ritual' (Givner 1999: 126). But where is the 'truth' of confession inscribed other than in a convincing performance? And what if the confession were performed differently? Rather than assuming or subscribing to the 'truth' that confession reveals, one might deliberately use the confession to challenge that foundational assumption, making what Irene Gammel terms 'confessional interventions' (1999: 8). As I aim to show, Bobby Baker strategically deploys multiple interventions as she exploits the confessional apparatus.

Bobby Baker has been creating and touring performance and installation works internationally for over twenty-five years. Her pieces share two important features – to varying degrees they all incorporate household products (often food) as artistic material, and they all focus on aspects of the quotidian.[2] Though Baker trained in fine art at St Martin's College of Art, she found herself unable to communicate her ideas through paint, 'because it had been appropriated in other ways by other voices, particularly the male voice' (Baker 2001). Baker instead found her own language in food (Tushingham 1994), and in 1972 she made her first cake – a carved and iced baseball boot: 'When I thought of carrying it into college, as a sculpture, sitting on my grandmother's cake plate, it was as if the heavens opened and light fell on it – it was so funny and rebellious' (Warner 1998: 74).

Her turn to live performance was equally borne out of frustration. Baker had used food as sculptural material, and had on occasion placed herself within such sculptures, as an object, but 'it became obvious that I couldn't get across the range of ideas that I had connected with the pieces that I had made' (Oddey 1999: 268). Baker's 'ideas' came from her own interests or experience. As a young artist she made the decision that she would 'examine things from the inside out' (Tushingham 1994: 31), having an intuitive sense that 'rather than stepping outside and presenting a third person view of life, I would work from myself' (Baker 2001). This subjective engagement led Baker to focus on the details of her everyday life – the daily events, rituals, and actions that are so often unacknowledged. For Baker, even the minutiae of daily existence have their place within the social world, and as such matter. Only 'by examining the small and personal and day to day does [one] get a chance to change things. Unless you address those details you can have no wider change' (ibid.). While all of Baker's work comes from this consciously subjective perspective, some of it is more directly confessional than others in its revelation of aspects from her own life, including the two pieces of work discussed here, *Drawing on a Mother's Experience* (1988) and *Box Story* (2001).

In 1976, at the same time that Baker made her first public art work, *An Edible Family in a Mobile Home*, Foucault pronounced that Western man had 'become a confessing animal' (Foucault 1990: 59). If we were already con-fessing animals in the 1970s, Foucault's statement begs us to consider what we are now. The number of confessional spaces available for occupancy in the mass media, and the sheer quantity of confessions elicited, is phenom-enal. The embracing of opportunities enabled by digital technology, includ-ing weblogs, webpages and live webcams, reveals that our fascination with confession is far from abating.

Jon Dovey, in his survey of various instances of 'first-person' media, by which he is predominantly referring to television, offers the conclusion that the proliferation of publicly mediated individual, subjective experiences operates as a 'new regime of truth' (Dovey 2000: 25). The subjective experience becomes the 'guarantor of knowledge' (23), and the offering up of intimate detail 'has come to signify authenticity' (ibid.). Dovey reads these mass-mediated confessional instances as moments of production of 'norm-ative identities' and 'coherent subjects'. In the docusoap, for example, char-acters are fixed in time – they do not change or develop, nor do they display contradictions or ambiguities. As Dovey comments, 'they are cast for a particular set of two-dimensional qualities', with the confessional moments themselves determined by 'the overarching narrative drive' (152). Anything that would contradict, or unsettle the 'character representation' remains unshown (150). The world in such docusoaps is accepted as it is given and there is no notion of reality as 'social, contested, constructed' (ibid.).

Dovey does admit that the huge variety of places in which one can now confess, combined with the different types of self-speaking that are available, makes it impossible to 'contain [such moments] within a single concept of "the confessional"' (113). It is also my opinion that context remains imper-ative; place and mode may make all the difference. While in the mass media there are increased spaces in which to offer up confessions, there are 'very few spaces ... for an autobiographical mode in which the author of the representation is also its subject' (110). It is worth remembering that in autobiographical performance art, by contrast, the author and the subject are more typically the same. As such, the 'author' potentially has far more control over the subject of representation. Moreover, such control over the construction of work is often combined with an awareness of the relationship between performance and the construction of the performed self. Given the context of the performance of autobiographical confession, one might also assume a matched 'knowingness' on the part of the spectator; seeing is not necessarily believing and witnesses of performance art are rarely asked to suspend their disbelief.

How does Bobby Baker stand up beside Dovey's confessing subjects – those who are claimed to be in the business of shoring up coherent identities through their confessional addresses? Who is the Bobby Baker that is pro-duced in these works, and what is her identity? Attempting to provide answers to these questions is surprisingly difficult, and that struggle is one sign of Baker's resistant mode of confession. Her unravelling identity is one means by which she resists becoming the confessing subject, even as she appears to be confessing.[3]

The various stories that Baker shares in *Drawing on a Mother's Experience* and *Box Story*, are all drawn from the life of Bobby Baker, and the person who performs these stories is Bobby Baker, so in classic autobiographical form, the 'writing' subject is also the subject of the story – subject and object are one. In *Drawing on a Mother's Experience*, the subject matter of the performance, as suggested by its title, is Baker's own experience of becoming a mother. This piece was the first work Baker made following a break of eight years, during which time she had two children. In the performance, she not only metaphorically draws on her experience of mothering, but literally makes a drawing out of those, applying various foodstuffs to a Persilwhite sheet, somewhat mimicking (or at least quoting) Jackson Pollock's action paintings. Over the course of the performance, the white sheet becomes transformed by the addition of fish pies, imprints of roast beef, dribbles of milk, spillages of Guinness, and a splattering of cake mix, to name just a few of Baker's 'artistic materials'.

Baker's stated embarrassment regarding the confessional nature of her performance reveals a self-reflexive mode of practice, further evidenced by her direct acknowledgement, within the piece, of its autobiographical status:

> I'm afraid something else I must point out ... is that this is slightly autobiographical. Totally autobiographical, and I mean that, and I thought that was all right because I felt I needed to get something off my – out of my system you might say.
>
> (Baker 1988)

Her claiming of the autobiographical act has a deliberate uncertainty within it – is this performance 'slightly' or 'totally' autobiographical? Whilst the subject matter of the performance is drawn from Baker's own life, and Baker performs this, there is a layer of complexity missing from my rendering of the subject-object equation. Between the Baker who performs, and the stories being performed, there are at least two other Bakers: the Baker who is performed and the non-performing Baker.[4] (The last of these Bakers will remain outside of this discussion.)

In each performance there is what is best described as a *persona*, and it is this persona that Bobby Baker, the performer, performs. In the construction of her performed 'self', Baker self-consciously observes herself, and with the security of some distance, is able, in a theatrically 'knowing' way, to make fun of what she sees. Her very process, then, admits to the gap between who she is outside of performance, and who she plays: 'I step on stage, I start performing, I become something else'. Of course, the moment anyone is on stage, they arguably become something else. However, Baker also admits to 'sort of develop[ing] that persona' (Baker 2001), or developing a style of presentation.[5]

Complicating matters, this persona is presented *as* Bobby Baker. Whose stories are these, then, that are being shared with us – Bobby Baker the performing subject's, or Bobby Baker the performed subject's? Who, if anyone, is confessing here? And if the Bobby Baker who offers up these stories is a persona, how referential or stable or truthful can these confessions be presumed to be? For Baker's confessing subject to trouble the act of confession, the presence of this persona must be evident and in fact the same persona appears in all of Baker's performances, although the 'eruptions' that she/Baker stages are different. This endurance of her persona, from show to show, is one of the means by which the persona becomes easily readable.

Informing Baker's persona is her 'trademark' costume, which up to *Box Story* has been a white, just-above-knee length overall, as might be worn by a cookery demonstrator or home economics teacher. The white overall might also refer to the professional 'authority' figure, such as a doctor or a scientist, adding to the humour of the piece. Baker is extremely 'authoritative' with regards to her 'advice' and 'instructions' on 'being a good mother'. The image is largely that of 'sensible', 'responsible' and 'professional'. (Tellingly, in *Box Story* Baker's overall is blue, like the blue typically depicted on the Virgin Mary's robe.) Baker also has a number of character 'traits' that signify her status as a character, in that they are immediately recognisable as 'stock' mannerisms, and taken together represent a (stereo)type: the middle-class (and in the late 1990s, as she deliberately foregrounds, 'middle-aged'), female. Such mannerisms include 'thriftiness', ecological awareness, domestic skill, embarrassment, self-punishment, self-deprecation, continuous apologising and chaotic activity. The parodic display of the good housekeeper/wife in *Drawing on a Mother's Experience* is most blatantly inscribed in the repetitive manner in which Baker cleans up after her every action, and references that fact as she does so. She repeats, for example, the refrain: 'Clear up as I go along', 'So let's just clear this up'. As she lays a protective plastic sheet on the floor, Baker advises us that: 'This is to avoid mess. Extra mess. Because one discovers quite early on, as an intelligent mother, that if you think ahead, you can save yourself a lot of work' (1988). Appropriate to this image, Baker also repeatedly references and uses a 'damp J-cloth'. A similarly instructive gesture is the habitual avoidance of embarrassing subjects, including giving birth, breast feeding and the more euphemistic 'women's problems', all of which Baker's glides over: 'I don't want to embarrass you too much with sort of nasty details about childbirth', 'I had – women's trouble –', 'We'll move on quickly'.

Reading the signs of Baker's persona, it is evident that in her performance of herself (and she *is* a middle-class mother of two), Baker performs an exaggerated, cultural (rather than strictly personal) version. The Bobby Baker that we see performed is one whom, through repeated cultural circulation, we 'know', but who in all probability does not actually exist.

There is, admittedly, a danger in playing this role of the parodic mother/housewife, for there is no guarantee that the spectator will recognise it as parody. However, the presence of multiple layers of activity and representation in *Drawing on a Mother's Experience* might minimise any threat of reinscription of Baker as a subjected mother/housewife. Whilst Baker at times does perform a passive, apologetic mother, other 'identities' and attitudes puncture that representation. Baker can be self-deprecating and authoritative; controlled and unpredictable; respectable and outrageous; revelatory and secretive; logical and intuitive. In effect, the culturally inscribed image of the 'housewife/mother' is simultaneously undermined by that character, as one prescribed image of 'Bobby Baker' – neat, tidy, clean, calm, organised, resourceful and self-effacing – clashes with other, more challenging images. Evidently, the most disruptive aspect of *Drawing on a Mother's Experience* is Baker's inappropriate use of food. Whilst the food might signify and reference domesticity, Baker's actual use of it – throwing it around, creating a mess, rolling herself up in it, making art from it – simultaneously undercuts this. Baker's use of the food places both it and her outside of prescribed cultural contexts. As Lucy Baldwyn writes:

> Apparently acquiescing to the repressive stereotypes proliferated within misogynistic culture – by identifying herself as a mother/housewife and discussing shopping and cooking – [Baker] simultaneously undermines them by contravening their limits.
>
> (1996: 37)

It could of course be argued that the Baker who resists the cultural position of the passive housewife/mother is the performer, Baker, and not the housewife/mother, Baker. However, such a separation of the two Bobbys is not straightforward. For it is also the neat, tidy, clean, calm, organised, resourceful and self-effacing persona of the start of the show that then proceeds to splatter food onto the white sheet, that bursts tinned, stewed blackcurrants by dancing on them in her bare feet, that rolls herself up into the sheet like a 'human Swiss roll', or as one who is 'mummified'. This is not to deny that there are troubling moments when we might determine two Bobbys. The performed Baker may present herself as apologetic, passive or self-deprecating, but the reality is that Baker is actually a woman with enough confidence to deliver a full-length solo show. Whilst it might appear to us that the performed Baker is chaotic and not really in control of what she is doing, Baker the performer is evidently a skilled artist. At such moments, there is an incongruity between the performer and the performed. It is these uncertainties regarding which Baker is being represented that run throughout the entire performance, and arguably they are deliberate.

The identity so far constructed in Baker's stage work appears far removed from Dovey's first person mediated identity, and as such seems something of a rhetorical strategy that both works with and resists the confessional apparatus. Confronted by Bobby Baker playing Bobby Baker, I have no idea who Bobby Baker is. Moreover, it would be more accurate to refer to the identities constructed here, since there is no single, cohesive subject being represented. Aside from the doubling of Baker (performer and performed), there is also a multiplicity within the parodic representation, as the representations of Baker shift, and each version competes with other versions. These contradictions and ambiguities are crucially important devices in undercutting the stereotypical representation and suggesting the inherent complexity of subjectivity, of 'being' a person. If the confession is an apparatus through which identity is produced, Baker uses this to her advantage to construct an identity that is multiple, complex and perhaps ultimately unknowable. As Gerry Harris writes, in relation to another of Baker's performances, *How to Shop* (1993):

> Baker performs a subjectivity which is at the same time not Bobby Baker and not not Bobby Baker, both a hyperbolic, theatrical character and the 'real thing', an ideological construct and a situated historical object, both entirely socially constructed and unique.
>
> (1999: 137)

For Harris, this 'doubled' positioning results in a 'hiatus in iterability' – a moment of unintelligibility or unreadability (of both the performance and the performer), producing a moment and space of agency for Baker. Such 'unreadability' necessarily affects the status and effect of this supposed confession.

Alongside her constructed persona, Baker employs other strategies that may use the confessional apparatus differently. Her work self-consciously acknowledges the contemporary appetite for consuming others' lives, through what might be referred to as modes of refusal. First, to what, precisely, is Baker confessing? Dealing with the everyday, her confessions are also of the quotidian. For example, she reveals that after giving birth (and in fact she reveals very little *about* giving birth: 'moving swiftly along') her own mother provides her with nourishment, in the form of fish pies. In many ways, then, Baker's so-called confessions confess very little, or very little that is deeply personal.[6] This is a clever strategy. Her performances appear to offer insights into her personal, private life and yet, in fact, such offers are withheld. Those moments which might be more revealing, more painful, more private, are rushed over, denied, as she moves us quickly along to the next section – away from childbirth, illness, depression. In this sense, Baker frustrates our desire to know, to own, her life. Similarly, Baker denies the spectator final consumption by holding something back, keeping her own secrets. The final food material that Baker uses to complete her action painting is white flour, sifted over the entire sheet, effectively 'blotting' out all the imprints, or graphic testimonies, that she has previously made. The referent of this white flour is only hinted at:

> There is one more thing which I find it very difficult to talk about but it is important and that's an element of my life, of life, that is sort of

like a, sort of peaceful and happy, and it's sort of symbolized by white
light.

(1988)

Tim Etchells captures the feeling well when he reflects that Baker 'builds up
to this moment where you feel she's going to "tell you everything" and then
she refuses ... and I'm left wondering what it was that she might have said'
(1999: 79). I too am left wondering. Thinking. But I am also engaged in my
own acts of 'making things up'. Baker's 'secrets' are not only moments of
refusal, moments of 'privacy in public' (ibid.); they also perform spaces in
which I, in the role of spectator – even confessor – can bring myself into
(the) 'play' as I fill in her gaps with my own stories.[7]

It is moments such as these that stage interventions into the 'confessional
mode'. Just as the blur between the real Bobby Baker and her performed self
makes it impossible to ever 'know' Baker, or know who is the subject of the
confession (perhaps then disrupting Phillipe Lejeune's 'autobiographical
contract' (1989: 5)), her strategy of keeping secrets similarly acknowledges
and refuses the voyeuristic gaze. In 'her' place, we see ourselves. Again, then,
who is confessing here? On the one hand, it would seem that Baker uses the
confession, but at the same time she refuses to confess appropriately,
strategically encoding 'significant distances, disruptions, and warnings'
(Gammell 1999: 11).

Whilst we may not be certain who the subject of confession is in *Drawing
on a Mother's Experience*, we are in no doubt as to what the subject of confession is. Baker's confessed experiences of motherhood do not so much 'show'
or produce a coherent representation of 'the mother/Baker', or even of 'mothering', as reveal the discursive forces that have resulted in certain experiences
– not least the experience of transforming (or having to transform) the everyday materials of the domestic sphere into objects of aesthetic beauty. The
questions that surface during Baker's acts of confession (confessions of anger,
of depression, of coping mechanisms) are why these experiences should be
experienced in this way and what alternative experiences might it be possible to imagine, to will? Her acts of self-revelation become, in actuality,
acts of social revelation. In contrast to Dovey's conclusions regarding mass
mediated first person narratives, in Baker's work the world is not just given.
Instead, it is a world that we are demanded to engage with, and to witness.
Baker's 'social confession' is made possible by her confessing to her inability
to live up to cultural expectations. As Sidonie Smith writes of the female
autobiographer:

> writing her experiential history of the body, the autobiographical
> subject engages in a process of critical self-consciousness through which
> she comes to an awareness of the relationship of her specific body to the
> cultural 'body' and to the body politic.
>
> (1993: 131)

Baker's recent performance, *Box Story* (2001), invites a more explicit reckoning with confession, sited as it originally was in her own local church in London. This embracing of religious iconography is not a new departure. In *Kitchen Show*, Baker confessed to a daily recitation of the Lord's Prayer. In *How to Shop*, she takes John Bunyan's *Pilgrim's Progress* as a sur-text, though her own 'quest' is tied to ' "shopping for life" or "shopping for enlightenment" ' (Harris 1999: 113).

In her illuminating essay on Baker, Marina Warner claims that the 'principles and disciplines' of Baker's Christian faith remain 'intrinsic to her pieces'. One principle of this Protestant faith, writ in the resurrection of Christ, is the demand 'that sacrifice take place before rebirth and renewal can happen'. For Warner, Baker 'uses the idea of suffering and humiliation as a resource' (Warner 1998: 79). Baker's very public suffering and humiliation perhaps can be linked to the pre-oral confession of sins, by way of the act of *exomologēsis*, 'recognition of fact', which is linked to penance. As Foucault writes, penance was 'not nominal but dramatic ... Symbolic, ritual, and theatrical' (Foucault 1988: 43–4). The exhibition of sin is the punishment, as well as an act of self-revelation: 'To prove suffering, to show shame, to make visible humility and exhibit modesty – these are the main features of punishment' (1988: 42).

Warner also reveals that Baker's father was a Methodist, and that the performer herself went to a Methodist school; also, on 'her mother's side there are "strings of vicars" ' (Warner 1998: 79). Though Baker is not herself a practising Methodist, there are nonetheless reverberations between *Box Story* and certain aspects of Methodism. For Methodists, as for Puritans, 'man' is born in original sin (and presumably one needs this sin in order to attain everlasting peace through forgiveness), but faith in Christ assures salvation. The experience of this new found faith results in the 'birth' of a new person. As one 'reborn' Methodist woman significantly reported, 'I found myself quite another' (Abelove 1990: 89).

Whilst Methodism is open to anyone, Abelove comments that historically 'once admitted, members were expected to make some kind of *public relation* of their spiritual experiences at least once a week' (1990: 94, my emphasis). Such self-expression might include self-criticism and self-scrutiny. At meetings, turns were taken to describe experiences and feelings, hopes, successes and failures. An account from 1833 of one of these meetings is notable in relation to its evident theatricality. Writing of the way in which one speaker would present his experience in the form of a prayer, the writer records that, 'when he got his heart warm, he would continue his prayer for 15 or 20 minutes; and thereby prevented others from *exercising their talents*' (cited in Abelove 1990: 105, my emphasis). This explicit theatricality appears to have been recognised by the Methodists themselves since they sometimes rented empty theatres as preaching houses. Though these buildings were used as a matter of necessity (they were available), the fact that these theatres provided the appropriate environmental conditions for 'preaching' is nevertheless notable (Abelove 1990: 106).

Methodist practice of self-scrutiny and public revelation – or confession – sits firmly within the Christian tradition. As Foucault notes:

> Christianity is not only a salvation religion, it's a confessional religion ... Christianity requires another form of truth obligation different from faith. Each person has the duty to know what is happening inside him, to acknowledge faults, to recognize temptations, to locate desires, and everyone is obliged to disclose these things either to God or to others in the community and hence to bear public or private witness against oneself. The truth obligations of faith and the self are linked together. This link permits a purification of the soul impossible without self-knowledge.
>
> (1988: 40)

Of course, this search for and disclosure of 'self', publicly or privately, carries with it an assumption of sin or guilt, accompanied accordingly by shame. Without guilt and shame, there is no contrition, and without contrition, there can be no forgiveness or absolution. Another shared feature of the confession, irrespective of its institutional location, is that it is generally considered to unburden, to cleanse, to release or lighten. As Peter Brooks writes, 'from Saint Augustine onwards, writers of personal confessions have claimed the need to expose their state of sin and error in order [to] regain the path of righteousness' (2000: 72–3). This purported 'effect' of confession can be found in the realm of the contemporary legal confession.

In this context, Brooks notes that 'Confession of misdeeds has become part of the everyday pedagogy of Western societies, normally with the understanding that recalcitrance in confession will aggravate punishment, while full confession will both cleanse the soul and provide possible mitigation of sanctions' (45). Brooks also suggests that whilst it is generally thought that confession admits guilt, in actual fact it might be the very act of confessing that produces guilt in the confessant (to use the religious term), rather than any action or referent outside of the confession. The confession, then, performs guilt. Thinking about Baker's literal performance, I want to propose that the confession might also contain within it the possibility of performing innocence. Just as Baker uses the confessional apparatus to construct multiple identities, and to make uncertain the 'truth' status of both 'herself' and her stories, might Baker use the confession as a way to acknowledge that feelings of guilt are sometimes unfounded? Further, I will argue that it is the opportunity afforded by confession to create stories that has a liberating effect, rather than any admission of sin.

Box Story begins with Baker entering her church carrying an enormous cardboard box that she then empties at the altar. From this large box fall ten smaller boxes, including a box of cornflakes, a box of matches, a packet of washing powder and a tin of mustard powder. As in *Drawing on a Mother's Experience*, Baker's artistic materials are 'domestic' and 'familiar'. During the performance, Baker will create a world in ten actions, telling a story and then using the contents from each of the smaller boxes as illustration. As she tips the contents directly onto the floor, Baker builds up a graphic image of a world – the planet Earth – beset by disasters of global proportion (the Methodist's apocalypse perhaps).

Each of Baker's confessions documents a sorry tale, for which Baker claims agency. The final story is of Baker trying to do a good turn for the benefit of her son, who is upset. They are in her car, and in an endeavour to cheer him up, she attempts to play a cassette tape. Momentarily distracted, she inadvertently causes three cars, including her own, to crash. At this point in her life story Baker claims responsibility for everything: 'It's all my fault. Everything is all my fault'. This claiming of ultimate blame resonates with the 'performance' of Catholic confession: 'Through my fault, through my most grievous fault'.[8] Within the context of Baker's vision of cataclysmic disasters and her sense of guilt in relation to these, *Box Story* importantly alludes to the myth of Pandora. Pandora, disobeying specific instruction, opened a box, thereby releasing its contents into the world, including diseases, sorrows, vices and crimes. Before this time, no one on earth had even experienced pain. Pandora, like Eve then (and, it would seem, like Bobby) is to blame for everything. It is all her/their fault (if the pervasive cultural myths are to be believed and internalised).

After claiming ultimate responsibility, Baker sweeps up her stories, depositing them back into the large box. She then climbs into the box after them, but with cunning use of a hand saw, cuts out holes in the box for her head, arms and legs, so that she can stand up in it, wearing the box in a way that resembles a crucifixion. Baker appears to rise again from the coffin-like box. In accordance with general notions of the confession, it does indeed seem as if by admitting her guilt, she has now achieved redemption, or absolution, and that her act of confessing appears to afford her some liberation, or re-birth. There is little about this that is 'resistant'.

But what of her confessions? Again, these are largely confessions of the everyday, and more importantly, they are confessions of the accidental, the mistake: the breaking of inherited heirlooms, the bad haircut, the over-indulgence in sugar resulting in rotting teeth. The event which leads Baker to the final claiming of blame – that everything is all her fault – arises because she was simply attempting to cheer up her son. 'Judging' the stories that Baker has shared (and as spectators our role here is arguably that of confessor) it is apparent that she has nothing to feel guilty about, that she is not to blame, that things do just happen, and that it is no one's fault (particularly in the case of her father's drowning during a family holiday, when she was fifteen). Could Baker's 'rising up' be her transcending unfounded guilt (a guilt women too often unconsciously carry)?[9] In respect of the content of her confessions, and in contradiction to her final statement, it is possible that Baker uses the confession as a 'quest for innocence' (Brooks 2000: 165), and that *Box Story* performs this innocence, rather than guilt.

In the closing moments of the performance, still wearing the large cardboard box, Baker dances out of the space taking her swept-up confessions with her. As in *Drawing on a Mother's Experience*, in *Box Story*, Baker, in spite of it all, has come through. But what needs to be remembered here is that the confessions that Baker shares are both carefully moulded, and then told and retold, first in rehearsal and then in performance. Though there is similarity here to the deliberate crafting of the written confession, and its desired effect, the fact that Baker's confessions are live (and ephemeral), renders them always available to be re-enacted, enabling a continual rewriting, or revising, of the confession.[10] For example, Baker has been confessing in *Drawing on a Mother's Experience* for some fifteen years, and over 200 times. The 'unburdening' that is supposedly enabled by confession might have less to do with admitting guilt (and being absolved), than with the opportunity that confession provides to craft a tale – to deliberately select, order, edit and perform. In confessional performance, the act of telling is most often an act of retelling, and it might be this that pulls Baker through at the end.

Of course, the belief that equates 'confession' with 'well-being' is found in non-religious contexts, such as psychoanalysis and other forms of counselling. In his seminar, 'Technologies of the Self', Foucault traces such 'technologies' in 'pagan and early Christian practice' (1988: 17). In both instances, Foucault contends that the focus was not on 'knowing oneself', but 'taking care of yourself'. Such 'taking care of oneself', within a Pagan context, might include 'writing activity' (27), guidance by a master, silence, retreating into oneself, examination and review of conscience (based on 'stock taking' rather than on judgement and/or punishment). What is fundamental for Foucault is that the Pagans' activities were pragmatic, focused on finding appropriate methods for self-care, whereas he perceives psychoanalysis as appropriating (ancient) methods in order to unearth some 'truth' about the self which will then lead to 'well-being'.

Baker, although admitting that her views may be unpopular, has stated that she sees 'the making of art ultimately as therapy'. Not wishing to pathologise art making, she clarifies that 'it's just the process that people adopt to *respond to life* ... An element of what I'm doing is sort of like going to a therapist, but I choose an audience' (2001, my emphasis).

Baker's act of confession – or perhaps *craft* of confession is more appropriate, given the evident awareness and skill with which she practises it – may be, as she states, simply the act of '*making* stories up to *make* sense of the world' (Baker 2001, my emphasis). Such stories are intended to neither provide a truth about the world, nor about the person who tells the story. They are merely one pragmatic response to the actual lived, messy, experiences of life: experiences that include, in this instance, such nonrationalisable tragedies as a parent being swept out to sea and drowning. Baker's confessions are, first and last, as her title acknowledges, stories. The private confessional box is knowingly reconfigured here as a story box. Returning to that other story that continuously ghosts Baker's, it is worth remembering that what is left in Pandora's box at the end is Hope. And perhaps it is hope that Baker is, finally, offering us. I use the plural pronoun 'us' deliberately.

One marked difference between the witnessed live performance and the read written text is that the former is experienced 'collectively', whereas the latter is more typically a private event. Though each spectator undoubtedly has their own individual experience, engaging with the performance in variable and unpredictable ways, the experience of spectatorship is shared. Baker has worried that her performances might be considered 'self-indulgent' (2001). However, capturing the paradoxical dialogic property adhering to this supposedly 'monologic' form, Baker reflects that the:

> audience actually don't come away from the show very often talking about my life ... They actually relate to it as people, they've had that experience, or similar experiences ... I heard some sort of fantastic stories about people leaving the show and then standing on the pavement for a long time telling each other stories.
>
> (2001)

The environment of performance then, its dependency on its audience, on its witnesses, in shared time and space, encourages the production of other confessions, the telling of other potential 'unburdenings'.

Post-script

And yet, and yet ... The ending, my ending, to this story, is too neat. Too easy. Too convenient. For this story has not, of course, reached its conclusion. The life, and the performance, continue. So let me 'end' here by resisting an ending, and offering instead two potentially contradictory possibilities:

1   In suggesting that it is the performing of her stories that has pulled Baker through I am in danger of forgetting that she is also performing that moment of coming through. In reality, Baker may feel far from dancing out of the church. (But the show must go on.) When asked about the extent to which making autobiographical works had affected her actual life trajectory, in wondering about the degree to which the process did not only take from the life lived, but perhaps impacted on the life yet to be lived, Baker admitted to 'a sneaking suspicion that it's sent me on a trajectory spiralling towards madness in a sense' (2001). During my own act of considering confessional performance as a mode of pragmatic therapy, I am confronted by its limitations, as I learn that the body of Spalding Gray has been found in the River Hudson (March 2004). Though the cause of death remains under investigation, it is common knowledge that Gray had attempted suicide on previous occasions. Spalding Gray, like Baker, had been publicly confessing his life since the 1980s.[11]

2   After completing this chapter, I learn that Baker's latest project, which will premiere at the end of 2004, is called *How to Live*. According to the publicity, this project will 'challenge perceptions of mental health and the

whole notion of "ordered/disordered" behaviour'. I catch myself smiling when I read that Baker is creating a 'whole new "therapy"' that is 'focused on the examination and transformation of the self' (Baker 2004).

Notes

This research has been supported by the AHRB, and develops work first published in *M/C: A Journal of Media and Culture*, 'Performing the Self', 5.5 (2002), http:www.media-culture.org.au/0210/Heddon/html. Earlier versions of this chapter have also been presented at Edge Hill University Symposium on Autobiography, Exeter University Feminist Research Network, and Colloque 'Confessions', Université de Provence. Thanks to all who offered useful critical responses to these earlier thoughts.

1 All citations of Baker's performances are transcripts taken from documentary video recordings.
2 Performances include: *Drawing on a Mother's Experience* (1988), *Cook Dems* (1990), *Kitchen Show* (1991), *How to Shop* (1993), *Take a Peek!* (1995), *Spitting Mad*, *Table Occasions*, *Box Story* (2001).
3 Baker's original name was Lindsey but when she was little she wanted to be a boy, so changed it to Bobby. Already, then, Bobby Baker is not quite Bobby Baker (see Warner 1998: 83–4).
4 Of course, arguably everyone is always performing and I do not wish to suggest here the presence of any 'essential' core.
5 Baker works with director Polona Baloh Brown.
6 Thanks to Rachel Jury for discussing this so eloquently with me.
7 Thanks to Elaine Aston for drawing my attention to the relationship between the spectator's stories and Baker's secrets.
8 I am grateful to the reviewer for pointing this out to me. Of course, confessions within the Catholic faith are now largely conducted in private. The actual institution of the oral confession dates back to the Fourth Lateran Council of 1215. Canon 21 of Lateran IV, makes confession to one's parish priest an annual obligation. The Council of Trent introduced the 'black box' only in the sixteenth century.
9 As I write this, I am reminded of how often I apologise for bad weather, for delayed trains, for events over which I have neither control nor personal responsibility.
10 Baker's performance scripts are unpublished. However, video documentation of her performances exist. Watching a video recording of a performance from ten years previously, and comparing it with a more recent performance of the same show, does enable one to see the 'rewriting' process. This perhaps bears similarity to the confession which has been scribbled over or revised. Earlier versions remain legible.
11 Gray's staged performances include *Sex and Death to the Age 14*, *Booze, Cars and College Girls*, *Swimming to Cambodia*, *Monster in a Box* and *Gray's Anatomy*. The majority of these have also been published, and some are available on video and DVD.

Bibliography

Abelove, H. (1990) *The Evangelist of Desire: John Wesley and the Methodists*, California: Stanford University Press.
Baker, B. (1988) *Drawing on a Mother's Experience*, National Review of Live Art: Glasgow.

—— (1994) *Kitchen Show*, Magdalena Project: Cardiff.

—— (2001) *Box Story*, LIFT: London (2001). Interview with the author, London, 29 November.

—— (2004) Available online at: http://www.bobbybakersdailylife.com/news.htm (accessed 29 May 2004).

Baldwyn, L. (1996) 'Blending In: The Immaterial Art of Bobby Baker's Culinary Events', *The Drama Review* 40 (4) (T152): 37–55.

Brooks, P. (2000) *Troubling Confessions: Speaking Guilt in Law & Literature*, Chicago: University of Chicago Press.

Dovey, J. (2000) *FREAKSHOW: First Person Media and Factual Television*, London: Pluto Press.

Etchells, T. (1999) *Certain Fragments*, London: Routledge.

Foucault, M. (1988) 'Technologies of the Self', in L.H. Martin, H. Gutman, and P.H. Hutton (eds) *Technologies of the Self: A Seminar with Michel Foucault*, Amherst: The University of Massachusetts Press.

Foucault, M. (1990) *The History of Sexuality, Volume One: An Introduction*, trans. R. Hurley, Harmondsworth: Penguin.

Gammel, I. (ed.) (1999) *Confessional Politics: Women's Sexual Self-Representations in Life Writing and Popular Media*, Carbondale and Edwardsville: Southern Illinois University Press.

Givner, J. (1999) 'TV Crisis and Confession: The Hill-Thomas Hearings', in I. Gammel (ed.) (1999) *Confessional Politics: Women's Sexual Self-Representations in Life Writing and Popular Media*, Carbondale and Edwardsville: Southern Illinois University Press.

Harris, G. (1999) *Staging Femininities: Performance and Performativity*, Manchester: Manchester University Press.

Heddon, D. (2002) 'Performing the Self', *M/C: A Journal of Media and Culture* 5 (5). Available online at: http:www.media-culture.org.au/0210/Heddon/html (accessed 3 December 2002).

Howell, J. (1979/1980) 'Solo in Soho: The Performer Alone', *Performance Art Journal* 4 (1) and 4 (2): 152–8.

Kalb, J. (2000) 'Documentary Solo Performance: The Politics of the Mirrored Self', *Theater* 31 (3) 13–29.

Larsen, E. (1995) 'Questions of Feminism: 25 Responses', *October* 71: 5–47.

Lejeune, P. (1989) 'The Autobiographical Pact', in J.P. Eakin (ed.) *On Autobiography*, trans. K. Leary, Minneapolis: University of Minnesota Press.

Munk, E. (1997) 'Brainchild of a Lesser God', in M. Roth (ed.) *Rachel Rosenthal*, Baltimore: The Johns Hopkins University Press.

Oddey, A. (1999) *Performing Women: Stand-Ups, Strumpets and Itinerants*, London: Macmillan Press.

Smith, S. (1993) *Subjectivity, Identity and the Body: Women's Autobiographical Practices in the Twentieth Century*, Bloomington: Indiana University Press.

Tushingham, D. (ed.) (1994) *LIVE 1: Food for the Soul*, London: Methuen Drama.

Warner, M. (1998) 'Bobby Baker: The Rebel at the Heart of the Joker', in N. Childs and J. Walwin (eds) *A Split Second of Paradise*, London: Rivers Oram Press.

Weisberg, R. (1980) *Artweek*, November 22; reprinted in M. Roth (ed.) (1997) *Rachel Rosenthal*, Baltimore: The Johns Hopkins University Press.

9   Death sentences

Confessions of living with dying in narratives of terminal illness[1]

Ruth Robbins

Death: not, first of all, annihilation, non-being, nothingness, but a certain experience for the survivor of the 'without response'.

(Derrida 2001: 203)

Language reveals the other, the ' "vision" of the face is inseparable from this offering language is'.

(Eaglestone 1997: 122, quoting Levinas, *Totality and Infinity*)

In the summer of 1997, the *Observer* colour supplement, a magazine then entitled *Life*, ran a sporadic series of columns entitled 'Before I say goodbye ...' by the journalist Ruth Picardie. In the midst of glossy advertisements for expensive consumer items, solid features on a range of subjects, a lifestyle section peddling yet more expensive consumer items, and just before the television listings pages, these articles appeared as if they might have been yet more fluff for the lazy Sunday-morning reader. Indeed, the first sentences of the first article did nothing to dispel that illusion:

> You're 32, a stone-and-a-half overweight, depressed by the stains on the sofa, and have never come to terms with having piggy eyes, but still, life is pretty great: you've got a husband who can make squid ink pasta and has all his own hair, your one-year-old twins are sleeping through the night, and, as for your career – well, you might be interviewing George Clooney next week.

(Picardie 1998: 38)

There was, however, a very large 'but' looming over this cheerful sentence. In it, Picardie announced that she was dying, aged thirty-two, from a horrifyingly aggressive cancer that had spread from her breast to her lymph system to her bones and lungs and liver, and which would finally reach her brain. 'Before I say goodbye ...' over the next two months intermittently documented her dying, finally trailing off into silence on 24 August 1997, when Ruth's sister, Justine Picardie, then editor of *Life* magazine, who had commissioned the articles, took over the narrative. Ruth Picardie was then in a hospice, incapable of writing. She would rally briefly to celebrate her twins' second birthday in September; she would live long enough to hear of, and gossip in emails with her friends about, the death of Princess Diana at the end of August. But on 28 September, Justine Picardie announced her sister's death the previous weekend. In the midst of *Life*, we were indeed in death.

A year later, these few brief columns were collected together by Justine Picardie, and Ruth's husband, Matt Seaton. To bulk out the collection of Picardie's own words – which would certainly have been too brief to make a book – husband and sister also collected Ruth's email correspondence with her friends, and a selection of the letters that her columns had elicited from the *Observer*'s readers. They added a foreword and 'After Words', and published the collection under Ruth's original title: *Before I Say Goodbye*. My first confession here is that I was one of the original readers of the columns, which I found desperately painful and moving; and when the book was published, I bought it, read the story again, and was again moved, even unto weeping. The experience, in other words, of reading this sad story of a young woman's dying and death, was an emotional and a bodily one: it produced a lump in the throat, a discomfort around the eyes. But I am a literary critic and theorist, and that bodily response was uncomfortable in more ways than one; how was it, the critic in me wanted to ask, that the account of a woman's life and death, a woman whom I only knew as a textual sign, so affected my subjectivity that I cried when she died? Even more oddly, how is it, many years after the event, that her words, as well as those of her husband, still produce emotional affect? What is it about the fact that this book documents not *A Life*, but a life, that makes it a potent and unsettling experience to read? In setting out to answer these questions in relation to Picardie's text, and by an analysis of a very different textual 'confession' of terminal status, by Gillian Rose in *Love's Work*, I want to suggest something of the possible limitations of high theory, and tentatively to propose that we must make a space within theoretical thought for the subjective – and even for the humanistic – response.

Theory and criticism propose a number of possible answers to these kinds of questions. In the case of Picardie's collage text of collected articles, informal emails and readers' responses, for instance, part of the answer as to how the writing produces emotional affect is to do with generic incongruity and instability. 'Have you read Diary of Bridget Jones?', Picardie asks one of her email correspondents: 'Brilliant' is her considered verdict (1998: 36). Like the readers who proclaimed, 'Bridget Jones, c'est moi!', Picardie's own readers recognize the ordinary, contemporary 'everywoman' life that she was leading, in which one is always too fat, never the perfect mother or housekeeper that the magazines insist one should be, and where there is never enough time or money to live up (or down) to the consumerist dream of the privileged West. At the same time, her life is, on the surface, for those same readers, an aspirational life. Not only might Picardie be interviewing

George Clooney next week, but in her professional capacity as a consumer journalist for broadsheet newspapers and glossy magazines, she also gets to try out expensive and glamorous consumer products on behalf of her readers. As her friend Carrie writes in an email, 'you are 99% of the glamour in my life' (1998: 11). The emotional affect produced by the text might well be a function of the fact that our generic expectations lead us to presume that the boundaries between laughter and sorrow will be more carefully policed, that chick-lit and trauma do not belong together in the same textual space.

This category error is disturbingly demonstrated in the article originally published in *Life* on 27 July 1997, where Picardie bemoans the fact that her fate is to die fat. Terminal cancer has not had, in her case, the presumed effect of making her, in the words of one of her readers, 'look "wonderful in an anorexic translucent fashion"' (1998: 48). She has, in fact, no chance of leaving this world in anything less than a 'size 16 urn'. That thought brings her up short, shocked by her own triviality in the face of her mortality:

> I'm not happy. Why? For a start, having a terminal illness is supposed to make you extremely wise and evolved, turning you into the sort of person who thinks, 'What is being 11 stone compared with the joy of seeing my children running through a flowery meadow as if in a junior Timotei ad?' Unfortunately, I just can't get my head round Zen meditation, and seem to be stuck in, 'Why did I eat the fishfingers that Lola spat out when I can't fit into my jeans any more?'
>
> (1998: 48)

Picardie's article constructs itself around the binary opposition of fat and thin, a binary which is very much at the forefront of Western women's self-identity: thin women are translucent and gorgeous whilst fat women are self-indulgent piglets. When people tell Picardie that she is looking 'well', despite chemotherapy, she is sure that they really mean that she is looking fat. And, in one way, she is not surprised that she looks so 'well'. Her support group, presumably as some kind of (highly inadequate) compensation for the horror of dying, always has the best biscuits to sustain its members through their emotional meetings; she kills time waiting for hospital appointments by eating sandwiches from the upmarket sandwich chain, Prêt à Manger; friends keep taking her out for lunch. Consumption – both consumption of consumer goods and the consumption of food – is a significant indicator of identity in this society, and Picardie is part of that consumerist dream/nightmare, carefully placing the products with which she wishes to be associated in the article. Timotei shampoo, for instance, is associated with youthful, blonde and healthful innocence in its advertising campaign. Consumption, however, is a rather vicious two-edged sword. On the one hand it marks your identity and elevates your social standing; on the other, it makes you fat, and to be fat is to be bad in this media-constructed world. The article grumbles on in much the same manner of any other first-person newspaper column in which the self itself is commodified for public consumption, except that its subject is terminal cancer and the diets it describes are the vegan, organic, dairy-free, gluten-free diets prescribed as a possible panacea for the disease, until it reaches its 'punchline', which comes like a blow to the guts: 'One of the women at my support group recently lost a lot of weight. On Monday night, she died. I'm glad I look well, after all' (1998: 50).

In the end, though, Ruth Picardie might never have lost weight, but in her dying she did not look 'well'. In the 'After Words' penned by her husband, Matt Seaton creates a haunting and nihilistic image of his wife's dying and death. He narrates the horror of her loss of self as tumours spread to her brain, attacking her frontal lobe, and partially excising her personality. On the night before she died, he narrates their last joint performance of going-to-bed rituals for their two-year-old twins, Joe and Lola. The children drink their bedtime bottles of milk, one seated on each parent's lap, and they sing nursery rhymes together in the half-light of the bedroom:

> After a few minutes, Joe simply got off Ruth's lap, came over and lay down on the bed by me and Lola. The sight of Ruth's poor, hunched silhouette, half-lit by a shaft of light from the door, still faintly finishing the lines of our song, was the saddest thing I ever hope to see. I knew then that, like Eurydice, she was lost to the Underworld, and that the true meaning of dying is its absolute loneliness.
>
> (1998: 115)

The pure diurnality – the ordinariness – of putting one's children to bed, is juxtaposed with the extraordinariness of doing so in the knowledge that it is almost certainly for the last time. Seaton has no choice but to retreat into myth. One might say that it is the craftiness of the writing, the writer's manipulation of event and metaphor in the organization of experience into narrative, which produces emotional affect in the reader. And some might equally say that the reader's experience of emotional affect is an intellectual failure – a refusal to accept the self-evident truth that the people in this story are pure textual signifiers. If I stand so accused – if I have been manipulated, if I have put my critical faculties to sleep – so be it. My point is that there are times when it is an ethical failure on the part of the reader to dismiss emotional and bodily response to textual materials as a mere effect of the hollowed out, repeated gestures of writing, or as an affectedness in the reading process.

To come at this from another direction, Gillian Rose's *Love's Work* is perhaps a more cerebral encounter with a 'confession' of mortality. In contrast to Picardie's narrative, this is a text which displaces the reader's sentiment. Like Picardie's, it is a collage, drawing together very different narrative strands which are juxtaposed, but which are not placed in a framework of causality. The problem Rose raises in *Love's Work* is that of the ways in which representation and narrative demand interpretation. Her view appears to be that all explanations are explanatory fictions – that they risk explaining away fear and terror, or pleasure and enjoyment, rather than permitting those emotions to be experienced in and of themselves. Its patchwork of narrative elements is placed at the service of a meditation on what happens when we are deprived of our connective frames of cause and effect. It is also unusual as an autobiography or thanatography in that it displaces the reader's attention from its central theme. Rose tells many other stories before she comes to her own, and she defers the text's *raison d'être*, her diagnosis of terminal ovarian cancer, until the sixth chapter of a short (eight chapter, 135-page) book. The other stories she tells along the way demand to be read, retrospectively, as a meditation on the body that has betrayed her and on the mind that has sustained her. In their sum, however, these various narrative strands, are not explanations: this is not a conventional *apologia* or confessional text which provides a ready-made interpretative strategy. Her theme is rather the proliferating mystery of the human condition.

The book opens with an account of a journey Gillian Rose took in the early 1990s, to New York, to visit a friend, Jim, who was then dying of the late twentieth century's keynote disease, AIDS. Another friend has arranged for her to stay in the apartment of a nonagenarian woman named Edna, slightly older than the century, who is, incidentally (or so it appears at first), suffering from a cancer that has attacked her face. In an image that uneasily poises between the comic and the grotesque, Edna owns a prosthetic nose which 'lacked any cosmetic alleviation ... with thick spectacles on top, this proboscis could have come from a Christmas cracker' (Rose 1997: 4). The comedy of the nose juxtaposed with the reasons for Edna's wearing of it, produces its own generic incongruity. But Edna's story also raises for Rose a massive rhetorical question, for it later transpires that Edna has suffered from various cancer episodes for almost the whole of her life – that she was first diagnosed with a tumour in 1913 at the age of sixteen. Edna is a mystery: 'How can that be – that someone with cancer since she was sixteen exudes well-being at ninety-six?' (1997: 6). Especially how can that be when Jim, the reason for Rose's trip, is dying at the age of forty-seven?

Answer comes there none. The unwillingness to impose meaning on the random contingencies of living and dying is the point of Rose's book. Before she gets to own story, she documents other deaths and dyings, some of which are local and personal to her (the deaths of her friends Yvette and Jim); and some of which are historical and universally interpreted as significant (the 'unnumbered but nameless dead in Poland', the Holocaust deaths of Auschwitz (Rose 1997: 30)). In chapter four, she also produces the most nearly traditional autobiographical part of the book, in an account of her own life that turns out to be a doomed attempt to explain how the woman Gillian Rose came into being through the excavation of her fragmented childhood. The fact that the project is doomed, however, is not a reason for despondency. For autobiographical explanations are at best only partial, and at worst are deliberate falsifications. In addition to the narrative of familial experience, the woman Gillian Rose became must also be explained in relation to the particular body that she inhabited: subjectivity is a function of biology as well as culturally specific experience. Her preference for difficult German texts (Rose became a philosopher) is partly explained, therefore, in relation to a resistance to her family's Jewish diasporic history: it is a refusal to accept the prohibitions on speaking and reading German that her émigré and refugee maternal and paternal grandparents imposed. But it is also explained by poor eyesight, diagnosed in childhood as a lazy eye, eventually cured by an operation, but which rendered the child Gillian dyslexic. Her early experience of the confusions of the written word, and the development of strategies to cope with her confusion have made her stubborn and dissident. Her confusions are a state of mind, culturally produced, certainly, but also, materially the result of physical facts about her own body, the locus of a very specific subjectivity.

One example of Gillian Rose's sense of impossibility of interpretation is her allusion to Peter Weir's film of Joan Lindsay's novel, *Picnic at Hanging Rock*. The story is apparently a simple one. On Valentine's Day 1900, during a school trip to a rock outcrop in Australia, three girls mysteriously disappear, two of them for good. The one schoolgirl who has been excluded from the trip kills herself (in the novel she is murdered); and the headmistress of the school, whose business and reputation have both been destroyed by the scandal at the eponymous rock, also kills herself, by jumping from it to her death. Neither novel nor film offers any explanation of the central mystery at the heart of the story: what happens to the three girls? The event is given consequences, but no cause. This story, says Rose, 'offers us no solace of psychology or melancholy, which we yearn to find in it. It presents the pattern of a doom and a consummation' (1997: 49). The reader's/viewer's desire for explanation, for reward and retribution, is the requirement for reassurance – usually vouchsafed by narrative if not by life itself – that the world is indeed a just place, and that its workings are predictable. But in life, poetic justice is often absent: things might just happen without significance. Thus, we live at least as much in the Lacanian realm of the 'Real' as we do in his more ordered Symbolic and Imaginary realms. For Lacan, the 'Real' is the space of contingency, of non-interpretation, that 'falls entirely and irretrievably outside the signifying dimension … the Real is that which lies outside the symbolic process' (Bowie 1991: 94).

The aetiology of the cancer that eventually killed Gillian Rose is as mysterious as the events in the film: it is, as it were, an effect without a cause, or at least, it has no cause that (scientific) narrative can as yet recover. Rose begins her 'confession' of her terminal status, as I've suggested, very late in the day, and very tentatively. She asks her readers what they would think of her if she now told them, this late in the book, that she was suffering from full-blown AIDS? She constructs a possible answer: 'I would lose you to knowledge, to fear and metaphor. Such a revelation would result in the sacrifice of my art, of artistic "control" over the setting as well as the content of your imagination' (1997: 70). This loss of control would be the result, she suggests, of both the unspeakable nature of death itself, and of the fact that the particularities of AIDS-related deaths have a well-developed narrative structure in Western culture – that they have been 'overspoken'. The admission of terminal status from another cause, cancer, produces a similar loss: the very word cancer 'overdetermines' the reader's response. Rose hypothesizes that readers will have their own narrative and imaginative version of what cancer does to a body, and she also knows that some readers might well see her diagnosis as 'a judgement, a species of ineluctable condemnation', though she will go on to disavow any such interpretation. But she wishes to offer an alternative possibility. 'To the bearer of this news, the term "cancer" means nothing: it has no meaning. It merges without remainder into the horizon within which the difficulties, the joys, the banalities of each day elapse' (72).

In discussing her own disease, in other words, Rose offers a very different kind of diagnosis; she argues that intellectual knowledge may be very far removed from experiential reality. Intellectual knowledge – theory, philosophy, any metalanguage – works on the basis that narratives of various kinds will 'tell'; that by placing events in a certain order as we retell them, we will be enabled to deduce patterns of cause and effect which reassure us of a minimal justice in the order of things. Experience does not behave so politely, as a medical example suggests. Rose narrates her own experience of undergoing a failed operation to reverse an earlier colostomy, following the discovery that her original ovarian tumour had begun to spread to her bowels. The two consultants responsible for her care could not reconcile their two very different accounts of what they have found inside her body. Mr Wong 'informed me that there was considerable progression of the disease', whereas Mr Bates opined: 'You look just the same as you did when we closed you up in April. No less cancer, but no more either' (Rose 1997: 91, 93). Both, clearly, cannot be right. No matter the context, interpretations conflict.

This local, personal and specific example of the failure of interpretation to produce answers then becomes an analogy for much larger historical example. Discussing the work of the Dutch Holocaust historian Robert Jan van Pelt, Rose observes that not all the deaths at Birkenau and Auschwitz were produced by the enactment of Nazism's murderous fantasy. On the one hand, we tell ourselves a story about the ruthless efficiency of industrialized slaughter in the concentration camps; on the other, we cannot bear to recognize that the camps were 'designed with lack of foresight regarding the organization of sanitation, and this resulted in much *unplanned* death' (Rose 1997: 85, original emphasis). Rose is exercised by the fact van Pelt has been attacked for pointing out that some deaths in the camps happened because of inefficiency rather than because of Nazi will. What cannot be borne, and is therefore resisted, is the meaninglessness of random dying. It is as if planned, motivated murder is more bearable than deaths that were not quite murders, where, as it were, no one cared enough to be the cause.

Gillian Rose has a different narrative fate from Ruth Picardie. She chose her own ending for the story, if not for the life it recounts. Her final chapter considers what might be an appropriate response to the messy, uninterpretable, meaningless contingency that is life, and her answer is that one must accept that the human condition is made up of (mostly) benign confusion. Her chosen route is that of *euporia* – the cheerful acceptance of the existence of melancholy and perplexity. Subjectivity is defined in the end by the personal (experiential) and philosophical (theoretical) responses one is able to construct to these conditions. *Euporia* is a process rather than an endpoint, and the subject must constantly renegotiate the terms of existence and acceptance. *Euporia* cannot exist without a 'minimal just order' (Rose 1997: 134): there are some things, like the Holocaust, that one neither can nor should accept cheerfully as part of the normal vicissitudes of living and dying. But despite the injustice of a premature death Rose's text offers a modus vivendi. Her last words, knowing she was dying, speak lyrically of the making of subjectivity out of mind and body, individual and wider culture, and the interplay between what are usually constructed as binarisms: 'I will stay in the fray, in the revel of ideas and risk; learning, failing, wooing, grieving, trusting, working, reposing – in this sin of language and lips' (135).

Dying is the condition of living. And foreknowledge of death is one of the traditional definitions of the category of the human animal. Death is universal, and is ordinary. Yet, whilst we know this abstractly, we who live in a world of relative material privilege, insulated from the daily confrontation of mortality that others less lucky have to cope with, we generally live in the denial of this knowledge. The grammatically possible sentences, 'I will die; I am dying; I will have died', have almost come to seem as if they are impossible, mere linguistic tricks. This is a modern phenomenon because it is only relatively recently, even in the privileged West, that death has begun to retreat from the standard experience of most people. As early as the 1930s, in hideously ironic ignorance of the trick history was about to play on him, Walter Benjamin observed that even amongst his contemporaries death had started to feel very remote. Cultural organization and social institutions had already made it possible 'for people to avoid the sight of dying'; dying, which had once been a public process, had increasingly disappeared from public view: 'Today people live in rooms that have never been touched by death, dry dwellers in eternity, and when their end approaches they are stowed away in sanatoria or hospitals by their heirs' (Benjamin 1992: 93).

It is perhaps because of this apparent remoteness that what was almost a 'vogue' for cancer narratives was discernible in Britain in the mid-to-late 1990s, an appetite possibly provoked by ignorance and consequential fear, possibly by the cult of personality and the commodification of the self that has also been observable in this time and place. Ruth Picardie's story was one such example; but there was also John Diamond's *C: Because Cowards Get Cancer Too*, which also originated in a newspaper column, and which charted, over a very long period, the mundane diurnality of dying, its ordinariness rather than its strangeness. For both Picardie and Diamond, the focus was not on erecting the meaning of life and death through narrative patterning (the episodic, almost diary-like structure of weekly newspaper columns would, in any case, tend to preclude such a shaping), but rather on the failure of meaning and on the multiple failures of language itself to make meaning possible. The concretion of the dying experience certainly appeared to evade the neatness of abstract thought – both for the dying subject, and for their inter-subjects, the readers who scanned the texts.

Despite their many differences, however, Diamond, Picardie and Rose all shared one striking similarity. They all presented a case against interpretation. Long ago, Susan Sontag (in *Against Interpretation*) proposed that the making of meaning is always a mode of fictionalization. In her two polemical pamphlets, *Illness as Metaphor* and *AIDS and its Metaphors*, she returns to this theme, arguing through a cultural history of fatal diseases that the metaphors and meanings that accrue to various diseases are already potentially deadly. In the case of tuberculosis, she notes the ways in which it had a cultural reputation as a rather glamorous ailment: it made women thin, pale and sexy, and it only, the story went, attacked sensitive men of genius such as poets, composers and artists. The cultural representation was obviously a misrepresentation of a disease that was largely the by-product of extreme poverty, and which caused excruciatingly painful deaths. By way of contrast, cancer proliferated meanings which apportioned blame, not glamour. Cancer sufferers have either done something to deserve their suffering (for instance, they smoked); or, more insidiously, cancer sufferers exhibit certain personality traits: the defeated, disappointed and neurotic get cancer, and therefore they produce responses of disgust in others, and feel shame at their own condition (Sontag 1991: 97). The metaphors of cancer are metaphors of invading armies, of aggressivity, terrorism and violence. The patient must 'battle' against the disease, and if they do not 'win', they did not fight hard enough. Her insight in these brief texts is one that the cancer writers named here have all bought into. John Diamond explicitly despised the clichéd descriptions of the cancer patient in popular culture: 'I despise the set of warlike metaphors that so many apply to cancer. My antipathy has ... everything to do with a hatred for the sort of morality that says that only those who fight hard against their cancer survive it or deserve to survive it – the corollary being those who lose the fight deserved to do so' (1999: 10). Picardie, in different vein, railed against the euphemism (of which metaphor may be just one example) that surrounds her disease: 'Cancer is all about fear, secrecy, euphemism – palliative care, advanced disease – all are euphemisms for dying. Oncology is the biggest euphemism in the world' (1998: 13). And Gillian Rose rejected the idea of the 'cancer personality' 'described by the junk literature of cancer' because 'it covers everyone and no one. Characteristics: obesity, anorexia, depression, elation ... lack of confidence, no satisfying or challenging work, poor relationships' (1997: 78).

Presumably the euphemisms and the metaphors are a defence mechanism, rendering the unspeakable invisible. And the language of battle, in particular, may have been developed as a method to reassure both the patients and the well that a minimal just order exists, that one will be rewarded for putting up a fight. But for Sontag and thence for Rose, Picardie and Diamond, this is scant consolation. Sontag's purpose in writing the original pamphlet, *Illness as Metaphor* was:

> Not to confer meaning, which is the traditional purpose of literary endeavour, but deprive something of meaning: to apply that quixotic, highly polemical strategy, 'against interpretation', to the real world ... To the body. My purpose was, above all, practical. For it was my doleful observation ... that the metaphoric trappings that deform the experience of having cancer have very real consequences ... The metaphors and the myths ... kill ... [I wanted] to regard cancer as if it were just a disease ... Not a curse, not a punishment, not an embarrassment. Without 'meaning'.
>
> (Sontag 1991: 100)

Disease does not mean: it just is. Metaphor offers no comfort and narrative cannot pattern the event into significance. Any theory of meaning attaching to disease involves a dangerous forgery.

When Roland Barthes announced, somewhat prematurely perhaps, the death of the author, these are not quite the kinds of text he had in mind. His own examples from that essay, with their trawl through canonical poets (Baudelaire), composers (Tchaikovsky) and artists (Van Gogh), stayed with those who were already safely dead, and who were already securely 'great' (Barthes 1977: 143). Perhaps it is somewhat unfair to drag him into this discussion given that his rhetorical flourish was placed at the service of an important argument, one that demanded a less simplistically biographical or simplistically humanistic account of the making of writing than had been common in the metalanguage of criticism. Nonetheless, autobiography generally, and thanatography in particular, make particular demands of theoretically inclined readers. Texts such as Picardie's in particular, resist theory because of an implicit demand that they make of their readers that we should suspend our critical judgement. There is, in *Before I Say Goodbye* ... the written trace of a speaking voice that says to its readers: these things happened, they happened to me. It seems churlish, inhumane even, to doubt that voice which is insistent and seductive. On the other hand, it is precisely because the narrative voice constructs its readers (and thereby also instructs them) to be complicit and uncritical, that autobiography demands theory. It is, however, a moot point whether Barthes' observation that 'the book itself is only a tissue of signs, an imitation' of previously written words, itself provides any adequate account of what actually occurs in the reader's encounter with the autobiographer (1977: 147). The sense that writing is finally empty, non-referential, is not what the reader experiences; and despite the dangers of a simplistic empiricism, experience does count for something.

Part of the problem is that the word theory itself, a word whose ghostly origins in the Greek word for 'way of seeing', implies a necessary distance, perspective and a (probably illusory) sense of objectivity. Theory will enable us to see things clearly and see them whole: that is its promise. But clashes with life and death, with their messy contingency and intimacy precisely deprive the reader of distance and anyway, the patterns we seek might not be there. Any attempt to conjure them out of material which states as its premise that there is no shape, no answer, no interpretative model, is to do unwarranted violence to the text. Other theoretical approaches exist, of course. It is certainly possible to read these texts as exhibiting and dramatizing the effects of what Julia Kristeva defines as abjection: those moments when the speaking subject is forced into an awareness that she or he inhabits a body, and is therefore, an object, powerfully subjected *to* forces that it can neither control nor resist. Indeed, Kristeva uses the proliferation of cancer cells in a previously healthy body as a metaphor for the process of abjection (Kristeva 1982: 11). But once I have said this much, identified an interpretative strategy that defines the effects of the text as exemplifying the Lacanian Real, the Barthesian sign, or the Kristevan abject, I have only accounted for a small part of the effects of the texts. The risk of such strategies is the risk of explaining away, of displacing emotion and bodily response into an arcane vocabulary of distance and pseudo-objectivity.

The two epigraphs at the head of this chapter signal something of the reading strategy I want to propose as a necessary compromise with the quasi-Cartesian dualism (this female body that cries at a sad story, this supposedly critical mind that wonders whether I should) of encounters with textual others who were also real people. Another confession then: the subjectivity with which I am most concerned, perhaps, is my own. This is not a strategy for every occasion, for I would wish to avoid any totalizing pronouncements. The Derrida quotation is taken from his 'Adieu' to Emmanuel Levinas. It is an ambiguous statement. On the one hand, the 'without response' refers of course to the dead and therefore absent other, who cannot respond; on the other, the grammar implies that the experience of surviving a friend's death is that survivor might also be 'without response' – unable to respond, just as much as the absent other. If death is defined by the 'without response', then these narratives of dying speak only to 'dead' readers if the response is not forthcoming. The reference to Levinas is included because the central statement of Levinas' ethical philosophy is that ethics depends on face-to-face encounter, whether real or imagined. The ethical subject is the subject who recognizes and responds to the face of the other, perhaps narcissistically because the subject sees itself in the other, though that need not be the worst of crimes. Borrowing, somewhat against the grain, from Gayatri Spivak, there may be moments when a strategic humanism (her phrase is 'strategic essentialism' (1991: 205)) makes a kind of sense.

The two narratives with which this chapter has been chiefly concerned appeal to different kinds of reader (though I am both kinds of reader). Rose's philosophical, shrewd and slightly rueful voice is both an academic voice and a lyrical one; it appeals to the theorist and the critic. Picardie's journalistic, informal prose twists emotions with consummate ease, produces a bodily response and an appeal to the emotions. In their various constructions of textual subjectivities and inter-subjectivities, each creates and demands a different kind of reader, despite the base line that their narratives share in the dying of their authors. It is a *face-to-face* appeal; and my view in the end is that we (or maybe just I) need to be both kinds of reader, and we need to read both kinds of text, otherwise we leave the various binarisms that these texts subvert appallingly intact. The capacity to respond to the demands and needs and requests of the (textual) other as if that other were present, face-to-face, is close to what I mean by strategic humanism.

Note

1 This chapter is dedicated to the memory of a woman I never knew, but whose dying has left an enormous hole in the lives of many people I know very well and by extension, therefore, in mine. To Mary Randle.

Bibliography

Barthes, R. (1977) 'The Death of the Author', trans. S. Heath, *Image, Music, Text*, London: Fontana.

Benjamin, W. (1992) *Illuminations*, trans. H. Zohn, London: Fontana.

Bowie, M. (1991) *Lacan*, London: Fontana.

Derrida, J. (2001) *The Work of Mourning*, eds P.-A. Brault and M. Naas, Chicago and London: Chicago University Press.

Diamond, J. (1999) *C: Because Cowards Get Cancer Too ...*, London: Random House.

Eaglestone, R. (1997) *Ethical Criticism: Reading After Levinas*, Edinburgh: Edinburgh University Press.

Kristeva, J. (1982) *Powers of Horror: An Essay in Abjection*, trans. L.S. Roudiez, New York: Columbia University Press.

Lindsay, J. (1998) *Picnic at Hanging Rock*, London: Vintage.

Picardie, R. (1998) *Before I Say Goodbye*, Harmondsworth: Penguin.

Rose, G. (1997) *Love's Work*, Harmondsworth: Penguin.

Sontag, S. (1991) *Illness as Metaphor; AIDS and its Metaphors*, Harmondsworth: Penguin.

Spivak, G.C. (1991) *In Other Worlds: Essays in Cultural Politics*, New York and London: Routledge.

10 Cultures of confession/cultures of testimony

Turning the subject inside out

Susannah Radstone

> *Testify*: bear witness, proclaim ... To bear witness to, or give proof (*of a fact*); to assert the proof (of a statement) ... to serve as evidence of.
> *Testimony*: Personal or documentary evidence or attestation in support of a fact or statement.
> *Confess*: To declare or disclose (something previously held secret as being prejudicial *to oneself*), to acknowledge, own, or admit (a crime, charge, fault, or the like).
> *Confession*: A making known or acknowledging of *one's* fault, wrong, crime, weakness etc.
>
> (Oxford English Dictionary, my emphases)

Literary and cultural theory continues to demonstrate an interest in confessional discourse. Contemporary cultural criticism suggests that confession continues to mark Western culture and that it remains of interest both to academics and to cultural critics. Recent conference literature refers to the continuing 'compulsion to confess' (Ashplant and Graham 2001) and to the 'imperative to speak out ... evident in popular culture ... such as confessional television' (Ahmed and Stacey 2001: 1).[1] Peter Brooks's recent treatment of the subject opines that confession is 'deeply ingrained in our culture' (2000: 2) and is to be found everywhere, though especially in the 'everyday business of talkshows' (Brooks 2000: 4; Elsaesser 2001: 196). A recent edition of a British radio series on literature examined the significance and value of confessional literature and poetry ('Off the Page' 2000). Like Brooks, the 'Off the Page' broadcast noted confession's contemporary move from the more rarefied arenas of poetry and literary prose, to the public (and more downmarket?) spheres of television chatshows, televised courtrooms and presidential addresses. Meanwhile, the popularity and marketability of popular literary confessions was still being remarked upon in broadsheet journalism of the late 1990s (Bennett 1995; Wurtzel 1998).

Alongside the continuing interest in confession, the recent development of interest in trauma and witnessing in the humanities places particular emphasis on the concept of 'witness testimony', as exemplified by the title of perhaps the most seminal work in the field, Shoshana Felman and Dori

Laub's *Testimony: Crises of Witnessing in Literature and History* (Felman and Laub 1992).² Since *Testimony*'s publication, there has been a rapid rise of interest in witness testimony. Linda Anderson's recent study of autobiography includes a concluding section entitled 'Testimonies' which draws on Felman's assertion that testimony has become increasingly important in '"recent cultural accounts of ourselves"' (cited in Anderson 2001: 127), because it issues from and relates to the traumas of contemporary history. Anderson points out that for Felman, autobiography constitutes a 'form of testifying, to be distinguished from confession' (Anderson 2001: 127). Yet there remains a marked tendency to associate or even conflate testimonial texts and discourses with those of confession. Peter Brooks's recent book *Troubling Confessions* (2000) asserts that testimony is a confessional mode by including in his discussion of confession Victim Impact Statements (130–40) and a parallel move is found in the editorial of the recent 'Testimonial Cultures' special issue of the journal *Cultural Values*, which includes the confessions of 'public figures, such as the late Princess Diana or President Clinton' (Ahmed and Stacey 2001: 1) amongst its examples of contemporary testimony. Similarly, the publicity for a recent conference on testimony suggested that confessional texts including spiritual narratives of the seventeenth century, feminist consciousness-raising narratives, and coming-out stories are all forms of testimony, before going on to associate testimony with the impact upon journalism and television of the 'compulsion to confess'.

Before I embark on a comparison of confession with witness testimony, I will offer some preliminary suggestions about why this comparison matters – about what is at stake, that is, in establishing witness testimony's specificity and its difference from other first-person texts and discourses. First, though both confession and witness testimony have long histories, the contemporary proliferation of testimonial discourses *and* of writing and criticism on testimony suggest that discourses of testimonial witness may now be superseding confession's dominance in literature and other media. This is of significance for what it suggests about the shifting cultural contexts within which confession and witness testimony have their places. To use Raymond Williams's terms, the emergence into the cultural limelight of witness testimony may be related to wider shifts as cultures emerge, gain dominance and retreat into residual modes (Williams 1977). In these circumstances, both the specificity of witness testimony and its inter-texts need to be carefully delineated. I want to suggest a number of research questions that might aid in the future clarification of witness testimony's specificity. First, there is the question of witness testimony's inter-texts: what *are* the cultural contexts of the present-day 'rise' of witness testimony? Second, how do testimonial witness discourses construct their subjects, their objects and their audiences? Third, what forms of recognition does witness testimony seek? Fourth, what are the broader cultural implications of these constructions and appeals? Fifth, what psychical drives and fantasies are implicated in witness testimony? And finally, what is the relationship between the theories that are currently being applied to witness testimony's analysis and the culture within which discourses of witness testimony are proliferating? In what follows, it will not be possible to address each of these questions. However, in this essay I will offer some preliminary suggestions concerning the differences between these two discursive modes, focussing, in particular, on what theoretical approaches to confession and to testimony might reveal about the wider cultural shifts that underpin the emergence of testimony within culture and its take up by literary, cultural and historical studies.

One means to address the difference between confessional and testimonial witness discourses is via an analogue with the law: in a court of law, both the discourses of the defendant and of the witnesses may be referred to as testimony. Yet there are crucial differences between the discourses of witnesses and of defendants – differences that can help in the explication of the differences between other forms and genres of confession and witness testimony. In a court of law, the defendant may acknowledge their guilt. In such cases, they place themselves in the position of the confessant. The defendant/confessant's responses to the questions directed to them by the defence and the prosecution will concern *themselves* – their actions, their motivations. At stake in the discourse of the confessant is the question of their guilt or innocence. In another place in the courtroom, witnesses provide 'witness testimony'. This testimony will have a direct bearing *not* on themselves, but on the defendant or on a certain event. The witness gives testimony, not about themselves, but about something external to them that they have witnessed and about which they can speak. Or the witness may describe something that has happened to them – an attack, for instance, but for which they are held to have no responsibility or agency. Witness testimony may concern an act perpetrated upon or against the witness, or it may simply concern an event at which the witness has been present. The witness testimony elicited by the prosecution has the aim of proving the defendant's guilt, while that elicited by the defence has the aim of disproving it. In the case of the witness whose testimony concerns an act that has allegedly befallen them, the testifier supplies evidence of that which has been done to them and seeks to describe witnessed events in order to clarify who is guilty of what. In the case of the defendant/confessant, their discourse concerns whether or not it was they who were the perpetrators of that act. In a court of law, questions of agency, perpetration, guilt or innocence are directed towards the defendant. It is the defendant whose guilt or innocence is in question and for whom much, even their lives, may be at stake. As Leigh Gilmore has pointed out, confession is 'a form in which telling the truth or not telling the truth can meet with dramatic and occasionally fatal results' (Gilmore 1994: 112). In the case of witness testimony, on the other hand, the catastrophe, injury or fatality about which the witness provides testimony has already occurred.[3] Witnesses are those that have innocently been 'done to' or those who have witnessed the perpetration of a crime.

The domain and discourses of the law are neither directly equivalent to nor comparable with those of literature and other media. Yet there is something to be gained by bearing the legal analogue in mind, since if nothing else, it problematises the inclusion of confession within the category of witness testimony. It reminds us that the witness and the defendant occupy different positions and that the subject positions constructed by witness testimony and confession are not equivalent. The boundaries between witness testimony and confession may not be as watertight as the legal analogue suggests and meanwhile, even in the law court, witnesses sometimes turn out to be guilty and confess. However, though there may be shifts between confession and witness testimony in a court statement or a work of literature, or a television programme, for instance, the two modes of discourse are nevertheless discrete: in confession it is the self that is scrutinised and implicated – the self that is the subject and object of confession. Witness testimony's object, on the other hand, is always an event or an other that is external to the witness.

One example of shifts between testimony and confession can be found in Primo Levi's *The Drowned and the Saved* (1989). I would describe this work as a text of witness testimony, in which Levi describes his experience in the concentration camp of Auschwitz and speaks of the atrocities he witnessed committed upon others and upon himself. Yet the text nevertheless contains some shifts from witness testimony to confession and back again. For Primo Levi, the scientist and the man of reason, religious faith was an anathema. For Levi, religion was simply not an option, since it provided nothing but false hope. Thus, when, in *The Drowned and the Saved* Levi discusses the one moment in which he felt tempted to beg God for help, there is a discursive shift from witness testimony to confession: 'I must nevertheless admit that I experienced (and again only once) the temptation to yield, to seek refuge in prayer ... For one instant I felt the need to ask for help and asylum; then, despite my anguish, equanimity prevailed' (Levi 1989: 117–18). At this point, what is at stake becomes the witness and their 'guilt' and the focus shifts from that of an external other to that of the subject themselves:

> A prayer under these conditions would have been not only absurd (what rights could I claim? And from whom?) but blasphemous, obscene, laden with the greatest impiety of which a non-believer is capable. I rejected that temptation: I knew that otherwise, were I to survive, I would have to be ashamed of it.
>
> (1989: 118)

How can the shift from confession to testimony – both in culture and in criticism and theory be understood? How can we understand this shift (to put it crudely) from the dominance, in first-person literature and culture of a self-incriminating inward-turning, reflexive exercise in self-transformation to the rise in outward-turning, other-oriented discourse, in which the testifier speaks from a position of innocence and it is the 'other' whose wrongs are witnessed? Elsewhere, I have linked the shift from confession to testimony with the further intensification of pressures on the 'modern' subject. Whether regarded from a Foucauldian or from a psychoanalytic perspective, the modern, confessing subject is constituted through what I call a related division, in which one element of the subject whether understood as the conscience, the super-ego, or the internal exerciser of power, has the task of scrutinising that very same subject in the interests of preserving 'civilisation' or 'order'. Confession, self-implication and the production of conscience can be construed, therefore, in relation to the sustenance of social order and the orchestration of individuals into a larger unit (Radstone 2001: 67). The 'turning of the subject inside out' that I refer to in my title relates to the breakdown of this internal related division. This related division is central to confession but not to witness testimony.

It is important to state before continuing that my perspective does not mean to imply that sufferings do not happen to people . But in this essay my aim is to offer some preliminary thoughts about the emergence into the cultural limelight of a culture of testimony alongside or even in place of the dominance of confessional culture. In testimony the subject is no longer in struggle with itself, but constitutes itself as innocent or 'done to' in relation to implicated other/s or events. In literary confession it is the subject's *own* violence or sexuality that troubles the narrator. In witness testimony it is the violence or sexuality of another, or the shock of an event, that disturbs the witness. In literary theory it is the split between the narrator and the subject of confession that 'troubles' the confessional text, whereas the object of study of testimony criticism is the 'traceless text' (Elsaesser 2001: 199) that results from the unrepresentability or unrememberability of traumatic events or actions. In what follows, I want to look a little more closely at what literary and cultural theory have understood as the 'impossibilities' of confession and of testimony, since these discussions shed further light on the cultural contexts of the two discourses.

Though autobiography and confession are interwoven, closer studies of the history of confession reveal that a discrete and particular history can be traced. It is generally agreed that the confessional mode first became dominant within autobiographical writing during the mid to late nineteenth century (Stelzig 1984: 26), while for Peter Axthelm the publication of Dostoevsky's *Notes from the Underground* in 1864 marked the emergence of the first truly confessional novel, characterised by the impulse towards not self-exposition, but 'sincere and single purposed self-analysis' (Axthelm 1967: 8). In an analysis of confession that begins with St Augustine, Axthelm usefully points out that it is not the inwardness of the modern confession's quest which differentiates it from St Augustine's: St Augustine's quest, like Dostoevsky's was directed inwards. But whereas the *Confessions* describes an inward journey to find the truth of God within the self – to find, slightly differently put, an inner self moulded in the image of God (Brooks 2000:

96; Lloyd 1993: 20), Dostoevsky travels underground 'where the light of revelation cannot enter ... to seek his primary causes in the depths of his own being' (Axthelm 1967: 5). The 'inward turn', then, signifies not simply an inward quest, but a search for the inner truth of the self. This 'inward turn' (Kahler 1973) identified by Axthelm as at the very heart of the modern confessional novel, registered a turning away from older confessional modes within which the confessant sought absolution and salvation from an outside power, and a turning towards a belief in salvation via introspection as an end in itself.

Literary theory attributes confession's 'impossibility' to two of the mode's defining features: its mode of narration and its construction of 'becoming-ness'. The confession's apparent 'projection of an inner life before the world' (Edel 1955: 16) together with the illusion that it is offering access to the most private and personal areas of its central protagonist's mind is constructed, as Stelzig has pointed out, via a splitting of central protagonist and narrator, whose relationship to one another he describes as 'the paradoxical one of identity and difference' (Stelzig 1984: 27). Unlike the confession's protagonist, its narrator knows how the story goes on (Lloyd 1993: 70). The narrator's confessions concern the activities, thoughts and feelings of a central protagonist who is separated from that narrator by time, age and experience – a separation between the narrating and the narrated 'I' that was arguably foregrounded from the 1960s onwards (Waugh 1989: 26). Though as Porter has argued, this mode of narration 'multiplies implicit distinctions between protagonist and implied author' (Porter 1976: 150), the confession mobilises a range of strategies to compound or confound the distance between the two. Thus while an ironic narrational tone implies distance between narrator and central protagonist, a more sympathetic tone implies closeness. A relationship of absolute identity between the two is unlikely, however, for a temporal distance must separate central protagonist and narrator in order for the narrator to confess earlier activities, thoughts and feelings. Furthermore, since confession produces self-transformation, each confessional act both adds to and alters the view of the central protagonist offered to the reader: as Stelzig has pithily concluded: 'the signified self is changed in the process of transformation; confessions are Janus faced' (Stelzig 1984: 27). The confession, moreover, presents the telling itself as the source of self-transformation: the confession describes and performs the *becomingness* which constitutes its very heart. For William Howarth, what I am calling 'becomingness' constitutes an essential feature of the confessional: 'only the process of becoming is essential ... if the book reveals that process, it endures, like a poem, for ever' (Howarth 1974: 381).The trope of 'becomingness' produces a central protagonist characterised as in process. At the heart of the diegetic movement of the confession is a subject on his or her way, a subject 'becoming', a subject characterised, indeed, by this forward movement towards becoming someone identical with yet markedly different from his or her former self. The unfinished or incomplete self – the 'self on the way', is a commonplace, one might say, of contemporary confessional fiction.

Critical approaches to confession exceed identifications of the mode's characteristic features. Literary and cultural theorists have sought, also, to understand confession's contemporary salience in relation either to the mode's cultural instrumentality and/or to the forces which have produced confession. Liberal humanist literary criticism assumes that 'subjectivity, the individual mind or inner being, is the source of meaning and of action' (Belsey 1980: 3). It finds in autobiographical confession reflections of essential human truths (Finney 1985: 21; Olney 1972: 3). More recently, however, alternative understandings of confession's determinations and of its agency as a cultural force in its own right have been proposed. These discussions deploy models of cultural instrumentality ranging from reflectionisms of various kinds to models which grant greater autonomy to confession.[4] Where reflectionism is concerned, approaches suggest that confession reflects an essential or a historically changing subject, or that it reflects what might be termed the psycho-social *zeitgeist*. Other critical approaches, however, grant to the confession a degree of autonomy and agency lacking in the reflectionist approach. On this account, confessions are construed not simply as reflections of actuality, but as having actual effects on readers and on subjectivities. Perhaps the most dominant form of such an approach within literary criticism distinguishes between texts which uphold and those which interrogate the unified subject of classic realism. Within this perspective, autobiography and confession emerge as limit-texts of classic realism, since their foregrounding of the relation between narrator and narratee – between the subject of the enunciation and of the enunciated puts the illusory unity of classic realism's subject in question.

By far the most influential theorist of confession is Michel Foucault, who, in the first volume of his seminal *The History of Sexuality*, argues that 'since the Middle Ages at least, Western societies have established the confession as one of the main rituals we rely on for the production of truth' (Foucault 1981: 59). Foucault's refutation of the 'repressive hypothesis' in relation to sexuality consists in a counter-history which replaces the history of repression's gradual erosion with a genealogy of those discourses through which, over the last three centuries in particular, subjects have been incited to speak, or confess the truth of their sexuality. For Foucault, literary confession constitutes but one instance of confession's central role in procedures of 'individualization by power':

> Whence a metamorphosis in literature: we have passed from a pleasure to be recounted and heard, centering on the heroic or marvellous narration of 'trials' of bravery or sainthood, to a literature ordered according to the infinite task of extracting from the depths of oneself, in between the words, a truth which the very form of confession holds out like a shimmering mirage.
>
> (1981: 59)

Unlike literary criticism which construes confession as a mode of literary autobiography, for Foucault, literary confession constitutes but one mode of a revised 'pastoral power' (Foucault 1982: 777–8). In 'The subject and power', Foucault argued that although, since the eighteenth century, the ecclesiastical institutionalisation of this power lost its vitality, its function has spread and multiplied outside the ecclesiastical institution (1982: 783). Essential to Foucault's argument is an understanding of the modern state's dependence upon the production of 'individuality'. It is pastoral power, exercised through confessional practices, which 'categorises the individual, marks him by his own identity, imposes a law of truth upon him which he must recognise and which others have to recognise in him. It is a form of power which makes individuals subjects' (1982: 780). This is an argument that has been expanded by Nikolas Rose, who has commented that:

> (T)hrough self-inspection, self-problematization, self-monitoring and confession, we evaluate ourselves according to the criteria provided for us by others ... The irony is that we believe, in making our subjectivity the principle of our personal lives, our ethical systems, and our political evaluations that we are freely choosing our freedom.
>
> (Rose 1990: 11)

Foucault's focus on confession as practice rather than as text produces a history that diverges, at points, from that found in the literary critical sources which tend to link confession's ascendance to dominance with the modern 'inward turn' of the late eighteenth and nineteenth century. Though Foucault does cite this period as the moment at which pastoral power broke free from its ecclesiastical insitutionalisation, he locates the moment of formation of confessional techniques in the penitential practices of medieval Christianity and points to two especially productive moments in the genealogy of the power techniques of confession: the development in the six-teenth century of 'procedures of direction and examination of conscience; and at the beginnings of the nineteenth century, the advent of medical tech-nologies of sex' (Foucault 1981: 119; see also Rose 1990: 219–20). Though this periodising sweep throws less light than one might want on the confes-sional practices of the twentieth century, its emphasis upon the nineteenth century's medicalisation and psychologisation of sex arguably fits with literary criticism's foregrounding of a nineteenth century shift towards psychologised confessional introspection.

Though Foucault stresses confession's role in tying the confessional subject to truth, he also points to the transformative nature of the act, which, as Stelzig has pointed out, changes the signified self in the process of signification. Thus, though confession produces a central core of truth, the act also suggests a certain mutability, or unfixity at the heart of subjectivity. Poststructuralist and Lacanian-inspired theories of autobiography celebrate the foregrounding of this unfixity by modernist autobiography, claiming that it reveals as illusory the coherence and unity of the bourgeois subject of classic realism. Foucault proposes, conversely, that the subjection produced by pastoral power's injunction to confession relies upon its operation upon an apparently 'free' subject. It would be erroneous to conflate the unfixity of the subject with bourgeois notions of freedom. The poststructuralist view of the subject's unfixity and incoherence constitutes a challenge, indeed, to bourgeois notions of the coherent and unified 'free' subject. Nevertheless confession's relation to the apparent freedom and autonomy of the subject is underscored – though not from within Foucauldianism – by Peter Brooks, who argues that though confession is predicated upon 'freedom', confession 'rarely appears to occur without some form of constraint "propelling" its utterance' (Brooks 2000: 69). For Foucault, it is the simultaneous fixing and unfixing of subjectivity found in the discourse of the confessing subject which is central to the efficient operation of power by individualisation. This power is exercised upon an unfixed subject who can be made subject to individual truth. The confession's simultaneous fixing and unfixing of subjectivity – a process I have previously termed its 'becomingness' – constitutes the 'agonism', which, for Foucault, lies at the heart of the operation of pastoral power while also constituting the means for its subversion. Whether couched in terms of 'freedom'/'constraint' or 'fixity'/'unfixity' what emerges, then, is the radically ambiguous nature of confession and the absolute centrality of related dividedness to all accounts of this mode of discourse.[5]

Literary critics have also focused on confession's relation to 'individualisation' and truth. These interventions, mainly from liberal humanist perspectives, start from the premise that the modern confessional novel constitutes a literary response to 'the disintegration and uncertainty of the modern condition' (Axthelm 1967: 97). Like Foucault, this criticism foregrounds the cultural work of confession and lays stress on the individualisation that underpins modern life. Unlike Foucault, however, for this criticism confession constitutes not the motor of power by individualisation, but the means through which the sufferings of the individual can be healed. According to this critical tendency, it is the confession's capacity to heal that explains its contemporary popular appeal. P.M. Spacks points out, in this regard, that the ability to tell one's own story coherently has been regarded as 'an index of mental health' (1976: 528), while Axthelm insists that confession answers to a need to find within the self 'new principles of order and meaning' (1967: 97) in a disintegrating world. This position is rather dramatically exemplified by G.K. Hongo, who argues that in confession 'something cathartic occurs, the expulsion of some psychic poison which has absorbed whatever had been previously retarding the growth of the soul towards its rightful splendour' (1985: 118). Though this criticism attends to the confession's text-reader relations, its conclusions diverge markedly from those that a Foucauldian-inspired critique of literary confession might draw, for it emphasises not the power lodged in the reader's hermeneutic function but the trust confession places in the reader (Stelzig 1984: 23) and the cure that confession might effect not only in its writers but also in its readers.[6] The parallels between psychoanalysis and literary confession implied by this critical tendency only serve to underline its overturning of Foucault's thesis, within which psychoanalysis is positioned at the heart of modern pastoral power – a position echoed in Jeremy Tambling's Foucauldian association of modern confession with the space of the clinic (Tambling 1990: 9–10).

Whether confession is understood, as much humanist criticism of the 1960s and 1970s understood it, as 'cathartic' and a mode of healing, or along Foucauldian lines, as a mode of self-regulation and micro-power within which the subject operates power upon itself, or within literary theory, as a first-person mode concerned with the tensions, or even impossibilities of the relation between the speaking and spoken of 'I' it is the intense and tense relation between discrete though related aspects of the subject which is emphasised. Although confession does address itself to a reader/confessor whose task it is to bear witness to the transformation effected *by* confession, criticism of many perspectives concurs that confession is nevertheless a fundamentally intra-subjective discourse aimed at achieving self-transformation and an end to self-scrutiny by confessing the past. Confession speaks from isolation and seeks re-entry into the world. For literary critics, the debate concerning confession's 'impossibility' concerns whether the subjective relatedness and coherence that it both rehearses and challenges was always illusory or whether, rather, that coherence has been put under strain by historical shifts. For Foucauldians the focus falls on the genealogy of confession and on demonstrating that its discursive strategies form part of a wider micro-politics of power exercised by subjects upon themselves.

Debates concerning testimony's 'impossibility' concern themselves not with the incoherence or tensions of the subject – and with the illusory status of the 'knowledge' the confessant claims regarding their former self, but with the impossibility of containing and communicating to others that which has been experienced or witnessed by the testifier. Theories of testimony's impossibility link it not to the impossibility of complete self-knowledge, but to the impossibility of communicating – even to the self, sometimes – an experience of an event. Epistemological doubt shifts, then, from the arena of self-knowledge, to that of 'events' and the central question posed by testimony concerns whether any meaningful sense can be made and communicated of traumatic experience. Whereas confession's 'impossibilities' are primarily associated with the tensions of intra-subjectivity, testimony's impossibilities are linked with the struggles of inter-subjectivity. Theories of testimony dwell on the difficulties attendant upon transforming the registration of significant events of suffering or shock into meaningful experience that can be communicated to others.

This understanding of testimony's impossibility has risen to dominance due to the influence in the humanities of trauma theories such as those of Cathy Caruth (1995, 1996) and Shoshana Felman and Dori Laub (Felman and Laub 1992). Influenced by new developments in US psychoanalysis, these theories replace older 'depth' models of the inner world with 'flat' models in which dissociation replaces repression.[7] According to this revised psychoanalysis, it is the nature of traumatic events and their qualities that prompts the mind's integrative capacities to shut down. Under the impact of trauma, events too shocking to be assimilated, integrated and remembered are consigned to an area of the mind where they become dissociated from ordinary memory and recall. Thus witness testimony of such events becomes all but impossible. On this account, the term 'witness' may be applied both to the original witness of the event – the testifier – and to the testifier's addressee or the analyst of the testimonial text. The task of the addressee or the analyst of testimony becomes that of searching for the absent traces left by trauma and dissociation. Confessional texts concern themselves with the sins perpetrated by the self and confessional theory focuses on the splits between speaker and spoken of or on the internal divisions constitutive of the operation of pastoral power. Texts of testimony are held to bear invisible witness to unrepresentable traumas, and theories of testimony concern themselves with the processes of bearing witness either to the horrors of history or to specific sins perpetrated by another. To me, what is most striking here is the movement of that which troubles the subject and the text from its place within the confessional subject to a location external to the traumatised subject. In this sense, testimony represents the 'turning inside out' of the confessional self so that the trouble which resided within and even constituted the subject is now deemed to be positioned outside the self. This is a fascinating shift which arguably 'cleanses' the testimonial subject of all sin at the expense of history or perpetration. This is, *inter alia*, a move which enhances the significance of the listener/academic at the expense of the testifier: on this account of testimony's impossibility, the proposed, all but impossible 'witnessing' occurs, if it occurs at all, in the dialogic relation between testifier and addressee.

There is a great deal that could be said about the shift from theories of the impossibility of confession to theories of the impossibility of testimony. But in the space which remains, I simply want to raise a question about theories and their cultural contexts. The period between the 1960s and the 1980s saw the publication and rise in popularity of large numbers of confessional novels. These novels concerned themselves with the (usually) sexual 'sins' of their male narrators, or with the troubled lives and sexuality of their incipiently feminist narrators (Radstone 1989). Their endings promised self-transformation if not absolution. Confessional theory wrote against the grain of confession's surface. It sought to reveal confession's mobilisation of the hidden incoherence of the bourgeois subject, or the illusory nature of bourgeois 'freedom'. In Foucault's terms, for instance, the sexual confessions and so-called sexual 'revolution' of the 1960s and 1970s to which confessional novels of the period were related were better understood as subjects operating pastoral power upon themselves. What is striking about the relation between theories of testimony and their cultural context is that this reflective distance between a cultural mode and a body of theory about that mode appears to have contracted to invisibility. On the whole, theories of testimony tend to avoid the analysis of the politics of testimonial culture.[8] Instead, testimony theory focuses on amplifying or rendering representable and narratable testimony's virtually unnarratable stories.

In *The Drowned and the Saved*, Primo Levi proposes and exemplifies a mode of testimony that raises profound questions about current theories of testimony's impossibility and about its allocations of innocence and implication – questions that are strikingly absent from current theories of testimony. *The Drowned and the Saved* constitutes an act of testimony that eschews judgements of guilt and innocence in the interests of acknowledging a morally equivocal 'grey zone' (Levi 1989: 22–51). At the same time, Levi contests the now accepted view of terrible experience as incommunicable. Throughout his writings, Levi insists that experiences of catastrophe and horror are communicable – a fact to which his writings bear testimony. In this chapter I have pointed to some key differences between confession and testimony and to some differences of perspective found in theories of confession and theories of testimony. For me the most striking difference between these two bodies of theories consists in the absence of a critical distance in testimony theory's treatments of its objects of study. Whereas theories of confession question the place of confession in the sustenance of dominant power relations and dominant modes of subjectivity, for instance, these questions tend to be absent in theories of testimony. Perhaps Levi's writings might prompt the development of a reflective distance from current theories of testimony and their subject matter. For it might now be time to produce a more critical analysis of the politics of testimony.

Notes

1 Both the conferences referred to here were on the theme of testimony, rather than confession, however.

2 New collections on trauma edited by Karyn Ball and E. Ann Kaplan are presently in press, adding to the already voluminous publications in this area.

3 Here I am raising a question about the different temporalities of confession and testimony, which I take up further in *On Memory and Confession: The Sexual Politics of Time* (Routledge, forthcoming).

4 For an accessible and informative discussion of models of cultural instrumentality in cultural theory, albeit in relation to science fiction cinema rather than the confession, see Annette Kuhn's *Alien Zone* (Kuhn 1990).

5 Peter Brooks's view of the ambiguous nature of judicial confession's relation to freedom and constraint is clearly expressed:

> (W)hat I think may be most peculiar about voluntariness in the confessional situation is the paradoxical conditions created for it by the law. On the one hand, the court's insistence that the subject's will remain free, uncoerced; on the other hand, all the efforts of the police interrogators to break the will.
>
> (Brooks 2000: 81)

6   For an alternative view, see Dennis Foster, who argues along apparently Nietzschian lines, that the confessional narrative undermines the reader's quest for truth: '(t)he writers pose as masters of their texts, but only to disclose finally the illusory nature of the category, for both writers and readers. For it is only the desire for a masterful author that makes one into a slavish reader' (Foster 1987: 19).

7   For an extended development of this point, see Susannah Radstone (2000).

8   But see Karyn Ball (2003) for an example of a critical engagement, from a feminist perspective, with testimony theory.

Bibliography

Ahmed, S. and Stacey, J. (2001) 'Testimonial Cultures: An Introduction', *Cultural Values* 5 (1): 1–6.

Anderson, L. (2001) *Autobiography*, New Critical Idiom Series, London and New York: Routledge.

Ashplant, T. and Graham, E. (2001) Call for papers, 'Texts of Testimony: Autobiography, Life-Story Narratives and the Public Sphere' conference, Liverpool John Moores University.

Axthelm, P. (1967) *The Modern Confessional Novel*, New Haven: Yale University Press.

Ball, K. (2003) 'Unspeakable Differences, Obscene Pleasures: The Holocaust as an Object of Desire', *Women in German Yearbook* 19: 20–49.

Belsey, C. (1980) *Critical Practice*, London: Methuen.

Bennett, C. (1995) 'True Confessions', *Guardian* ('G2' section), 7 July: 2–3.

Brooks, P. (2000) *Troubling Confessions*, Chicago and London: Chicago University Press.

Caruth, C. (ed.) (1995) *Trauma: Explorations in Memory*, Baltimore: The Johns Hopkins University Press.

—— (1996) *Unclaimed Experience: Trauma, Narrative and History*, Baltimore: The Johns Hopkins University Press.

Edel, L. (1955) *The Psychological Novel*, Philadelphia: J.B. Lippincott.

Elsaesser, T. (2001) 'Postmodernism as Mourning Work', *Screen* 42 (2): 193–201.

Felman, S. and Laub, D. (1992) *Testimony: Crises of Witnessing in Literature, Psychoanalysis and History*, New York and London: Routledge.

Finney, B. (1985) *The Inner I: British Literary Autobiography of the Twentieth Century*, London: Faber and Faber.

Foster, D. (1987) *Confession and Complicity in Narrative*, Cambridge: Cambridge University Press.

Foucault, M. (1981) *The History of Sexuality: Volume 1: An Introduction*, Harmondsworth: Penguin.

—— (1982) 'The Subject and Power', *Critical Inquiry* 8: 777–95.

Gilmore, L. (1994) *Autobiographics: A Feminist Theory of Women's Self-Representation*, Ithaca and London: Cornell University Press.

Hongo, G.K. (1985) 'Sea and Scholarship: Confessional Narrative in Charles Olsen's "Maximus for Himself"', *New England Review and Bread Loaf Quarterly* 8 (1): 118–29.

Howarth, W.L. (1974) 'Some Principles of Autobiography', *New Literary History* 5 (2): 363–82.

Kahler, E. (1973) *The Inward Turn of Narrative*, Princeton: Princeton University Press.

Kuhn, A. (ed.) (1990) *Alien Zone: Cultural Theory and Contemporary Science Fiction Cinema*, London: Verso.

Levi, P. (1989) *The Drowned and the Saved*, London: Abacus.

Lloyd, G. (1993) *Being In Time: Selves and Narrators in Philosophy and Literature*, London and New York: Routledge.

'Off the Page: Confession' (2000) BBC Radio 4 broadcast, 15 October.

Olney, J. (1972) *Metaphors of Self*, Princeton: Princeton University Press.

Porter, L.M. (1976) 'Autobiography Versus the Confessional Novel', *Symposium* 30 (2): 144–59.

Radstone, S. (1989) *The Women's Room: Women and the Confessional Mode*, Unpublished Ph.D. thesis, University of Warwick.

—— (2000) 'Screening Trauma: *Forrest Gump, film and memory*', in S. Radstone (ed.) *Memory and Methodology*, Oxford and New York, Berg.

—— (2001) 'Social Bonds and Psychical Order: Testimonies', *Cultural Values* 5 (1): 59–78.

Rose, N. (1990) *Governing the Soul: The Shaping of the Private Self*, London and New York: Routledge.

Spacks, P.M. (1976) 'Only Personal: Some Functions of Fiction', *Yale Review* 65 (4): 528–43.

Stelzig, E.L. (1984) 'Poetry and or Truth: An Essay on the Confessional Imagination', *University of Toronto Quarterly* 54: 17–37.

Tambling, J. (1990) *Confession: Sexuality, Sin, The Subject*, Manchester and New York: Manchester University Press.

Waugh, P. (1989) *Feminine Fictions: Re-Visiting the Postmodern*, New York and London: Routledge.

Williams, R. (1977) *Marxism and Literature*, Oxford: Oxford University Press.

Wurtzel, E. (1998) 'Memoirs are Made of This', *Guardian* ('G2' section), 27 October: 5.

11 How we confess now

Reading the Abu Ghraib archive[1]

Leigh Gilmore

At the end of April 2004, over a year into the US occupation of Iraq, an explosive series of images depicting the torture of Iraqi detainees by US personnel at Abu Ghraib prison began circulating.[2] When I began writing this essay on confession in June 2004, the news brought daily revelations about how early the Bush administration sought legal arguments for the use of coercive interrogation techniques in its war on terror; the extent to which practices that violate the Geneva Conventions were vetted by Secretary of Defense Rumsfeld for use in the war on terror in Afghanistan and Iraq, and the creation of extra-jurisdictional spaces of detention where such methods could be practised outside national and international law. Sharp concerns had also been raised about when the abuse at Abu Ghraib was first reported and to whom; the implications of using multiple, uncoordinated groups to interrogate prisoners, including military police, military intelligence and private contractors with corrections backgrounds; and the connections between abusive techniques at Abu Ghraib and the approved interrogation practices that have been and are currently being employed at Guantánamo Bay and detention centres in Afghanistan. Confession, interrogation, investigation and torture appeared in this crisis in tense, convoluted relations. Draped in secrecy and loaded with violence, events at Abu Ghraib cast the Bush administration's war on terror in a disturbing light.

Reporters, international humanitarian agencies like the Red Cross, and military attorneys for those accused in the Abu Ghraib scandal are continuing to find information produced by the Bush administration in secret as they labour to construct retrospectively who knew what when and who did what where.[3] The fruits of this reporting include Seymour Hersh's book *Chain of Command: The Road from 9/11 to Abu Ghraib* (2004), which collects and expands on the reporting he did for *The New Yorker*; *The Abu Ghraib Investigations: The Official Reports of the Independent Panel and the Pentagon on the Shocking Prisoner Abuse in Iraq* (Strasser 2004), as well as the *Taguba Report* (Zimmerman 2004) and two other reports generated by official investigations and reviewed recently in the *New York Review of Books* by Mark Danner (2004); Danner's own reporting on the subject and his forthcoming book on torture; and the current near daily reporting, including front page *The New*

York Times stories by Tim Golden (2004), on the Bush administration's secret meetings and directives generated in response to the attacks of 11 September the aim of which was nothing less than the rewriting of military law, an unprecedented expansion of wartime powers and the consolidation of those powers in the executive. In their efforts to structure a story in the face of so much secrecy masking as security, journalists face the challenge of their own belatedness. For the story they seek to tell has already been told even as the conditions for its hearing are not fully present.[4]

Warnings and reports by the Red Cross, military inspectors, officers, enlisted soldiers and others were circulating within the US military and the Bush administration by January 2004. Yet problems within Abu Ghraib were under investigation by General Taguba in January 2003. His comprehensive and scathing report on the abuse was delivered in November 2003 (Elliot 2004). In terms of comparative explicitness, the reports say what the photos show. How, then, did the publication of the images alter the production of truth concerning the US war on Iraq? What does this case reveal about confession in the current context of overlapping, and unequally observed, national and international laws governing detention, interrogation, human rights, the fragility of truth and the vulnerability of justice to power? Despite the graphic nature of the images, their power did not reside solely in their content. The verbal reports of prisoner abuse already warned of sexual humiliation, abusive interrogation techniques and the migration to Abu Ghraib of interrogation tactics approved by Rumsfeld for use at Guantánamo, and were, in fact, compounding over time from various sources. Indeed, as the revelation of a series of secret memoranda now make plain, President Bush endorsed the findings by lawyers for the White House, the Department of Justice, and the Pentagon that prisoners captured on the battlefield in Afghanistan have no legal rights under federal law or the Geneva Conventions. As one official reported, the 'gloves had come off' early on in the war on terror. The case in point is the treatment of John Walker Lindh, branded the 'American Taliban', and photographed naked and duct taped to a board in a disturbing preview of the Abu Ghraib iconography.

Yet it is the images from the Abu Ghraib archive that are now indelible: Lynndie England, cigarette dangling, fingers pointed like pistols at the genitals of a hooded prisoner; a naked human pyramid of Iraqis behind which Charles Graner and Sabrina Harmon grin, hooded naked Iraqi men forced to simulate sex with each other. Certainly, the images confirmed for many the notion that 'seeing is believing' and 'a picture is worth a thousand words'. However, as soon as seeing begat believing and words began to flow, disputes over what the images proved followed immediately: did the grins on the soldiers' faces reveal their lack of concern about repercussions and indicate, therefore, that they were acting under orders? Or was the abuse the wretched work of 'a few bad apples', an instance in the fraying of discipline, in other words, an aberration? Did the acts photographed and the photographing itself constitute torture under the Geneva Conventions, or were they, in the characterization of a caller to Rush Limbaugh's radio show echoed by other conservative talking heads, no worse than a fraternity prank? The images alone cannot answer these questions; instead, they underline the complexity surrounding the truths we seek, both in this case and beyond its frame of reference. The images, and our attempts to interpret them, expose fissures in the rhetoric of confession itself, its relationship to interrogation and force, as well as to truth, the bureaucratic techniques of power that underlie it, and its differing audiences and modes of dissemination.

As reports warning of abuse made their way through the labyrinth of containment mechanisms known as 'channels', the images were not so readily managed. They spoke in an explicit visual language of bound and posed naked bodies, grinning abusers and lunging attack dogs. They displayed the banal iconography of power: a uniformed guard slouches against a wall passing time, another holds the end of a leash attached to a man who has been stripped naked and lies on the prison floor. The images produced a response that the reports and counter-memos did not. They provided verification of abuse. They constituted evidence. They erupted across the Internet. Whether or not responsible individuals in the Bush administration can or will be made to stand trial in The Hague for violating the Geneva Conventions remains to be seen.[5] But if the purpose of the torture was to elicit confessions from the detainees, to force them to give up secret knowledge, its revelation has to be considered a massive derailing of those energies into their unintended opposite. For instead of representing the scene of successful intelligence gathering, the images constitute the accidental confession of US torture.

The documented torture and abuse at Abu Ghraib occurred within the context of the Bush administration's global war on terror and its effort to remap the war zone as potentially everywhere a terrorist is, and a terrorist as potentially anyone. Indeed there is no battlefield per se anymore, only multiple intensifications in an ongoing global war against enemies who are not necessarily soldiers when they are fighting nor prisoners of war or criminals when they are captured, but susceptible to being classed as enemy combatants outside the protocols and protections of law. Under the conditions of open-ended detention and interrogation and the perilous expansion of enemy combatant status to cover anyone in detention, some of confession's more disturbing dimensions come into focus. If the purpose of the abuse at Abu Ghraib was to 'loosen up' prisoners before interrogation (as those charged have claimed), then the torture and sexual abuse reveals the problematic quality of the truth confession would produce.

Confession, torture and truth exist in a triangulated relation: torture names the implicit threat that elicits confession, truth names its goal, and the successful production of truth via confession sanitizes the threat that impels it. Not only, then, is confession in this logic the means to truth in which causality flows in a single direction, but torture is also the means to confession, and the presence of these prior energies raises disturbing questions about the twinning of torture and truth. Torture and truth are mediated by confession, yet the intermediary, formalized and presumably salutary act of confession itself obscures their close relation. It is less the case, then, that torture as the most explicit form of coercion is but one technique among many, albeit extreme, for extracting information. Instead, torture and the truth it would produce are both always implicit in confession. Within the Bush administration's global war on terror, all persons who happen to be in Iraq, in Afghanistan, or indeed anywhere on this non-linear battlefield, can be designated as enemy combatants, held without benefit of legal process and enter into an open-ended confessional scene.[6] Interrogation extends to cover the entire duration of detention, saturates the identity and use of the one detained, and makes him or her perpetually about to be interrogated, always in the need of 'loosening up', always in possession of secret knowledge, even as it remaps the globe as an extra-jurisdictional battlefield with proliferating partners in, and sites of, interrogation. Indeed the relation between this spatial remapping and law was exemplified early in the war on terror when the Bush administration described its detention centre in Guantánamo Bay, Cuba, as a site outside the jurisdiction of US and international law.

The brutality of interrogation in all its hyperbolic degradation is on display in the Abu Ghraib photographs, but let us not fail to mention some of the nuances of coercion it exploits. Because accusation and detention are inherently coercive situations, to what extent is any confession uncoerced? Certainly, they are motivated and not all motivation is properly understood as coercion. The very possibility of willingness, of confessional agency and desire, underwrite the prospects of exoneration (in legal proceedings), atonement (in the Christian confession) and self-representation (in literary acts). But the law is mindful of its bind in regard to confession and the effects of coercion. It recognizes its reliance on the paradoxical speech act known as a free and voluntary confession, even as a body of case law documents its problems. Police are given instruction in how to question prisoners (and how and when not to); courts remain dubious about confessions even as they rely on them. Given the pressing need to gather information that could win battles and save lives during wartime, one might be tempted, as the Bush administration has been, to accelerate the process, and to use as much force as permissible toward this end. Yet, paradoxically, in the case of criminal investigations and war, coercive interrogations and torture prove notoriously unreliable for extracting accurate and actionable information. Prisoners of war are routinely unable to offer the kind of battle-shifting, life-saving information their captors desire. In the context of combat, those captured provide the most reliable information in the hours immediately following their capture. What makes Guantánamo and Abu Ghraib such glaring failures at producing the information they are supposedly designed to extract is that they do so many things wrong. The consequences are apparent: of the thousands rounded up in Afghanistan and Iraq, no one has been convicted of anything. Only the US soldiers in the Abu Ghraib archive are already under prosecution. Jeremy Sivits and Ivan C. Frederick II have been convicted and are serving sentences.[7] What to make, then, of the current abuse in the war on terror given the ineffectiveness of torture in yielding the kind of information that might result in lives being saved and battles won? What to make of the extensive sweep into detention of civilians given their dubious potential as informants and their ostensible identity as bearers of the hearts and minds the US seeks to win?

Although torture is not a particularly effective technique for gathering information, it has been used repeatedly in conflicts ranging from war to more intimate settings because it embodies an extreme form of dominance over another: it is the means through which to unmake a person's truth and identity and remake it into what the torturer says it is. The use of torture in the Bush administration's far flung war on terror, its multiplying detention centres, and its contracting of interrogation to civilians and nations that will allow CIA interrogators' leeway for acts that would otherwise place them in violation of US law were they to take place within the jurisdiction of the US, suggests that a broader project than intelligence gathering is underway. Coercive techniques and the legal fine-tuning of where, when and who can employ them is less about construing torture as the technique of last resort in interrogation than it is about shrugging off any pretence of acknowledging procedural constraints that recognize the reflexivity of prisoner of war status. One of the historical arguments against the use of torture during captivity is to deter enemies from torturing one's own troops. If there are no prisoners of war in the war on terror, and if those who are detained are civilians and not enemy soldiers, then what reciprocity, what law on one hand and what fear and humility on the other, binds the interrogator? As Staff Sergeant Frederick testified when asked why he had abused detainees, 'I just wanted to humiliate them'. The use of torture marks the point at which the purpose is no longer to gather information, but to render a person thoroughly under the control of the torturer.[8] It also marks the loss of reflexivity built into military protocols around interrogation and detention. Torture marks a crucial shift in the status of the person being abused by rendering him or her abject not only through threat, entreaty or bribe but, crucially, force. It also marks a loss of the subject's self-constitution and institutional identity in relation to that person and within the context that binds them together in an unequal power relation.

Legal historians of confession pull together the religious, military and judicial contexts of confession in order to remark on the disturbing continuities among them. In a study of coerced confessions, inquisitions and loyalty oaths, Haig Bosmajian (1999) points to the hard-fought battle to secure the fragile right not to speak. He details the dynamics of institutional power that bring heretics of many sorts before a variety of interrogators. Sometimes interrogations are tenuously authorized, quasi-official or surreptitious; sometimes they bear the full support of the state. It is both odd and troubling to consider how one can be compelled to testify against oneself. Those compelled to name names and to profess oaths of loyalty in the US during the Cold War, speak of the shame and humiliation of this coercion. The 'truth' produced by such confessions (naming names) and the humiliation of interrogation coincided. The Fifth Amendment offers protection against self-incrimination in courts and the humiliation it imposes. It preserves a subject before the law who does not bow to the interrogator's demand and remains a subject. The Fifth Amendment draws on an older common law right even than the First Amendment and its protection against self-incrimination was secured even before the freedoms of speech, press and religion (Levy 1968: viii). We can think, then, of the right not to speak as preceding the protection of free speech and the two crucial arenas of speech that mark the interpenetrated site of privacy and the public sphere: religion and the press.

In Bosmajian's survey of the historical terrain, he argues:

> Over the centuries, the issues have changed, but the demand to speak has not. Roman authorities demanded that Christians 'revile Christ'; Henry VIII demanded that Thomas More take the loyalty oath; the church demanded that Galileo recant; colonial authorities demanded that colonists baptize their children and disavow transubstantiation; state and federal governments compelled Reconstruction-period attorneys and teachers to sign loyalty oaths; state officials required students to salute the flag; a variety of un-American activities committees coerced citizens to reveal political and religious beliefs and affiliations.
>
> (1999: 14)

In his delineation of these activities, Bosmajian sees the shifting alliances of power consistently relying on and linking coercion, power and confession. We might ask if we risk painting with too broad a brush when such disparate activities are linked? Certainly, confession and interrogation name related but not interchangeable practices. They are embedded within different histories and rely on different arguments about necessity and expediency, but if we look at each instantiation outside the frame of torture, confession and truth, we fail to grasp the critical insight Bosmajian's links reveal and we perpetuate a crucial problem identified by Peter Brooks: 'Rules governing the conditions of confession may never be wholly adequate to the problem: they address only the context, not the nature of confession' (2000: 31). The profoundly intimate coercion of substituting one's truth and identity for the one power requires is consistent across a range of confessional practices. Whether the penitent in question is to become a member of the faith, to exchange the identity of 'heretic' for 'orthodox', or 'accused' for 'guilty', or whether s/he has been swept up in Iraq, Afghanistan or a Chicago airport for that matter, the purpose of confession is strikingly similar. Indeed, confessional writing as practised by the poets Lowell, Plath and Sexton and a range of autobiographers and memoirists, among others, permits many writers to go to 'the nature of confession' by establishing a confessional scene that is extra-judicial and extra-ecclesiastical yet nonetheless fraught with the potentialities of confession, including the recognition that truth cannot be disclosed in speech in any simple way, nor that silence is without its confessional power (Gilmore 2001).

The images of torture at Abu Ghraib and the techniques they revealed prompt us to confront our investment in the truth of confession itself. In order to untie the relation between torture and confession, we will need to relinquish the falsely causal view of the relation between confession and truth. Confession produces unintended effects, including the exposure of the confessor, who is typically hidden within the logic and practices of confession. In the case of the Abu Ghraib photographs, I have claimed that the images constitute the unintended confession of US torture and abuse. The form this takes is revealing. The images confess, if obliquely, not only how US guards and interrogators saw their prisoners, but also how they saw themselves. I want to consider the sexual nature of the abuse in this context. Some of the images resembled pornographic *tableaux vivants* with prisoners stripped naked and placed in sexual positions. Interestingly, the prisoners were not only posed as life-size models in pornographic pantomimes with other prisoners, but the guards themselves played key roles in the scenarios. This interaction between prisoners and guards reveals the need the confessor has for the one confessing, highlights the sexual dimension of the confessor's need and his/her investment in confession and its target, and, in so doing, reminds us of the interwoven relation of sex and power in confession, as well as in institutions' views of individuals and their capacities. The desire to own the individual's truth and the development of techniques for relentlessly searching it out and compulsorily attending to its articulation – in the very words power wants to hear – echo through the grim romance citizens have with institutional power. When the MIs and MPs saw the prisoners as people to humiliate, on what forms of self-recognition did they rely? Did the scene of torture make them unrecognizable to themselves as torturers, or did it constitute them in precisely that way such that when deposed they would deflect responsibility for their actions onto their supervisors, seeking to distance themselves from acts they committed, or would they maintain the view that they had acted as lawfully-empowered abusers? As Charles Graner, who is a Pennsylvania prison guard in civilian life, told Sgt. Joseph Darby, who handed over the two CDs containing Graner's Abu Ghraib torture porn photos: 'The Christian in me says it's wrong, but the corrections officer in me says, "I love to make a grown man piss himself"' (cited in Higham and Stephens 2004: A01).

Though the circuits of power are not transparent in this situation, it does seem that many of those who observed, participated in, and/or criticized the torture at Abu Ghraib recognized their attachment to power, how power acted through them and how it might be refused. What some lost, however, was the sense of the detainee as prisoner of war that would bind the US soldier in a relation of reciprocity and restraint. We still have an either/or explanatory lurking here: *either*:

1   it was the Bush administration's policy on abuse that resulted in the catastrophic collapse of soldiers into torturers (i.e. the abuse represents the 'new normal') *or*;
2   the change in how the US characterized detainees led to some abuse, but these practices were still not approved of by the majority of people in the military (i.e. the abuse was an aberration practised by soldiers, like Graner, who had histories of sadistic behaviour, or the 'bad apples' defence).

This is an example in which a certain locution loses its capacity to coincide with a shifted reality even as it persists in this shifted context. The abuse is an aberration, if by aberration we mean serious, illogical and dangerous shift in US policy away from adherence to the Geneva Convention. The term aberration makes sense in this context, but it does not, strictly speaking, describe the particular acts of abuse. Those, unfortunately, appear now to be part of the US's new practices in its global war on terror. Our attention to the rhetoric of explanation reveals how and why the descriptions of the Pentagon's Abu Ghraib report resists the confession the Abu Ghraib photos make (even as Gen. Taguba decries the abuse): they insist on the abuse as aberrant behaviour even as they describe a situation in which detention, interrogation and abuse are the new norm. My effort here is to contextualize the either/or explanatory model within a triangulated model of truth, torture and confession that recognizes not only the violent but also the sexual potentialities within confession. Perhaps this will help us better understand why, when 'the gloves came off' in the war on terror, US personnel not only wanted to beat up Iraqis, they wanted to take their clothes off, chain them up and force them to simulate sex acts.

   The deployments of sex and deployments of power in the modality of sex consisted in inversions of power: women guards taunted male prisoners and male prisoners were forced into acts and poses intended to simulate homosexuality. Many US commentators, including Seymour Hersh, confidently cited the culturally specific nature of the torture, even as they deplored it, claiming that it targeted Arab sensibilities through the humiliations of nudity and sex acts construed as homosexual. Islamic law prohibits homosexuality, they reported, and nudity among men and before women is not only shameful, but uniquely so for the so-called Arab mind. A book by this title, *The Arab Mind* (Raphael Patai 1973), became highly influential with the neoconservative architects of the war on Iraq and Saddam Hussein. It's an old-fashioned, Orientalizing account of the so-called Arab mentality. In its reduction to stereotype lay its *raison d'être* for the neocons: mastery over this Other, knowledge of his secrets and the development of uniquely effective and gendered forms of humiliating him and 'his' women. Again, this rhetoric was previewed in the run-up to the war in Afghanistan to remove the Taliban from power. The Taliban were bad, proclaimed Bush, not only because they harboured al-Qaeda, but also because of the way they treated 'their women'. Laura Bush and Cherie Blair were launched nearly simultaneously to carry forward the same message in speeches of sisterly concern.[9]

But the techniques of abuse also derived from decades of the CIA's development of no-touch tactics including sleep deprivation, solitary confinement, stress positions, inducing disorientation with bright lights and blaring music, hooding and so on. These techniques aim at breaking down the psychic constitution of the person upon whom they are inflicted. An example of this is seen in one of the Abu Ghraib images in which a man standing on a box wears a hood, his body draped by what looks like a blanket. Wires are attached to fingers and genitals. He has been told that if he falls off the box, he will be electrocuted. Clearly, the use of attack dogs, beatings and sexual humiliation exceed the no-touch repertoire. Still, it was the apparent homosexuality of the abuse, homosexuality as torture, that was decried by a range of those who saw the photos, including the Senators who viewed them in a closed session, from which they emerged blinking, disoriented and grim-faced. What did they/we see?

When we in the US look at the photos, we participate in a history of disturbing trophy photos that includes snapshots of lynchings in which smiling white spectators look into the camera while the bodies of murdered African Americans hang behind them from tree branches. Some of these photos were turned into postcards, though their distribution through the US Postal Service was stopped. There is pleasure in the faces of some of those looking at the lynchings, pleasure, too, in their looking into the camera, even a presumed pleasure to be shared in the circulation of the images. The look behind the camera joins with those photographed in shifting ways: it seems to invite conspiracy with the spectators, or at least extends a sort of permission, even as it documents atrocities. The image provides evidence of pleasure, to the extent that pleasure can be represented, as well as evidence of terror. The *in extremis* simultaneity of pleasure with war crimes (all those smiles and thumbs up signs are archived on CDs that also have photos of the US personnel having sex with each other), or war crimes meant to simulate forms of sexual pleasure and the pleasures of coercion and brutality point to how scopophilic pleasure and horror can be twinned. The presence of the horror permits some distancing from the gruesome spectacle of pleasure. In looking at the Abu Ghraib images, many viewers did not acknowledge their pleasure, conflicted as it may have been, but only their outrage. In a repetition of claims in *The Arab Mind*, many viewers saw the homosexuality of the coerced acts as tantamount to torture itself. That is, the content of the abuse played into the homophobic spectacle of seeing naked men in sexual poses with other men. Could the conflation of homosexuality and torture be broken out of an already densely disturbing iconography of abuse? The problem with that spectacle and its proximity to the prisoner torture has yet to be fully absorbed.

Regulatory norms around sex and power are in effect when the photos are viewed: we enter the scene of confession bound already by its terms, by its norms around truth and torture, caught up in positions of confessor-penitent, prisoner-guard, torturer-tortured, guilty-innocent that are reversible and non-identical to the persons who occupy them. The confident parties to confession unwittingly document their own guilt. Confession's power lies in its capacities for making and unmaking subjects, even in the same act. Its power as power acts upon a body, forms a body, as if from the exertions of its external imposition; at the same time, power enables the internal constitution of subjects, makes their acts of torture permissible and knowable as within a legal framework that is already outside the law. How will we read these images once they have seduced us into thinking they are all we need know of the Bush administration's war on terror, that once we prosecute the people in the photos, we need go no further? Will the Abu Ghraib images become 'our' trophies, evidence of swift judicial retribution for acts of abuse (in fact, the only prosecutions to date in the widening war on terror have been on US citizens)? I hope not. For if the body in its subjection can also escape some aspects of subjection by being re-framed, then the subjects of these images have become something different from what power intended them to be. They refuse shame and become anti-confessional subjects as well as emblems of the confession US power could not avoid making.

Notes

1 I want to express my gratitude to those whose conversation and support enabled me to pursue this subject, especially Judith Butler, Chris Castiglia, Alejandra Kramer, Phil Lynch, Tom Pounds, Baram Sagari and Melanie Rae Thon. My thanks also to Michael Lucey, the Center for the Study of Sexual Cultures and the Department of Gender and Women's Studies at Berkeley for inviting me to present this work.

2 CBS aired some of the images on 28 April 2004, breaking the story to a wide American audience. The images were quickly disseminated worldwide via the Internet. A word on terminology: the images of torture were taken with a digital camera and stored on a CD. Although the images are not technically photographs, that is what they are called in many of the reports and in the media. They are also framed and reproduced in ways that theories of the visual, including those developed around photography and film, have taught us to think about (including the dynamics of the gaze and our responses to the images). Thus I will refer to 'images' mostly, but sometimes to 'photos', especially when I am describing their reception.

3 On the timeline, Tepperman (2004) summarizes the current view: 'The abuses seem to have been more than isolated actions. Instead, they now appear to be part of an explicit policy of coercive interrogations conducted around the globe and supported by Justice Department and White House lawyers, who argued in 2002 and 2003 that the Geneva Conventions and other domestic and international bans on torture did not apply in these cases'. But the timeline on the

Bush administration's inquiry into how far it could go in interrogating prisoners precedes Iraq. It begins in Afghanistan and issues from the same post 11 September rationale that had lawmakers rolling back civil liberties through their support of the USA Patriot Act. The war on terror makes a casualty of human rights and civil liberties in the name of protecting American freedoms at home and abroad. This logic is focused on the management of information and secrecy: on how it can be elicited (through interrogation and torture), who can elicit it, and who can take refuge behind official cover. For the early roll out of the interrogation methods currently drawing such concern in Iraq, see Serrano (2004):

> After American Taliban recruit John Walker Lindh was captured in Afghanistan the office of Defense Secretary Donald H. Rumsfeld instructed military intelligence officers to 'take the gloves off' in interrogating him. The instructions from Rumsfeld's legal counsel in late 2001, contained in previously undisclosed government documents, are the earliest known evidence that the Bush administration was willing to test the limits of how far it could go legally to extract information from suspected terrorists.

Indeed, Berkeley Law Professor John Yoo, then deputy assistant attorney general, reported to the Pentagon on 28 December 2001 'that Guantánamo Bay was a perfect place for detainees because it was not a part of the sovereign United States and therefore not subject to the federal courts'. But, Yoo cautioned, 'there remains some litigation risk that a district court might reach the opposite result' (Serrano 2004).

4   Scandals are characterized by disrupted temporality. In effect, they have multiple lives that require multiple corresponding narratives. The story of torture at Abu Ghraib unfolded in real time in a real place with people many of whose identities can be determined. Yet, it was being both hidden and recorded even as it occurred, known and ignored in official memoranda, and engaged in and unrecognized by many of the military participants. The reporting of the scandal is similarly marked by the burden of temporal disorganization consistent with the revelation of anything that was previously hidden or unknown, and raises questions about our limits of knowing and telling what happened. Deception throws a wrench into the works of narrative, but the genre of investigative reporting emerges with this constraint as its precondition. The result is that not only do stories of scandal often 'break' more than once, but they have to keep on breaking because the official discourse has such a powerful hold.

5   See Tepperman (2004) for an account of how and why senior officials in the US government can and should be held accountable for prison atrocities under the doctrine of command responsibility. Tepperman elaborates:

> This doctrine is the product of an American initiative. Devised by Allied judges and prosecutors at the Nuremberg tribunals, it was a means to impute responsibility for wartime atrocities to Nazi leaders, who often communicated indirectly and avoided leaving a paper trail. More recently, the principle has been fine-tuned by two other American creations: the international tribunals for Yugoslavia and Rwanda, which were established in the last decade by the United Nations Security Council at the United States' behest ... If this is now the standard in international law – which the United States and the United Nations are applying to rogue leaders like the former Yugoslavian president, Slobodan Milosevic – what does it mean for Washington? The rulings of the Nuremberg and Hague tribunals don't directly bind the United States at home. But given that these institutions were created with the support and approval of the United States, their judgments will be difficult for American officials to disown.

6 Jose Padilla was seized in a Chicago airport, designated an enemy combatant, removed to a Navy brig in Charleston, South Carolina, and held there. In *Rumsfeld v. Padilla*, the Supreme Court has begun to zero in on the jurisdictional dilemmas in the Bush administration's remapping of its power over those designated enemy combatants and its expansion of the territorial scope of its war on terror. In a related case, Yaser Hamdi, a US citizen, was seized in Afghanistan, designated an enemy combatant, and held without due process. In a showdown between the executive and the judiciary over the Bush administration's tactics in its war on terror, the Supreme Court ruled in *Hamdi v. Rumsfeld* that due process must be extended to a US citizen designated as an enemy combatant who is held in the US.

7 Both Sivits and Frederick were charged in May 2004 under the Uniform Code of Military Justice with a range of violations related to their abuse of prisoners at Abu Ghraib. Sivits was sentenced to a year in prison, demoted from specialist to private and given a bad conduct discharge. Frederick, who held the rank of staff sergeant, is the highest-ranking person to be convicted so far.

8 There are two positions here masking as alternate explanations of the prison abuse: one is torture-as-prelude-to-interrogation ('loosening up'), the other, torture-as-retaliation/entertainment/surplus violence. In the former, the abuse is consistent with Bush policy in the global war on terror. In the second, the abuse is the work of a 'few bad apples'. But the positions are not mutually exclusive, in a narrow sense, and, in fact, the insufficiency of the either/or rhetoric is part of what my triangulation of truth, torture and confession means to demonstrate. The differing explanations serve less to ease the mind about abuse in the prison than to underscore the vulnerability of the one in detention to violence *for whatever reason*.

9 I include here brief highlights of the BBC's reporting on 'First Ladies back Afghan Women' (2001):

> The plight of women under the Taleban is set to be highlighted in a new campaign fronted by Cherie Blair and US first lady Laura Bush ... The prime minister's wife will join female cabinet ministers at an event at Downing Street next week in order to 'lift the veil' on the treatment of women under the regime that banned their education and forced them to wear burqas ... Mrs Bush will tell America on Saturday that not only did the Taleban repress Afghan women but they tried to export their practices abroad. Mrs Bush's broadcast is the first time a president's wife has made an address entirely on her own, according to the White House.

Bibliography

Bosmajian, H. (1999) *The Freedom Not to Speak*, New York and London: New York University Press.

Brooks, P. (2000) *Troubling Confessions: Speaking Guilt in Law and Literature*, Chicago: University of Chicago Press.

Danner, M. (2004) 'The Logic of Torture', *New York Review of Books*, 24 June.

Elliot, A. (2004) 'Documents are Said to Show Earlier Abuse at Iraq Prison', *New York Times*, 19 June: A5.

'First Ladies back Afghan Women' (2001) Available online at: http://news.bbc.co.uk/1/hi/uk_politics/1660016.stm (16 November 2001) (accessed 15 December 2004).

Gilmore, L. (2001) *The Limits of Autobiography: Trauma and Testimony*, Ithaca: Cornell University Press.

Golden, T. (2004) 'Learning Nothing from Abu Ghraib', *New York Times*, 29 October: A1.

Hersh, S. (2004) *Chain of Command: The Road from 9/11 to Abu Ghraib*, New York: HarperCollins.

Higham, S. and Stephens, J. (2004) 'Punishment and Amusement', *Washington Post*, 22 May: A01.

Levy, L.W. (1968) *Origins of the Fifth Amendment: The Right Against Self-Incrimination*, London, Oxford and New York: Oxford University Press.

Nelson, D. (2002) *Pursuing Privacy in Cold War America*, New York: Columbia University Press.

Patai, R. (1973) *The Arab Mind*, New York: Scribners.

Serrano, R.A. (2004) 'Prison Interrogators' Gloves Came Off Before Abu Ghraib', *Los Angeles Times*, 9 June.

Strasser, S. (ed.) (2004) *The Abu Ghraib Investigations: The Official Reports of the Independent Panel and the Pentagon on the Shocking Prisoner Abuse in Iraq*, New York: Public Affairs.

Tepperman, J.D. (2004) 'An American in the Hague?', *New York Times*, 10 June: A5.

Zimmerman, W.F. (2004) *Basic Documents about the Treatment of Detainees at Guantánamo and Abu Ghraib* (includes the Taguba Report, Geneva Convention, Hamdi and Padilla cases), Online publication by W.F.. Zimmerman. http://www.wfzimmerman.com/staticpages/index.php/20040719145035123 (accessed 15 December 2004).

Index